Joyce ? Jai
from
gray ? Jessie

Warmest good wishes ! enjoy
this great read.

May 1997

City Unique

City Unique

Montreal Days and Nights in the 1940s and '50s

WILLIAM WEINTRAUB

M&S

The author thanks the University of Toronto Press for permission to quote
from *The Collected Works of A.M. Klein*, and DC Books for permission to
quote from John Glassco's poem "Montreal."

Canadian Cataloguing in Publication Data

Weintraub, William, 1926-
    City unique

Includes bibliographical references and index.
ISBN 0-7710-8991-0

1. Montréal (Quebec) – History. 2. Montréal (Quebec) – Social conditions.
I. Title.

FC2947.4.W45 1996   971.42'8   C96-931272-5
F1054.5.M857W45 1996

The publishers acknowledge the support of the Canada Council and the
Ontario Arts Council for their publishing program.

Typesetting by M&S, Toronto
Printed and bound in Canada

McClelland & Stewart Inc.
The Canadian Publishers
481 University Avenue
Toronto, Ontario
M5G 2E9

    2 3 4 5   00 99 98 97

Contents

For Magda

I

1939:
Summer Before the War

The soldiers were worried that their horses might panic if the crowd was large and noisy. And so, during the rehearsal, as these magnificently groomed steeds trotted down Park Avenue, the neighbourhood children were asked to make as much noise as possible, to help the animals get used to boisterous cheers, applause and patriotic outcry. Mounted on the horses, in gold-braided black tunics, were men of the Seventeenth Duke of York's Royal Canadian Hussars, who would provide an escort for the limousine bearing King George VI and Queen Elizabeth. Their Majesties would be arriving in four days – on Thursday, May 18, 1939 – and would drive twenty-three miles through the streets of Montreal, which presumably would be lined with crowds cheering so wildly that the horses might be dangerously alarmed.

But the *Gazette* was worried that the cheering might not be quite loud enough. "It is essential," the paper wrote, in a stern front-page editorial, "that we become for this once a little more articulate than is our wont, somewhat more free in the expression of our feelings, a little less careful of our emotions." It would be the first time a reigning monarch had ever visited Canada, and as Montreal prepared and rehearsed, anxiety was everywhere. The Province of Quebec Safety League was worried that balconies along the route of the royal motorcade might become overloaded with spectators. The League warned householders that they might have to face lawsuits in the event that their balconies collapsed, causing injury and/or death. The wives of dignitaries had other anxieties. When presented to the king and queen, should they perform an ordinary curtsey or a deep curtsey? When they asked Emile Vaillancourt, chief organizer of the festivities, he told them that he didn't know.

Nobody was more worried than the mandarins of Ottawa, who were responsible for the overall organization of the Royal Tour, which was going to go all the way across the country. Their most vivid nightmares involved the possible behaviour of certain officials in Quebec. For instance, when Premier Maurice Duplessis was presented to Their Majesties, would he be drunk or sober? After all, it was only a year since he had ordered his car to stop in front of the Reform Club, had rushed in and, to the astonishment of the members – all political enemies – had unbuttoned his fly and urinated into the fireplace, extinguishing the Liberal flames. And what about the equally unpredictable Camillien Houde, mayor of Montreal? It was only three months since Houde had said during a speech that if England were to go to war with Italy, Quebec would side with Mussolini. Had the king of England heard about this declaration of disloyalty, made by the man who would be welcoming him to Montreal?

Perhaps the greatest concern of all in Ottawa was how the French Canadian populace of the city would greet the English king. In London, the British government would be watching carefully. The unstated purpose of the Royal Tour was to bolster the Dominion's loyalty to the mother country. If war against Nazi Germany were to break out in Europe, as now seemed inevitable, could Britain count on Canada's all-out support? There had been growing doubts about this, and especially about French Canada, which in the past had always felt that it had no stake in England's foreign wars. If, during the Royal Tour, the crowds on St. Hubert Street or St. Denis Street were sparse, or tepid, or even hostile, it would be a bad omen indeed.

But now, just a few days before the arrival of Their Majesties, there were grounds for optimism. The whole city seemed to have broken out in red, white and blue. Houses, office buildings and stores were swathed in bunting and Union Jacks, and shields with the royal coat of arms hung precariously from apartment windows. On St. Catherine Street, huge portraits of George and Elizabeth looked out of the windows of department stores. And, as the *Montreal Star* noted with satisfaction, "Many of the very poorest in the city have somehow managed to provide themselves with small flags." For the poor, the purchase of even the cheapest flag entailed a sacrifice, in a city that was in the grip of the Great Depression, where people were often hungry. At Eaton's, a small Union Jack cost forty-five cents; for an unemployed man on the dole, forty-five cents represented more than two days of what the government gave him for food. In the newspapers, large advertisements welcomed the royal couple. As might be imagined, the ads were mainly from banks, insurance companies and department stores. But there were also a few smaller ads, affirming loyalty to the Crown, from enterprises like Tony Fuoco's shoeshine parlour on Guy Street and the One Minute Lunch on St. Antoine.

For Montreal, the Royal Tour would be the outstanding event in a year that marked the beginning of a new era. Within four months, Canada would be at war with Germany. With the war would come an end to the Depression that had impoverished the city for almost ten years. The year 1939 would usher in two decades of prosperity, growth and a flowering of the arts. Montreal would begin to think of itself as a city unique in the world – bilingual, cosmopolitan, exceedingly handsome and wonderfully odd. At the same time, these would be decades darkened by the repressive Quebec government of Premier Duplessis. The authoritarian fog engendered by Duplessis would dissipate only after his death in 1959, the year that marked the end of this era.

The 1940s and 1950s were years of ferment. They saw the growth of a sophistication which, by 1959, made it hard for Montrealers to credit how innocent their city had seemed only twenty years earlier, how colonial its exaggerated reverence for a king from across the ocean.

~

Now, on May 18, King George VI and Queen Elizabeth were on their way to Montreal aboard a glistening blue-and-silver train pulled by the Canadian Pacific Railway's most powerful locomotive, the mighty 2850. They had arrived at Quebec City the day before, having crossed the Atlantic aboard the *Empress of Australia*. They were due in Montreal shortly after two o'clock in the afternoon. Outside Park Avenue Station, the first spectators had taken up their positions before dawn, some of them wrapped in blankets against the unseasonable chill in the air. By the time the train arrived, there were an estimated 100,000 people waiting on the avenue leading up to the station.

As the train came to a stop, a resounding cheer arose from the crowd. Wearing his uniform of Admiral of the Fleet, His Most Gracious Majesty George VI, by the Grace of God, of Great Britain, Ireland and the British Dominions beyond the Seas, King, Defender of the Faith and Emperor of India, stepped out onto the red carpet, with Queen Elizabeth. Mayor Camillien Houde immediately sprang forward to welcome them. The mayor was a hugely fat man with a bulbous nose and bulging eyes, a man of surpassing ugliness and legendary charm. Little more than a year hence, with Canada at war, Houde would be arrested by the RCMP and locked away for advising Quebeckers not to register for possible military service. But today a bustling, smiling Houde was the picture of obeisance to the Crown. The day before, in Quebec City, Premier Duplessis had been cold sober and on his best behaviour. King George, a quiet, nervous man of forty-four, usually ill at ease at public functions, seemed to like these two rambunctious Quebec politicians.

A custom-built Lincoln touring car, with the top down, was waiting to take Their Majesties through the streets of Montreal. Mayor Houde and Mackenzie King, the prime minister of Canada, were in the second car of the motorcade, with lesser dignitaries and assorted lords and ladies of the royal entourage in the next three cars. As the procession moved down Park Avenue, the horses of the Hussars were calm and properly dignified, despite the clamour of the crowd. People stood three deep on the sidewalk, while others, waving flags, leaned out of the windows of the National Varnish Company and the Orange Crush bottling works.

Turning west into Van Horne Avenue, the king and queen

entered the Town of Outremont, where Lionel Albert, age eleven, was among the patriots lining the sidewalk. Like all the children at Guy Drummond School, Lionel was vociferously pro-British, singing "God Save the King" every morning before classes. The Guy Drummond boys had become anti-American, too, when, in 1936, King Edward VIII gave up the throne so he could marry Wallis Simpson, an American divorcee. On that occasion, the boys sang: "Who's that walking down the street? Mrs. Simpson's dirty feet." Now Lionel Albert and his friends were turning out en masse to cheer George, a much more admirable monarch than the weak, deluded Edward. Here, on Van Horne Avenue, was a *real* king, a sovereign who wasn't afraid to do his duty and reign firmly over the Empire.

Elsewhere in Outremont, Lea Roback had little enthusiasm for the authority symbolized by royalty. Lea was a militant labour organizer, and her house on Querbes Avenue, just a few blocks from the royal route, was subject to frequent raids by the police, who were looking for subversive literature. Montrealers were not allowed to possess books that admired Marx or Lenin, and the authorities could confiscate any such volume. Because of their limited grasp of the English language, the police were known to also seize books by such authors as George Eliot, Charlotte Brontë and Somerset Maugham, especially if the books had red covers. On nearby Stuart Avenue, also close to the royal route, Madame Bizanti, by contrast, had nothing to fear from the constabulary, despite the fact that she was the operator of some of the busiest brothels in Montreal and the employer of dozens of hard-working prostitutes. Madame Bizanti's payoffs to the police were always adequate and always on time, and this assured her that she would never have any trouble with the law.

During their visit to Montreal, the king and queen would not get to meet the likes of Madame Bizanti and Lea Roback, but at City Hall they would be presented with a number of citizens who lived only half a mile to the west, in the Outremont enclave of the French Canadian aristocracy. Here, on Côte St. Catherine Road and adjacent secluded streets, were the big houses and gardens of the elite – the Dandurands, the Beaubiens, the Gérin-Lajoies. And just up the hill, on McCulloch Avenue, was the house where Grace Elliott Trudeau lived with her nineteen-year-old son Pierre.

Emerging from the wealth of the Outremont slopes, the imperial cortege turned south and went down Park Avenue, past the long expanse of Fletcher's Field. This was the traditional park and playground of the city's less affluent Jews, the "downtown Jews" of St. Urbain Street, Esplanade and St. Dominique, as distinct from the "uptown Jews" of Outremont and Westmount. The uptowners were often the owners of the garment factories where the downtowners worked long hours for puny wages, all the while plotting strikes and dreaming of social justice, Soviet style. On this sunny Thursday afternoon, many of the cutters and seamstresses from the nearby sweatshops had a few hours off, and they crowded Fletcher's Field to see their king and queen, the very sovereigns who, during prayers every Saturday morning, were reverently blessed by Rabbi Bender and the congregation of Adath Israel Synagogue. Now, as the big maroon car finally came down the avenue, many of the garment workers cheered and waved their little flags, but others remained silent. "I was a leftist," one of the spectators recalled, half a century later. "I didn't have much use for the monarchy."

The motorcade now turned eastward and was soon going up St. Hubert Street. This was French Montreal, *pure laine*, and for the next hour the king and queen would be driving through streets where a word of English was almost never heard. It was an area of modest triplexes, with outdoor staircases going up to the second storey, the homes of garage mechanics, grocery clerks, bus drivers and workers in textiles, fur and leather. There seemed to be a church every few blocks here, and massive greystone buildings that housed convents and seminaries. There was no power in Quebec greater than that of the Church, and Cardinal Villeneuve, from the apex of its hierarchy, made it known that he wanted all Catholics to extend a warm welcome to the king and queen. After all, even though they were essentially *les autres*, they represented authority and stability; their grandeur would remind the masses of the virtues of respect and obedience. And so, in the east end of Montreal, the faithful turned out in substantial numbers, waving not only the Union Jack but also the Tricolour of France and the yellow-and-white flag of the Vatican.

A week later, in far-off Toronto, *Saturday Night* magazine would marvel at French Montreal's enthusiasm for the British sovereign. The magazine did not hesitate to entertain its readers with its parody of the French Canadian accent. "De King goes for to pass twenty-tree mile," it quoted one spectator as saying. "Dey sure did go over wit' a bang!" said another. Torontonians would not have been surprised at Quebec's appreciation of the monarchy had they read Wilfrid Bovey's book *Canadien: A Study of the French Canadians*, published a few years earlier. Writing with clear-eyed foresight, Bovey, an upper-crust Montreal Anglo, insisted that "in the British Common-wealth of Nations . . . he [the French Canadian] will be a loyal subject of the Crown. . . . He will stand beside his English-speaking fellow citizens a Canadian pure and simple."

From St. Hubert Street the motorcade went east along Mount Royal Avenue. Better planning, some people said, would have taken the royal visitors along Rachel rather than Mount Royal, so they could pass one of Montreal's major tourist attractions – the Palais des Nains, the Midgets' Palace. Visitors from far and near flocked to this establishment, to meet the little people who lived there and to see their little beds, their little bathroom, their little kitchen. The King of the Midgets would no doubt have been glad to compare palaces with the king of England. At the Delormier baseball stadium forty-five thousand Catholic schoolchildren were waiting, some of them English-speaking but most of them French. There was lusty cheering and flag-waving as the motorcade entered, and nine hundred children who had been supplied with red, white and blue jackets formed a huge Union Jack and shouted *"Dieu sauve le Roi!"* Gangs of English and French children sometimes fought each other in nearby streets, but today in the stadium all was peace, propriety and patriotism.

∼

As the motorcade crossed the Jacques Cartier Bridge on its way to St. Helen's Island, dozens of ships in the harbour unleashed a cacophony of sirens, whistles and horns. From the island, the king and queen could appreciate the skyline of the city, standing out against the green slope of Mount Royal, its outline resembling a lion couchant. The Port of Montreal lay before them now, the largest inland ocean port in the world, the port that had made the city Canada's metropolis. The ten miles of wharf here could accommodate more than a hundred ships at a time, and the four huge grain elevators could store fifteen million bushels of wheat from the Prairies. Downstream at the Vickers shipyard, the floating drydock could hold the largest ship in the British navy. And from the passenger terminals, liners were constantly leaving for Europe, ships like the *Ascania*, the *Andania*, the *Ausonia*, the *Duchess of Bedford*, the *Duchess of Atholl*, the *Duchess of York*. Crossing the Atlantic in an airplane was still years in the future.

Back on the Island of Montreal, the king and queen were soon travelling west on St. Catherine Street, through the main French shopping district, past the Dupuis Frères department store, the Ed Archambault music store, Sarrazin and Choquette's pharmacy. Swinging abruptly off St. Catherine and down St. Denis, the motorcade wisely avoided the red-light district. But on St. Denis Street, Their Majesties may have noticed a number of brightly painted young women cheering patriotically, off duty for a bit from Madame Mimi's on nearby Sanguinet Street, Madame Lola's on Mayor Street, Madame Lucienne's on St. Elizabeth Street. The motorcade was also skirting the lower reaches of St. Lawrence Boulevard – "the Main" – Montreal's tenderloin. In this area, if you were a sailor from the port, you could get inexpensively drunk in the Broadway Tavern or the Zig Zag Inn, but during the night Pierrette or Doreen would probably rob you of your wallet. A bed for the night, in a flophouse on the Main, could be had for only ten cents, but the bedbugs could be ferocious. The only permanent residents of these lodgings, it was observed, lived in the mattresses. For entertainment on this street, there were movie houses that offered "Six Shows for Six Cents," with a few vaudeville acts thrown in for good measure.

At City Hall, the queen, dressed in pale blue with a white fur collar, mounted the steps on the arm of Mayor Houde. The king followed with Madame Houde. Inside, the visitors signed the Golden Book and shook hands with 150 important people. Later the king, with the rotund mayor beside him, stood on the balcony of City Hall to acknowledge the cheers of the crowd that had assembled below. It was here that Camillien Houde made his most memorable remark of the day. "You know, Your Majesty," he said, to the Defender of the Faith, Emperor of India, "some of those cheers are for you also."

A few minutes later, the motorcade entered Place d'Armes, the symbolic heart of Montreal. In the middle of the public square stood the monument to Paul de Chomedey, Sieur de Maisonneuve, who had founded the city 297 years earlier. Facing the statue was Notre Dame Church, modelled after Notre Dame in Paris. When it was completed, in 1829, it was the largest structure of any kind in all of North America. Across the square from the church was the head office of the Bank of Montreal, housed in an opulent building whose facade had been inspired by the Pantheon of Rome. For French Canadians, Place d'Armes symbolized the essence of Montreal's soul, with French Catholics worshipping God in Notre Dame and English Protestants, in the bank across the street, worshipping Mammon.

Notre Dame's great bells pealed out as the motorcade drove through the square and into St. James Street. With the head offices of banks, trust companies, brokerage houses and other stately enterprises, this street was the financial heart of Canada. The royal visitors were once more in English Montreal, going from St. James Street up Beaver Hall Hill, with its echoes of the fur trade that had been the foundation of the city's commerce, a century and a half earlier. On St. Catherine Street they drove past lavishly decorated Anglo institutions like Eaton's, Morgan's and Simpson's department stores, the Honey Dew coffee shop, Macy's Drug Store and Hooley Smith's Billiard Academy. The sidewalks were crowded with spectators, many using cardboard periscopes to see over the heads of people standing in front of them. But the best vantage spots were the ones you had to pay for, like a seat in the window of the Hungarian Tokay Restaurant, which cost a hefty three dollars. All over the city, householders lucky enough to be on the royal route were selling seats in their windows. If you had a really wide window, you might take in enough money that afternoon to pay a month's rent. And in almost two hundred locations, entrepreneurs had put up wooden grandstands and were charging three dollars and up for a seat. On University Street, standing room on a lawn was offered at two dollars.

Driving through the McGill University campus, the royal couple was greeted not only by the governors and faculty in academic robes, but also by twenty aged veterans of the Montreal Garrison Artillery who had fought in the Riel Rebellion of 1885. In Percival Molson Stadium, fourteen thousand Protestant schoolchildren were assembled, waiting for the motorcade. They were noisy but orderly and well behaved, this being a time when Montreal children were taught to respect authority, to stand up when the teacher entered the room. The children had all been given souvenir bronze medallions bearing the portraits of the king and queen and the inscription *Regem et Reginam Canada Salutat*. As many of these children were studying Latin, they presumably would know what this meant.

After being cheered by the children, the king and queen were driven to the top of Mount Royal where, at the Chalet, the daughters of prominent families were waiting to serve them afternoon tea, with shrimp canapés and watercress rolls. From the Lookout at the Chalet, the royals could peer down on the city, stretching from the mountain to the St. Lawrence, thick with trees sprouting springtime greenery. In the clear afternoon air they could see all the way south to the Green Mountains of Vermont and the Adirondacks of New York. It was from this vantage point, the royal couple was told, that Jacques Cartier had gazed out on the valley of the St. Lawrence some four hundred years earlier. And it was this view that probably inspired Stephen Leacock's statement that "Montreal, in point of natural beauty of situation, is excelled by no city in the world." Only Rio de Janeiro and Sydney, Leacock wrote, could attempt to rival Montreal.

But gazing out on this verdant panorama, Their Majesties would not have known where Montreal's slums were concealed, mostly

French in the east, English in the southwest. They might not have been told that of all Canadian cities, Montreal had been hardest hit by the Great Depression and the unemployment it brought. In these slums there were families with fourteen children that were "on relief," trying to subsist on a dole of $1.20 a week per person. Here, in winter, people too poor to afford coal were known to burn the shutters of their houses to keep warm. Many of their children could not go to school because they had no warm winter clothing, while others were diagnosed as suffering from malnutrition. In Griffintown, little more than a mile from where the king and queen were now standing, a three-year-old girl had recently died and her parents were dismayed to find that the funeral home wanted twenty-five dollars for a child's coffin, a sum they couldn't possibly raise. A homemade box would have to do.

~

From the top of the mountain, the royal motorcade headed south and into Westmount, the abode of much of the city's wealth. Here, on the upper slopes of Westmount's own little mountain, was the domain of the Molsons and the Redpaths, the McConnells and the Southams – bankers, financiers, company presidents and tycoons of every stripe. They lived in grand houses built in a great variety of styles – Gothic Revival, French Provincial, Stockbroker Tudor. If they looked about them, the royal couple would be able to see crenellated parapets, French mansard roofs, Italianate towers, Queen Anne villas and mansions with a vaguely Southern antebellum flavour.

In the midst of this opulent Anglo-Scottish preserve, a number of wealthy Jews had established themselves, and now Westmount was also the domain of the Bronfman brothers – Sam, Harry, Abe and Allan – who lived almost within shouting distance of each other. And conveniently located for them, on Upper Belmont, was the residence of Aimé Geoffrion, who was perhaps Quebec's smartest lawyer. It was Geoffrion, with the help of eleven other expensive attorneys, who had won an acquittal for the Bronfmans, after they had been arrested by the RCMP for bootlegging. But that trouble-some trial was four years in the past. Now, in 1939, the Bronfman brothers were making considerable headway in their campaign to be thought of, by the public, not as racketeers but as solid citizens and philanthropists, to say nothing of being among the world's great-est distillers of legal booze. To show their admiration for the British Empire, the Bronfmans and their company, Seagram's, marked the year of the Royal Tour by creating a new brand – Crown Royal, a special blend of rye whiskey that came in an ornate cut-glass bottle. Each bottle reposed in a little purple velvet bag with a gold draw-string, and it became one of the most costly tipples on the market. Ten cases of Crown Royal, a gift from the Bronfmans, were put aboard the Royal Train for the trip across Canada.

Enthusiasm for the British Crown was nowhere stronger than on the elegantly shaded streets of Westmount, although this suburb did harbour at least one anomaly, Dr. Noel Decarie. Dr. Decarie's house, at 4375 Westmount Avenue, offered an unexcelled view of the royal motorcade as it drove by on its way westward, but the doctor would have much preferred to see Adolf Hitler in the big maroon touring car, rather than the British monarch. Dr. Decarie, a prosperous dentist, was an avid anti-Semite, much given to tirades about the likes of his next-door neighbour, Dr. Jacob Rosenbaum, and, of course, Harry and Abe down the street and Sam and Allan up on Belvedere Road. Dr. Decarie was the chief lieutenant of Adrien Arcand, the leader of Quebec's fascists, the Parti de l'Unité Nationale. Later that summer, Arcand, flanked by four of his Blueshirt storm troopers, would address an overflow audience at St. Thomas Aquinas Church and tell it that if war did come (it was only a few weeks away) it would be the result of a Jewish capitalist-communist conspiracy. And, the Quebec fuehrer urged, Canada should definitely stay out of any war of that kind.

Leaving Westmount, the motorcade headed back eastward, along Sherbrooke Street. Just after Guy Street, some two hundred Mohawks from the Caughnawaga reserve were assembled on the lawn in front of Lady Amy Roddick's house. Lady Roddick, a middle-aged poetess whose benefactions to the Mohawks were generous, would soon become an honorary Indian princess, initiated into the Iroquois tribe with due ceremony by Chief Poking Fire. She now looked on with pride as her guests, wearing beaded buckskins and feathered headdresses, held aloft their greeting to the royal couple, on a banner that read, "WELCOME TO THE GREAT WHITE FATHER AND MOTHER."

The king and queen were now passing through the Square Mile, legendary habitat of Montreal's old money, its really serious money. Although the area's decline had already begun, there were still Square Milers living here in mansions more grand than anything in Westmount, mansions built by men who, at the turn of the century, controlled three-quarters of the wealth of Canada. Cheered by crowds lining Sherbrooke Street, the motorcade passed the Ritz-Carlton Hotel. Although some of the rich had been ruined by the Depression, there were still many who could afford Sunday brunch in the Oval Room of the Ritz, at $1.85 plus tip.

One block past the Ritz, at the corner of Stanley Street, Izaak Walton Killam and his wife Dorothy waited for the motorcade on the steps of their flag-draped greystone mansion. That evening, with the help of their ten servants, they would entertain friends at a lavish formal dinner. For that occasion, Dorothy would have to decide whether to wear the pendant with the huge Briolet diamond that had once belonged to King Henri II of France, or the Astor pearls that Killam had bought for her not long ago. Those were the pearls that the late Mrs. John Jacob Astor had clutched as she jumped into one of the *Titanic*'s lifeboats. Izaak Walton Killam, once a newsboy in Yarmouth, Nova Scotia, had made his money in pulp and paper, utilities, movies, sugar and several other enterprises. Now president of Royal Securities, he was one of the richest men in Canada, and because Dorothy loved baseball as much as she loved diamonds, he once considered buying the Brooklyn Dodgers for her.

But even richer than Killam was Sir Herbert Holt, who lived just up the street, on Stanley, a few steps away from the royal procession. Sir Herbert, whose house had fourteen bedrooms, was generally believed to have more money than anybody else in Canada. He was president of the Royal Bank and of twenty-six other major corporations, and for French Canadians he epitomized the ruthless Anglo robber barons who, they felt, had been exploiting them since 1760. When he died, two summers after the Royal Tour, the baseball game at Delormier Stadium was interrupted so that his death could be announced on the loudspeaker. There was a moment of stunned silence, and then a prolonged outburst of cheers and applause. At the foot of Sir Herbert's street, some lesser millionaires were assembled on the steps of the Mount Royal Club to watch the king and queen go by. This was Montreal's most exclusive men's club, so exclusive that even Izaak Walton Killam was blackballed when he tried to join. The reason for this astonishing rejection was never disclosed, and it remains one of the enduring mysteries of Sherbrooke Street.

Many members of the Mount Royal Club were in attendance that night at the Windsor Hotel, for the banquet tendered to Their Majesties by the City of Montreal. Dinner was served to a thousand guests amid a lavish decor of palms, hydrangeas, crimson velvet and yellow satin. The *Gazette* called the evening "the most brilliant scene of fashion Montreal has ever witnessed," and it proceeded to devote two whole pages to a meticulous listing of what each of the ladies was wearing. Mrs. Jackson Dodds, the paper noted, was attired in a smoke green gown by Worth, the long bodice with halter neckline ornamented with a rosette of rhinestones at the decolletage. Mrs. T.J. Coonan was wearing a Schiaparelli model of periwinkle blue chiffon, while Mrs. T. Taggart Smyth was decked out in georgette, also periwinkle blue. In contrast, Mrs. L. deGaspé Beaubien was gowned in black chiffon and Mrs. Napoleon Courtemanche in Suez rose lace.

But nobody's finery attracted more attention than that of the queen, who was wearing "a gown of silvery brocade having its design traced with shimmering silver sequins and jewelled orders." There were many exclamations about the beauty of the thirty-eight-year-old queen, in her diamond tiara. Roger Champoux, writing in *La Presse*, carried the adulation about as far as it could go by saying that "her smile illuminated the entire room and, amid the gold of the decor and the gleam of silver and crystal, her eyes resembled the most beautiful jewels in the world."

Sitting between the king and the queen at the dinner was Mayor Camillien Houde, who had been born in an east-end slum, in a house that fronted on a lane so humble that it didn't even have a name. Now, Houde was not only drinking Pommery Brut 1929 and coping with a table setting of three forks, three knives and four spoons, but he was also making amiable chitchat with a monarch whose empire covered one-quarter of the earth's surface. Houde – *le p'tit gars de Ste-Marie* – soon had both the king and the queen laughing loudly, and they would probably long remember his final speech that night when he said to them, in his precarious English, "I thank you from the bottom of my heart for coming. My wife thanks you from her bottom too."

While Montreal's elite ate their turtle soup and squab with royalty inside the Windsor Hotel, thousands of commoners had assembled outside, in the floodlit Dominion Square, hoping for another glimpse of the magic visitors. The crowd stood for hours, clamouring for an appearance by the sovereign and his wife, who eventually obliged by leaving the dinner table to come out onto the balcony, where they waved a hand to these loyal Canadians, all apparently happy to be British subjects. "Those who didn't cheer," said the *Montreal Star*, "didn't cheer because they couldn't; they were crying." In a remarkable departure from the restrained journalism of the time, the *Star* reporter described the emotions of the crowd by saying that "here indeed was a prayer answered, a life ambition realized. People were so moved that they would have died for their monarch then and there."

Actually, only one person died during the excitement of the day, a man who suffered a heart attack while waiting for the motorcade on Peel Street. Less than half a dozen persons collapsed, and there were only sixty-four lost children. All these lost children, the police reported proudly, were returned to their parents by nightfall. There was much praise for the efficiency of the police on this difficult day. There had been rumours that certain malcontents might attempt to rush out from the curb to the motorcade and present the king with petitions pleading for action against the widespread poverty and hunger in the city, but no such embarrassments occurred, and the vigilance of the police may well have been instrumental in averting them.

In dealing with the Cypress Street problem, the police found a solution that was in the best traditions of the force. Cypress was only one block long, bordering the north side of the Windsor Hotel. This was where the Royal Suite was located, and the hotel's manager was painfully aware of the fact that if Their Majesties peered out their window, across the narrow street, they would be looking directly into the uncurtained windows of one of Montreal's busiest illegal gambling dens. They would see plenty of action around the barbotte tables, which were generally humming day and night. Barbotte, of course, was Montreal's unique, peculiar dice game. For years the hotel had been begging the police to close down the various barbottes located in streets around the hotel. After all, the Windsor was the preferred hotel of diplomats and other foreign dignitaries and it was embarrassing to realize what unsavoury comings and goings these notables had to witness during their evening strolls in downtown Montreal. Now the hotel manager appealed directly to Fernand Dufresne, Montreal's chief of police. Surely the presence of the king of England would be reason enough to finally close down this foul Sodom and Gomorrah across the street.

But the hotel manager was being naive. While the king was certainly important, he was not quite important enough to warrant the closure of a beloved local institution whose payoffs to the police were always generous. Police Director Dufresne, however, was a man of courage and imagination. Braving the wrath of the barbotte's operators, he ordered Cypress Street completely closed off, to both vehicles and pedestrians, for the duration of the Royal Visit. During that short interval, customers would not be able to gain access to the gambling den and so the dice would not roll. But the minute Their Majesties departed the Windsor Hotel, to resume their cross-Canada tour, Cypress Street would be reopened, and upstairs in the busy barbotte the cry of "trois-trois" or "six-cinq" would again be heard as Montrealers immersed themselves in one of their traditional pleasures.

~

Throughout the spring of 1939, while Montreal was preparing for the Royal Visit, there was mounting fear that war might soon break out in Europe. Nazi Germany had already swallowed up Austria and Czechoslovakia, and now Hitler was threatening to annex the Free City of Danzig, on the border between Germany and Poland. Poland's objections to this were strenuous, but Hitler was believed to be ready to use force if his demands were not met. On June 9, Prime Minister Chamberlain of Britain expressed the hope that Hitler would be willing to settle this dispute at the conference table. Meanwhile, in Danzig itself, there was a feeling that there would be no outbreak of war during the summer. After all, European wars traditionally did not start until the autumn, after the harvest was in.

In Montreal, war clouds did not blot out the summer sunshine, and on weekends the No. 17 streetcar to Cartierville was crowded with young families on their way to Belmont Park. Here they would ride the scenic railway, eat cotton candy and watch The Audacious Satanellos – "two men and a girl" – do their stuff on the high wire and the flying trapeze. The Ringling Brothers-Barnum and Bailey Circus came to town, and children were taken to see Gargantua, billed as the largest gorilla in captivity – "the world's most terrifying creature." Meanwhile, at Woodland Park in Verdun, there was a more gentle spectacle, the weekly community singsong, where the crowd sang "Flow Gently, Sweet Afton" and "Polly Wolly Doodle." Following the singsong, there was an ice-cream-eating contest in which the boys held out plates of ice cream and the girls attempted to feed it to them, a task rendered both difficult and messy by the fact that both the boys and the girls were blindfolded.

Relatively few people owned cars in 1939, but those fathers who did would often take the family out for a Sunday spin. Children would urge Daddy to fill up his tank at a station of the Joy gasoline company where, with every six gallons, Joy would give you a free, live baby turtle. For the unemployed and others too poor to afford Belmont Park, or to drive in a car, hot Sunday afternoons might be spent sitting on the balcony or the front doorstep, sipping Kik, the local economy cola – "six big glasses for five cents."

On June 18, Joseph Goebbels, Hitler's propaganda minister, went to Danzig and told an enthusiastic audience that the city must inevitably become German territory. "No amount of diplomacy or power politics can change this fact," he said. Ten days later, from London, Winston Churchill warned Hitler not to "plunge into the unknown." The British Empire, Churchill said, had reached the limit of its patience. That same day, it was reported from Warsaw that nearly three thousand German soldiers, in civilian clothes, had slipped into Danzig during the past week, heightening the fears of a coup d'état. Heinrich Himmler, head of the Gestapo, was also said to be in Danzig, to confer with members of the local Nazi Party.

In Montreal, on July 8, people gathered on the waterfront to wave goodbye to the *Nascopie*, the Hudson's Bay Company ship that was leaving for the Arctic with supplies for the company's remote trading posts. On board was a cargo ranging from drums of gasoline to canned peaches and babies' bottles. There were passengers, too – doctors, missionaries and red-coated Mounties. Some of these men would not come back south for five years. Captain Thomas Smellie, master of the *Nascopie*, would take his ship all the way up to Ellesmere Island, eight hundred miles from the North Pole, and bring her back before the ice closed in. Now, as she steamed out into the St. Lawrence, to start her annual ten-thousand-mile voyage, the horns and whistles of many other ships bade her a noisy farewell, the traditional acknowledgement of the *Nascopie*'s importance in the Canadian scheme of things.

Ten days later, officials gathered at St. Hubert Airport for another send-off, this time for an airplane, a silvery Lockheed Super Electra of Trans-Canada Air Lines. It was about to inaugurate the first daily service between Montreal and Toronto. With a brief stop in Ottawa, the trip would take only two hours and forty-five minutes. The plane, with a crew of three, could carry ten passengers. There was another aviation landmark the following month when the Imperial Airways flying boat *Caribou* put down on the river at Boucherville, seven miles from Montreal, to inaugurate a regular transatlantic airmail service. The flight, from England to Montreal, took thirty-three hours, with stops in Ireland and Newfoundland and a midair refuelling over the Atlantic from a tanker plane. This airmail flight raised hopes that passengers, too, might soon be able to fly to Europe.

The early weeks of July seemed to bring some respite from the threat of war. In a radio speech, Chamberlain warned Hitler that Britain would throw her whole weight against any aggression he contemplated. In response, a Nazi spokesman in Berlin assured the world that Germany would not resort to force. "We have no desire to go against the territorial integrity of Poland," he said. Meanwhile, in Montreal, a young German sailor, interviewed while his ship was in port, told a reporter that Hitler could not last much longer, and if he went to war over Poland the German army would revolt. Needless to say, the German sailor asked to remain anonymous.

There were other friendly sailors in port, midshipmen from the United States Naval Academy at Annapolis. The young women they had met during their visit to Montreal turned out in great numbers to say goodbye when the midshipmen boarded their train to go home. "Seldom has such a wide variety of femininity visited Windsor Station at one time," the *Gazette* reported. "There were girls of every size, description and standard of pulchritude. They ranged from tall, sophisticated peroxide blondes, with lips and fingernails of the same carmine hue, to gum-chewing lasses with turned-up noses." The young women's farewells to their "temporary sweethearts," the paper went on to say, were often tearful.

Temporary sweethearts could pose a grave menace, because of their lecherousness, according to Dorothy Dix, a syndicated columnist carried by the *Montreal Star*. "It is so nauseating, terrible, heartbreaking," she wrote that summer, "to think of girls who are willing to do things that revolt them, things they know to be wrong, things that would disgrace them if they became known, because that is the price that boys exact for their attentions." Miss Dix showed surprising tolerance for ladies who yielded their bodies to Lotharios who were rich, but she had no use whatever for the poor little shopgirl with round heels and little ambition. "There have always been women," Dorothy Dix wrote, "who sold themselves for money and the things that money buys – furs and jewels, fine clothes, soft and luxurious living. These women are understandable. But what one cannot understand is why the modern girl holds herself so cheaply, why she throws away all that a woman should hold dear for the price of an ice-cream soda or being taken to a movie." Dorothy Dix was but one among many who were concerned with a decline in morals. Preaching at Emmanuel Church, Reverend James W. Clarke deplored the breakdown of the home, the corruption of marriage and contempt for the law. The rise of the secular mind, he said cryptically, "reduces man to the status of an electric battery, flesh that pulsates for twenty-five years – then starts to decay."

But the sanctity of marriage was very much in evidence on July 23, in an event that rivalled the Royal Visit in terms of the public enthusiasm it aroused. It took place in the baseball stadium, the "Delormier Downs" of the sportswriters, this mass wedding of 105 Roman Catholic couples, before a crowd of twenty-five thousand family members, friends and well-wishers. The 210 brides and grooms, young and not so young, were all Jocistes, members of the Jeunesse Ouvrière Catholique, the young Catholic workers' movement. They had all taken a year-long course inspired by Pope Pius XI's encyclical calling for thorough preparation for Christian marriage. Now they were ready to take their nuptial vows, administered by the archbishop of Montreal and 104 priests. It was a colourful scene, under a hot midsummer sun, with all the brides gowned in white, all the grooms wearing blue suits. There were six bishops on hand, in scarlet robes, and the 104 priests wore the differently coloured vestments of their various orders. After the ceremony, Father Henri Roy, founder and chaplain of the JOC, suggested that the newlyweds postpone their honeymoons for three months or so. He said that they should get settled first, that they could get to know each other better at home than in a hotel room. But it seems that few of the couples took their mentor's advice, the vast majority opting for the hotel room, with an immediate departure from town.

A good many of them headed for resorts in the Laurentian

Mountains, north of Montreal. Those who ended up in the village of Ste. Agathe would have attended mass in the Catholic church there, on the Sunday after their wedding. Here they would have heard a sermon by Canon J.B. Charland in which he told his flock that the village should rid itself of Jews. Ste. Agathe was a favourite summer resort for Jews from Montreal, who rented cottages or came up for the weekend to the two Jewish hotels. There was a kosher butcher in the village, a delicatessen and a Jewish taxi. In his sermon, Father Charland stressed the importance of "remaining masters in our community" and said that French Canadians must be taught to rent their places in summer to other Christians and not to Jews. The Jews, he explained, had been persecuted through the ages because they had not recognized Jesus Christ. "You must not hate this race," he said, "but neither must we give up our best traditions."

The day before Father Charland delivered his sermon, Ste. Agathe had awakened to find, on telephone poles and elsewhere, some two hundred bilingual posters that said "*Les Juifs ne sont pas désirés ici. Ste-Agathe est un village canadien français et nous le garderons ainsi.*" "Jews are not wanted here in Ste. Agathe," said the English message, "so scram while the going is good." Herman Barrette, member of the Quebec Legislative Assembly for the area, added his voice to the warning. Jews in the Laurentians, he said, were getting "what they were asking for." They deliberately congregated on the sidewalks in large groups, he said, and obstructed traffic and laughed at the locals. In St. Faustin, not far from Ste. Agathe, Adrien Arcand, leader of Quebec's fascists, addressed a crowd of two thousand and warned about "the Jewish menace." Arcand was never reluctant to voice his admiration for the way Hitler was dealing with the Jews.

In Montreal, leaders of the Jewish community expressed alarm and indignation, but the Quebec government tried to reassure them. Colonel P.A. Piuze, commissioner of the provincial police, was sent to the Laurentians to investigate, and he issued a statement saying that after much travel in the region he had concluded that the situation was not serious.

While the police were not unduly upset by the utterances of Adrien Arcand and his homegrown Nazis, they were deeply disturbed by other ideas that were circulating. The doctrines and the proselytizing of the Witnesses of Jehovah, for instance, were offensive to the Catholic Church, and so one night the provincial police descended on several Montreal homes and arrested five Witnesses – two women and three men. They were charged with conspiracy to commit seditious libel. The idea of birth control was also repugnant to the Church, and when the latest issue of the American magazine *Look* carried an article on the subject, the police seized hundreds of copies. Meetings of an anti-fascist nature were highly suspect, as they might be tinged with Communism. Thus officers of Captain Jack Ennis's famous Red Squad arrested two young men on Fletcher's Field as they were handing out flyers inviting people to a rally to protest Japanese aggression in China.

That summer saw a great victory for the provincial police and for Premier Duplessis, who guided their work from on high. In Superior Court, Chief Justice Greenshields dismissed a challenge to Duplessis's Padlock Law and upheld its constitutional validity. The law, unique to Quebec, allowed the police to padlock any building or dwelling that they suspected served to disseminate Communist ideology. In effect, people could be barred from entering their own homes for periods of up to one year. In his lengthy and closely reasoned judgement, Chief Justice Greenshields found that the Padlock Law in no way interfered with freedom of speech.

~

The month of August brought increased tension in Europe. Early in the month, Polish authorities reiterated their determination to resist any German effort to take over Danzig. The German press reacted with a barrage of articles threatening to wipe Poland off the map. In Berlin, it was announced that every German between the ages of five and seventy must register so that appropriate tasks could be assigned to them in the event of war. And in Britain, 1,300 military aircraft took part in a huge exercise to test air-raid defences.

As the hot summer progressed in Montreal, the corn on Raya Gulkin's farm grew taller. There were tomatoes, too, and peas, carrots, cabbage, lettuce – food for the family for many months to come and food to share with unemployed friends in these lean Depression days. Mrs. Gulkin called it her farm, but actually it was a very large back-yard behind the family house on St. Lawrence Boulevard, just south of Duluth – agriculture not much more than a mile away from Peel and St. Catherine, the city centre, with its smart shops, hotels and nightclubs. It was not only Mrs. Gulkin's unflagging labours that made her urban farm prosper but also an abundant supply of free manure, for fertilizer, deposited by the horses that came to be shod by Israel Natovitch, the blacksmith, on St. Dominique Street, at the other end of the farm. These were the skinny nags that pulled the carts of the rag-and-bone men through the back lanes, as well as the better-fed horses of the milk wagons, the bread wagons, the ice wagons.

There were good movies to be seen in Montreal, that last summer before the war. Loew's was showing *Confessions of a Nazi Spy*, with Edward G. Robinson, while down the street at the Palace you could see Cary Grant and Jean Arthur – "together at last in a glorious romance" – in *Only Angels Have Wings*. The Capitol announced that it now had "the most elaborate air-conditioning system ever installed in this city," and it invited patrons to cool off while watching *It's a Wonderful World*, with Claudette Colbert and James Stewart. At night, at the Chalet on top of Mount Royal, there was open-air opera and "concerts under the stars." Victor Brault's Opera Guild drew a huge crowd with its performance of *Carmen*, as did the orchestra of Les Concerts Symphoniques, with a program featuring Mendelssohn, Debussy and Berlioz. Meanwhile, below the mountain, at street level, amateurs of more contemporary music would be dancing to the strains of Jack Bain's orchestra at Chez Maurice, Montreal's leading nightclub. They would also see a floor show featuring Houkane and Lolia, ballroom dancers, and Red Smith, the Musical Plumber, who was able to coax a tune out of anything from a wrench to a bathtub.

There were signs, in 1939, that the cruel grip of the Great Depression was relaxing a bit. In the first seven months of the year, permits were granted for the building of thirty-nine new apartment

buildings in Montreal, twenty-seven more than in the same period
the previous year. The number of tourists visiting Quebec, from the
United States and other countries, was up 22 percent. Among the
tourists was E.S. Price, an oil company executive from Kansas City,
who was outspoken in his praise of Montreal not only for its hos-
pitality but also as a place to make investments. "I have done considerable travelling," Mr. Price said, "but I know of no country that
appears to offer as great an opportunity to capital as does Canada,
and especially the Province of Quebec." Montreal's industrial future
was bright, even brilliant, according to George Mooney, director of
the Montreal Economic and Industrial Bureau, who told a Rotary
Club luncheon that the city was in no danger of ever losing its industrial supremacy to Toronto. There were new industries on the
horizon, he said, with the promise of many new jobs.

There were no official unemployment statistics for Montreal
during the Depression, but during the worst years, in the mid-1930s,
it was estimated that between a quarter and a third of the work force
had no jobs. By 1939 things were somewhat better, but there were
still over 100,000 people "on relief" in Montreal proper, excluding
suburban municipalities like Verdun. Being on relief meant getting
a minimal handout from the city, the dole for a single man amount-
ing to less than one-seventh of the average industrial wage. This
paltry sum was given grudgingly, amid suspicions that the recipients
often did not deserve it. There were many "fakers," it was believed,
who secretly held jobs but collected relief money at the same time.
To put an end to this, the city council in July proposed a scheme
whereby all persons receiving the dole would have to report to a
municipal office every day to prove that they were truly idle. And
they would have to report not just once a day, but twice a day. There
was immediate and vociferous protest from the unemployed. Scores
of them wrote letters to the city council, one of them observing that
"two-thirds of the unemployed are nearly barefooted. Are they to
waste the little footwear they possess to walk to relief offices and
then be unable to look for work?" In a matter of weeks the idea was
quietly dropped by the city council, municipal bureaucrats having
figured out that it would cost more to staff this form of inquisition

than might be saved by apprehending any fakers. Also, it dawned on the aldermen that the unemployed had votes.

On August 20, a quarter of a million German troops were massed in Slovakia, on the Polish border. Two days later, Montreal and the rest of the western world were stunned to learn that Europe's arch enemies, Nazi Germany and the Soviet Union, were about to sign a non-aggression pact. Hitler would now be free to invade Poland without any opposition from Stalin. Britain and France had had no inkling that this menacing development was in the offing.

In Montreal, troops of four infantry regiments were called into service and began guarding railway yards, bridges, power stations and other points that might be subject to sabotage. The Red Cross announced that it was ready for war service and could quickly organize the training of nurses and ambulance drivers. Church attendance on Sunday, August 27, was higher than usual, and most services included prayers for peace. In bars downtown, radios were installed so that patrons could listen to the latest news flashes. At the Palace Theatre, moviegoers watched not only Bette Davis in *The Old Maid* but also newsreels from Europe only four days old, thanks to the new transatlantic flying boats. In England, visiting Canadians hastened to book passage on ships that might get them home before the outbreak of war. Among the travellers were two young women from Montreal, Margaret Patch and Patricia Hale, who filled two knapsacks with heavy sweaters and warm clothing. "To wear in the lifeboat," they explained to friends. "In case we get torpedoed."

News that Germany had invaded Poland came on the morning of September 1. In Montreal, silent crowds stood on St. James Street to read the bulletin boards posted outside the offices of the *Star*. On the morning of September 3 they learned that Britain had declared war on Germany. Only hours after the declaration of war, a torpedo fired by a German submarine smashed into the British liner *Athenia*, off the northern coast of Ireland. The ship, which had been bound for Montreal, did not go down immediately, and most of the passengers managed to get into lifeboats.

One of the Montreal passengers was Mrs. Ella Pimm, who had gone to England to visit her daughter Trixie. After Mrs. Pimm was rescued and taken to Scotland, she wrote home to her husband Charles about her experiences in the lifeboat, bobbing through the darkness in the frigid waters of the North Atlantic. "We were eleven hours out," she wrote, "until dawn came and the destroyers came and picked us up. It was so cold, for I was only in a little cotton dress. It was drizzling, and the odd wave came over us. I had no hat or coat or even a handkerchief. . . ." But Margaret Patch and Patricia Hale, also passengers on the *Athenia*, were better prepared. They had all that warm clothing they had so prudently packed in their knapsacks, and in their lifeboat they shared some of it with other shivering survivors. There had been 1,417 passengers and crew on the ship and 112 lost their lives.

The *Athenia* had been a regular visitor to the harbour of Montreal. During the 1930s she had taken thousands of Montrealers to Liverpool, Glasgow or Belfast. For many there were memories of noisy farewell parties in the ship's cabins, of champagne corks popping, of coloured paper streamers unfurling from deck to dockside. Now, on September 4, 1939, the thought that this familiar, graceful ship was lying in cold blackness at the bottom of the Atlantic, a gaping hole in her side, brought this new war much closer to home.

2

War:
The Home Front

James McCann, twenty years old, was a very happy man. Canada had been at war for only three days and James had already passed his physical examination and had been accepted into the army. To celebrate, he went to a downtown tavern for a few beers. As his exhilaration mounted, he managed to break thirty-six beer glasses and a large mirror. When the tavern-keeper objected, James threw a few punches at him. The police arrived and the jubilant young recruit was arrested, but in court the next day Sylvain Desforges, the tavern-keeper, withdrew the charges, despite the fact that replacing the broken glassware would cost him a considerable amount. "I guess the boy was feeling pretty good," Mr. Desforges told Judge Monet. "He made me pretty mad last night, but I guess I can stand the loss, seeing he is taking a chance of giving his life."

For many older Montrealers, September 1939 brought back sombre memories of the First World War, which had ended little more than twenty years earlier. They remembered the slaughter in the trenches of France, and the veterans who came home maimed and broken. And now it was going to start all over again. Now it was their sons who would wear the uniform, who would be sent away to Europe, who would face the horrors of the battlefield. But the young saw it differently. For many of them, like James McCann, the outbreak of war brought elation rather than dread. During the Depression, their lives had often seemed aimless, but now there was a sense of purpose, and there was adventure in store. There were patriotic reasons for "joining up," and, of course, Hitler and his Nazis

27

had to be taught a lesson. Also, the money looked good. Single men who were unemployed quickly learned that in the army they could earn as much in one day as they received in a week on the dole.

Immediately after news came of the German invasion of Poland, hundreds of men started lining up at regimental armouries, anxious to be among the first to enlist, even before Canada officially declared war. A good many of the would-be soldiers were quickly rejected, especially boys of sixteen who were unable to convince recruiting officers that they were eighteen. In Westmount, at the headquarters of the Royal Montreal Regiment, a man who claimed to be thirty-eight was sent away when he finally confessed to being fifty-nine. Other older men turned up with their grey hair dyed black.

At lunchtime on a Friday, soon after the declaration of war, downtown office workers crowded around the Champ de Mars, the wide expanse of concrete behind City Hall, to see a demonstration by gun crews from six artillery units. On what had once been a parking lot, the gunners were manoeuvring their sixty-pounders and their six-inch howitzers – a display designed to attract recruits. The exercise was successful. Within days the artillery units received more applications than they could handle, and three infantry regiments announced that they had already attained full wartime strength. At Red Cross headquarters, the first twenty volunteer women were being taught how to change tires and adjust carburetors, skills they would need as ambulance drivers. And other young women were besieging the Red Cross to have their names put down as prospective nurses. Restaurant operators were worried about what would happen if all their waitresses became nurses.

But enthusiasm for the conflict to come was not universal. Britain had declared war on September 3, but Canada did not immediately follow suit. It was a decision that Parliament in Ottawa would have to make, and it was a week before that vote took place. In the interim, French Canadian nationalists in Montreal raised their voices against participation in the war. On the night of September 4, two members of the Quebec Legislative Assembly told a noisy mass meeting at Maisonneuve Market that there should be a referendum on whether or not Canada should go to war. The war, another speaker said, was the result of "the diabolical machinations of international finance." Any help extended to Britain, he said, should be on a strictly cash-and-carry basis, with Britain providing the transport. The huge crowd cheered and shouted, "*A bas les Anglais!*" The cheers were especially loud for René Chaloult, the member for Kamouraska, when he said that rather than die in Europe, French Canadians would prefer to fight in the streets of Montreal. Meanwhile, not far from where this mass meeting was taking place, other French Canadians were flocking to the colours at the armoury of Le Régiment de Maisonneuve, where its commanding officer, Lieutenant-Colonel Robert Bourassa, would soon announce that more than two thousand men had already presented themselves for enlistment. And in Lafontaine Park, three hundred recruits of Les Fusiliers Mont-Royal, most of them still in civilian clothes, were marching up and down, getting their first lessons in drill.

French Canadians must render whatever service they can to the British Empire, Vincent Dupuis, member of Parliament for Chambly-Rouville, told a meeting in the Queen's Hotel. "It is a sacred duty at this time to think of liberty," he said, "the liberty that was granted to the French-speaking people of this country in 1759, the liberty that was reaffirmed and extended by the great and good Queen Victoria." Another patriot, a man named Rodrigue Langlois, went even farther. He announced that he had mailed a white feather – the traditional symbol of cowardice – to René Chaloult and to each of the other men who had addressed the anti-war rally at the Maisonneuve Market.

It was immediately evident that the war would be costly, and Ottawa lost no time in announcing an array of new taxes. Income tax would eventually be increased by 20 percent, and there were new taxes on items like tea, coffee and soft drinks. A package of cigarettes would go up to twenty-five cents, and it was feared that the days of the five-cent glass of beer were numbered. Housewives were afraid that some commodities might soon be in short supply, and many of them started stocking up. Steinberg's Wholesale Groceterias announced that in the first week of September they had sold 350,000 pounds of sugar, five times the normal weekly amount. Henceforth, the company said, it would restrict the amount allowed to each customer. But there was no need to worry about food shortages, Steinberg's told its customers in an advertisement that proclaimed that Canada had "enough food . . . to feed the entire British Empire." Even imported delicacies were abundant, with Eaton's suggesting treats for Thanksgiving that included black walnut brandy jelly, English pheasant ($3.00 a brace) and Scottish grouse ($2.25 a brace).

But inevitably there would be some sacrifices. No girls would be making their debut this autumn at the St. Andrew's Ball, the *Gazette* announced. That lavish annual event was cancelled, as was the Victoria Rifles Ball, the IODE Debutantes' Ball, the Jewish General Hospital Ball and the Royal Montreal Golf Club's closing dinner dance. The social season was virtually dead. Instead of spending hours at dressmakers in preparation for their debuts, the daughters of the elite were advised to start knitting socks for soldiers. Young men also saw their activities curtailed. The Westmount Football Club decided to suspend operations for the duration, and the Westmount Athletic Grounds were taken over by the military. And it was on these grounds, covered with snow, that men of the first battalion of the Royal Montreal Regiment assembled, before dawn on the morning of December 6. They were on their way to England, part of the First Canadian Contingent. In the course of the war, 104 men of this regiment would give their lives.

The German conquest of Poland had been completed before the end of September, and now, in the autumn and winter months, there was no fighting of any consequence in Europe. There was some naval action on the high seas, but no major battles on land. In Montreal, the war seemed not only far away but also strangely unreal. Some people were calling it the Phony War, and some of the social events that had been cancelled were held after all. Then, in the spring, the Germans again unleashed their *blitzkrieg*. Early in April, they invaded Denmark and Norway, and the following month their armoured columns raced through Belgium and the Netherlands and into France. By mid-June they were in Paris, and France capitulated. Now the massive German war machine was at the coast of France, poised against Britain, only a short distance away, across the Channel.

In Montreal, as everywhere in Canada, the war was now much more real – and menacing. In the newspapers, there were disturbing stories about how, in Norway and the other conquered countries, local Nazi sympathizers had aided the German invaders, and now in Montreal an angry public wanted to know why Quebec's fascists were still free to preach their subversive doctrines. If German paratroopers ever rained down on Montreal, Adrien Arcand and his Blueshirt storm troopers would surely be waiting to welcome them with open arms. Since the outbreak of war, Arcand had been much more discreet in his activities, but he was still operating. His printing press had gone underground, but it was still turning out pamphlets blaming the war on the Jews. He was still recruiting "legionnaires" and holding meetings in private homes, where he extolled the virtues of the much misunderstood Adolf Hitler. Finally, belatedly, the government took notice and the RCMP arrested Arcand and ten of his followers, members of his Parti de l'Unité Nationale. On their premises, the police seized swastika banners, propaganda from Germany and a plan for a Canadian Nazi army of seventy thousand men. Under the Defence of Canada Regulations, Arcand and his chief aides were interned for the duration of the war.

Italian citizens and Canadians of Italian origin who were suspected of being fascists were also arrested. Italy declared war on the Allies on June 10, 1940, and an hour after the news reached Montreal the RCMP, aided by city and provincial police, descended on homes, factories, offices and social clubs to round up Italians on their list of possible spies and saboteurs. Some 2,400 persons were arrested, among them doctors, businessmen, journalists and former police officers. In the Little Italy district, around Jean Talon Street, the police seized firearms, ammunition and black shirts – the uniform of Mussolini's bully-boy legions. These items were taken to be evidence that their owners were members of fascist organizations sponsored by the Italian Consulate downtown. Most of those arrested were released within a month, but more than two hundred were considered to pose a danger to the state and, without trial, were shipped to internment camps. There, in Ontario and New Brunswick, they spent much of the war, in blue-grey uniforms with a red circle on the back, to serve as a target for their pursuers in case they attempted to escape.

In the internment camps, the Italians encountered Germans, Hungarians, Finns and men of seventeen other nationalities. The most famous of these, of course, was a Canadian – Camillien Houde, the mayor of Montreal. Houde once kept a photograph of Benito Mussolini by his bedside, but it wasn't his admiration for the Italian dictator that got him arrested, it was for an act that Ottawa considered tantamount to high treason. In the summer of 1940, the government decreed that all Canadians over the age of sixteen must register for possible national service. This was not, it was stressed, the first step toward conscription for the army, something that was anathema to most French Canadians; it was simply to create an inventory of manpower – and womanpower. But Camillien Houde saw it differently. The National Resources Mobilization Act, he said, was nothing more than conscription in disguise and he would personally break the law and refuse to register. And he urged his fellow Montrealers to follow his example. A few days later the RCMP arrived at City Hall just before midnight and took the mayor into custody. Without trial, he was bustled off to the internment camp at Petawawa, Ontario. There, and later at a camp near Fredericton, New Brunswick, he spent the next four years, a prisoner like all the others. In the camps, the corpulent, ebullient Camillien Houde joined work gangs, chopped wood and refereed hockey games. As referee, he never gave penalties, explaining that the internees were already in enough trouble.

With the exception of the anti-war nationalists, Montrealers displayed little sympathy for Houde. *La Presse* said that law-abiding French Canadians had been shocked by this latest flamboyant gesture by the mayor, and *Le Devoir* said that he had acted like a fool and had gotten what he deserved. Cardinal Villeneuve urged Catholics to comply with the law – and when the time came almost all of them registered without any fuss, coming away from the registration offices with the little certificate they would have to carry in their pockets for the duration of the war.

~

In the Piccadilly Lounge, they were drinking rye and ginger ale and speaking English in the accents of Australia, New Zealand, Canada, South Africa, Texas, Kentucky. They were talking about crash landings on Baffin Island, filthy weather over Greenland, deplorable cuisine in Scotland and, above all, their relentless pursuit of young women on several continents. They were civilian pilots employed by the Royal Air Force Ferry Command, men who flew bombers fresh from the factory across the Atlantic to Britain, delivering them to combat pilots who would take them into action against the enemy. The ferry pilots flew out of Montreal, out of Dorval Airport, and between flights their unofficial headquarters was downtown at the Mount Royal Hotel, in the Piccadilly Lounge. Here, in "the Pic," they would "check the stock," their inelegant term for looking over the ladies. For many of the women they accosted, the dashing young ferry pilots were unutterably romantic adventurers. Also, they earned an unheard-of thousand dollars a month, a small fortune that enabled them to show a girl a good time at the fanciest of Montreal's restaurants and nightclubs.

The Atlantic ferry service came into being in the summer of 1940 as a purely civilian operation managed by the Canadian Pacific Railway out of offices in Windsor Station. Britain had ordered large numbers of bombers to be built in the United States, and it was urgent that they be transported across the Atlantic in a steady stream. Sending them by ship was time-consuming and dangerous, with German submarines sinking far too many merchant vessels. And so it was decided to try to deliver the big bombers by flying them across the ocean. They would be flown to Montreal from the American factories, and Montreal would be the jumping-off place for the hazardous crossing to Britain.

Before the outbreak of the war, transatlantic flight was in its infancy, and the relatively few crossings that had been made had taken place in the good weather of spring or summer. Very little was known about weather systems over the North Atlantic, and many thought that fog, snow and ice on the wings would make it suicidal to attempt that route in the winter. But the men who conceived the ferry service were determined to try. Bush pilots, airmail pilots, barnstormers and amateur flyers were recruited wherever they could be found, as well as potential navigators, flight engineers and radio operators. Training proceeded at great speed at St. Hubert Airport, across the river from Montreal. The first seven Lockheed Hudson bombers took off from there on November 10, 1940. They refuelled at Gander, Newfoundland, and then headed out across the forbidding Atlantic. In less than ten hours the lumbering twin-engine craft put down near Belfast, without mishap, demonstrating convincingly that an Atlantic ferry was feasible.

The airport at St. Hubert soon proved to be too small for the great numbers of aircraft arriving from the American factories en route to Britain. A new and much larger airport was being built at Dorval, ten miles west of Montreal, and it was opened in September 1941. The management of the ferry service had by now passed out of civilian hands and was being run by the Royal Air Force. But most of its pilots would still be civilians, and by the end of the war they would deliver 9,027 planes – Hudsons, Liberators, Flying Fortresses, Mitchells, Martin Marauders and others that would rain down destruction on the German war machine.

For the pilots and their crews, the task was hazardous and uncomfortable. The warplanes they flew often had cockpits that were poorly sealed and heaters that failed, and for hours on end they would sit at the controls shivering in the Arctic cold. Also, electrical systems occasionally faltered, and radios failed, adding to the difficulties of navigation. Passengers were sometimes carried, usually important government officials, and with no seats for passengers in bombers they had to lie on the floor in sleeping bags, packed like sardines and, like the crew, enduring the freezing cold. But the experience gained in these flights did much to prepare the way for the regular airline passenger service that would begin flying to Europe out of Dorval Airport after the war. In time, the Ferry Command pilots were flying not only across the North Atlantic but also down through South America and across the South Atlantic to Africa, the Middle East and India. Flying west, they would cross the South Pacific to Singapore and Sydney. Back in the Piccadilly Lounge of the Mount Royal Hotel, these routes made for ever more colourful tales to recount, including adventures in exotic places like Madame Zee Zee's house of pleasure in Belém, Brazil.

In the months before the ferry service's first flight across the ocean, England had endured the ferocious bombing of London by the Germans, and in the Battle of Britain the Royal Air Force had lost some nine hundred planes. More aircraft were desperately needed, with Britain standing alone in Europe against the Germans. A few days before the departure of the first Hudson bombers from St. Hubert Airport, Lord Beaverbrook, Britain's minister of aircraft production, sent a telegram to ferry headquarters in Montreal in which he said, "Day to day we stand at our sentinel posts. . . . The enemy may still invade. . . . We have asked you for much, but we must ask for more. We will fight with pikes if we need, but we hope for guns and aircraft and ships and tanks."

Those guns, aircraft, ships and tanks would be forthcoming from Montreal factories in great numbers. The city would become Canada's biggest arsenal, and providing arms and ammunition would be its greatest contribution to the winning of the war. By 1941, the retooling of industry for war production was almost complete, and on May 22 of that year the first tank rolled off the assembly line at the Angus Shops, in the east end. With workmen and dignitaries assembled outside the shop doors, the twenty-five-ton Valentine tank lumbered out, the khaki paint still sticky on its flanks, to be officially handed over to C.D. Howe, the minister of munitions and supply.

For the previous sixty years, the Angus Shops had been making and repairing locomotives and cars for the Canadian Pacific Railway; now, during the war, it would turn out 1,420 tanks, which would see battle on fronts from North Africa to Russia. While the Angus Shops were producing their Valentines, the Montreal Locomotive Works was making medium-sized Ram tanks, as well as huge engines for ships of the Royal Canadian Navy. Nearby, on the river, at the Vickers shipyards, they were building dozens of frigates, corvettes and minesweepers for the navy, as well as freighters for the merchant marine. At United Shipyards Limited, landing craft for the invasion of Europe were being built, as well as scores of ten-thousand-ton freighters, some of them completed in thirty-eight days from the laying of the keel to the launching. Tugs, diesel barges and ammunition lighters came from Montreal Drydocks Limited.

"Brave men shall not die because I faltered," said an advertisement placed in the *Gazette* in January 1942 by the Department of Munitions and Supply. "Are you devoting your time and your talents," the ad asked, "your strength and your very life to the production of the thousand and one things so urgently needed to carry this desperate struggle to a successful conclusion?" Fortunately Montreal could muster the largest supply of labour of any manufacturing city in Canada, so the production of those thousand and one things proceeded at an ever-increasing pace. By early 1943, there were some nine thousand people working at the plants of Defence Industries Limited, producing ammunition for rifles, Bren guns and machine guns for fighter planes. Thousands more workers were employed at Dominion Textiles making camouflage cloth, gas-mask cloth, fabrics for uniforms, canvas for army tents and cloth for surgical dressings.

Montreal was the centre of Canadian aircraft production. At Canadian Car and Foundry they were making not only large-calibre shells but also airplane propellers and wings for Ansons and Hurricanes. Across the river, in Longueuil, seven thousand employees at Fairchild Aircraft were turning out Bristol Bombers and Cornells, as well as Helldivers for the American forces. Down the road, at Pratt and Whitney, they were making engines for aircraft ranging from Harvard trainers to Catalina flying boats. Noorduyn Aircraft, in business for only four years before the war, was, by 1943, completing more than three planes a day. It had twelve thousand workers in five factories making Harvard trainers, Mosquito

fighter-bombers and the renowned Noorduyn Norseman, the bush
pilot's favourite freighter, which Bob Noorduyn said he designed on
the back of an envelope.

This concentration of war industry in Montreal led to fears that
the city might some day be a target for German bombers. The Ferry
Command had demonstrated that flying the Atlantic was feasible,
and so German Heinkel 177s could easily reach Canada, via Norway
and Greenland. After dropping their bombs, the Germans would not
have enough fuel to return home, so they would land their planes
and surrender, ready to become prisoners of war.

In Montreal, the citizenry was urged to prepare for air raids. Every
household was advised to prepare a shelter in the basement, complete with first aid kit. Owners of apartment buildings were told to
create communal shelters. By the beginning of 1941, the Civilian
Protection Committee had signed up almost fifteen thousand volunteer wardens. Their leader, Charles Barnes, said they would be
involved in much more than just air-raid precautions. Patrolling the
streets in civilian clothes, unnoticed by the populace, they would
constantly be on the lookout for spies and saboteurs. They would be
watching for sabotage, Barnes said, "at its germinating point – in a
pool room, around a tavern table, in a plant where a seemingly care-
less worker is doing a lot of damage."

One defence against air raids that was kept secret from
Montrealers was installed in the third sub-basement of the massive
Sun Life Building downtown. Here 850 steel railway rails were put
in as beams to reinforce the walls, making this big chamber indestructible in any onslaught from the air. Winston Churchill had
decided that if the Germans overran Britain, the wealth of the
country must not fall into their hands but must be preserved to
finance the war from abroad. Thus the British treasury's great store
of gold and its paper securities were shipped across the ocean to
Canada, the gold going into the vaults of the Bank of Canada in
Ottawa and the paper into the Sun Life's basement in Montreal.
These securities were in nine hundred large cabinets which were
guarded by the RCMP, around the clock, until the end of the war. The

hundreds of people working in the building above had no idea of the gigantic treasure that lay beneath their feet.

The bombers might well come at night, and so in June 1941 the city prepared for its first blackout. At 10:20 p.m. on June 9, sirens would sound the alert. All streetcars would stop in their tracks and put out their lights. All trucks, cars and motorcycles would pull over to the curb and put out their lights. Horse-drawn vehicles would do the same, with their drivers being asked to stand at the horse's head throughout the blackout. All lights outside dwellings, stores and buildings of every kind would be extinguished and inside lights would also go out, or windows would be heavily curtained. People on the street would refrain from lighting cigarettes. And, of course, the lights on the big cross on top of Mount Royal, which would make a splendid beacon for German bombers, would be switched off for the first time in living memory.

This first blackout, which lasted only fifteen minutes, was deemed to be an almost total success, although a few lights here and there stubbornly stayed on. A crowd on St. Catherine Street, angered by lights in a men's clothing store, smashed the plate-glass window to turn them off. In its blackness, the city was an eerie place, with a ghostly, silver glow arising from streetcar tracks that reflected the moonlight. On the streets, people spoke in hushed tones, and the city had never been so strangely silent. When a young girl started laughing hysterically on a downtown street, voices from the darkness barked at her to shut up. In subsequent blackouts, air-raid wardens patrolling the streets took note of lights that persisted in a few windows, and in court the culprits were duly fined ten dollars.

For the city's children, the prospect of an air raid was always exciting, especially the one they knew was coming on Saturday, November 15, 1941. All eyes were on the sky that afternoon as eight bombers of the Royal Canadian Air Force came over the city, on schedule, dropping clouds of leaflets that urged people to buy War Savings Bonds, to finance the war effort. As the leaflets rained down onto the streets, children – and many adults – scrambled for them, often dodging perilously through traffic. Everybody hoped to scoop up one of the "lucky bombs," one of the few leaflets that bore a red star, which meant it could be exchanged for a four-dollar certificate.

Bombers flying out of Dorval, on the ferry route to England, were a common sight in the sky over Montreal, but on the morning of April 24, 1944, a Royal Air Force Liberator coming over Mount Royal attracted particular attention. Office workers downtown saw it losing altitude and watched in horror as it came roaring down over Peel Street, sinking ever lower and heading for the river. It narrowly missed the roof of the Bonaventure railway station, seemed to brush a wingtip against the giant chimney of the Dow Brewery, and finally crashed and burst into flames in the heart of Griffintown. Ten residents of this working-class district were immediately killed, as was the aircraft's crew of five. The leaping flames, the smouldering buildings flattened by the crash and the cries of people trapped in the ruins gave Montreal a small taste – its only taste – of the devastation that was commonplace in many of the war-torn cities of Europe.

Because of the war, there would henceforth be no icing on any cakes made by commercial bakeries, except for wedding cakes, and no dusting of sugar on cookies. The decree came from S.R. Noble, sugar controller for the Wartime Prices and Trade Board. It was another of the many edicts issued by the board in its effort to conserve scarce commodities. No detail seemed too obscure to escape government regulation. Even milk-bottle caps, those humble bits of cardboard, were subject to decree. In Montreal, the Guaranteed Pure Milk Company reluctantly had to dispense with the little paper collars that it proudly put on bottles of its premium Golden Jersey milk ("from prize Jersey herds, on selected farms"). In effect, the authorities said, these ornamental collars constituted a "double cap," and as of March 1942, only single caps were permitted.

To save cloth, there were stringent regulations for the design of clothing. Men's suits could no longer have cuffs, patch pockets or vests. Women's skirts, for a size sixteen, could not be longer than thirty inches, including hem and waistband. These rules applied not only to factory-made clothes but also to a dress a woman might be making at home, for herself. If she put more than nine buttons on it, she would be breaking the law. But the decree that caused most concern dealt with gasoline. Drivers had been paying little heed to pleas for restraint in the use of their cars, and so, on April 1, 1942, gasoline became the first commodity for which ration coupons were issued. Drivers of "non-essential" cars would get coupons allowing them to buy enough gasoline to drive about one hundred miles a week, while drivers who used their cars for business would get considerably more coupons. But it was not long before counterfeit ration coupons became available, and, despite the fact that oil tankers heading for Canada kept on being torpedoed, motorists who were prepared to break the law found it relatively easy to get extra fuel.

In 1942 housewives also acquired ration books, which were now required for the purchase of tea, coffee, sugar, butter and meat. There was a ration book for every member of the family, and in households like that of Georgette Bleau there was even internal rationing, with each of the children having a personal sugar bowl with his or her name on it. At the end of the week, if any bits of sugar were left over they went into a common pot, for the baking of a cake. Montreal traditionally had a massive sweet tooth, and the rationing of sugar, jam, honey and molasses was bothersome to many.

Others were unhappy about the fact that only two pounds of meat was being allowed, per person per week. But generally speaking the quantities of food available were adequate, and for housewives the highly complex rationing system was more of a nuisance than a hardship. And if there were shortages of some provisions, at least prices were reasonably stable. One of the main concerns of the Wartime Prices and Trade Board was to prevent inflation, and in this it was largely successful, constantly laying charges against violators of its edicts. In a typical day in Judge C.E. Guerin's court, he levied fines on three merchants, one for charging too much for onions, another for bananas and another for cooked ham.

The WPTB was less successful in controlling rents, with unscrupu-lous landlords finding many ways to get around the regulations. A young woman working downtown as a stenographer for sixty dollars a month might have to pay almost half of that amount to rent a small room in a building where she would have to share the bath-room, down the hall, with a dozen other people and where she would have to dry her washing on the radiator. The housing shortage in Montreal was acute all through the war years. There had been vir-tually no low-cost housing built during the 1930s, the Depression years, and now, with building materials under strict control, there was again almost no construction of new housing. At the same time, wartime industries were bringing ever more people to work in the city, from the countryside and small towns. In the spring of 1942, the City Improvement League declared that there was an urgent need for at least fifty-one thousand new dwellings for working people. In Ville St. Laurent, Wartime Housing Limited managed to put up four hundred units of "emergency housing" for workers in the expanded Canadair factory, but as far as the overall shortage was concerned, that was merely a drop in the bucket.

There was no equivalent housing offered to employees of the Canadian Car and Foundry Company, two of whose factory workers shared a dwelling on St. Antoine Street. This was in an old aban-doned store, and the men lived there with their wives and children – thirteen people in a single room, with three cats to protect them against rats. There was no bath, and people passing by on the street saw grubby children sitting in the storefront window, "as if they were for sale," as one observer noted. There were many families living in abandoned stores, and others in disused garages, ware-houses and sheds. In suburban Ahuntsic, Elzear Touchette lived with his wife and eleven children in a one-room tarpaper shack that had once been a pigsty. Because the room was so crowded, their three chickens were imprisoned in a cage that hung from the ceiling, over the table.

To alleviate the housing shortage, people who had spare rooms in their houses were urged to rent them to workers who needed them.

Government ads in newspapers declared that it was unpatriotic to have an empty bedroom in your house. But the campaign had a limited success. A registry set up on Park Avenue to match up would-be renters with would-be tenants managed, in its first month of operation, to find shelter for only one applicant in ten. Middle-class patriots, in big houses, might hesitantly tolerate a neat, single girl who worked in an office, but a grimy welder from a factory, with his brood of kiddies, was another matter entirely.

For the great majority of Montrealers, who had comfortable places to live, the war years were the best years they'd known for a long while, so much better than the thin times of the 1930s. Everybody now seemed to have a job, and there was plenty of money in circulation. Servicemen coming back from England, where they had seen the effects of the bombing and the really severe rationing, were struck by the feeling of peace in Montreal and the lavish displays in store windows. Summertime tourists from the United States were still coming in large numbers and were finding plenty of Indian moccasins to buy in the souvenir shops. In 1944, Canada Steamship Lines reported a record number of bookings for its six-day cruises down the St. Lawrence to the Saguenay. Passengers were probably not informed that a few freighters had been torpedoed by German submarines out in the Gulf of St. Lawrence.

Writing in *Maclean's*, Jim Coleman expressed wonderment at the amount of night-clubbing and boozing he found in wartime Montreal. "Night life in the Paris of America is booming like Big Ben on Armistice Day," he wrote. "From dusk until the milkman starts on his morning rounds the town sputters and fizzes like a Roman candle. Tired businessmen, expatriates who have fled briefly from the more arid sections of the country, money-heavy war-workers and young men and women of the armed services keep the merry wheels spinning. . . . Montreal is a bountiful oasis in a land of rationing. Demon rum may be rationed in other sections of the country, but there is enough medicinal spirits in Montreal to float the entire Atlantic Fleet up St. Catherine Street." Coleman was also highly appreciative of the fare being offered by the city's better restaurants, where there was no shortage of gourmet delights. At Café Martin, he noted, the supply of caviar was holding up well, and other items to tempt the diner included frog's legs meunière and unexcelled crêpes suzettes.

Life was also good for young people growing up in the city's residential areas, teenagers not yet ready for the downtown nightclubs and caviar. Instead they congregated in soda fountains and restaurants like the Prince of Wales in Verdun and Ma Heller's in Notre Dame de Grâce. The scene at places like these is described by Mary Peate in her excellent book about growing up in wartime Montreal, *Girl in a Sloppy Joe Sweater*. "It was the same situation at Heller's," she writes. "A boy would come in regularly for years and would perhaps miss a few days, then reappear dressed in Navy uniform. He would self-consciously remove his cap to reveal his white-walled head [a regulation brushcut] and suffer the good-natured kidding, then wouldn't come in anymore. It was noticeable in movie theatres, streetcars, offices, stores, and on the street too – the dearth of young men." When her own boyfriend left to serve in the air force, Mary Peate says that all the songs on the hit parade took on a new significance for her. "Their titles," she writes, "succinctly summed up wartime social life: *They're Either Too Young or Too Old* . . . so . . . *I Don't Get Around Much Anymore* . . . and that's why . . . *Saturday Night is the Loneliest Night of the Week* . . . and . . . *I'm a Little on the Lonely Side* . . . because . . . *There's No Love, No Nothin' Until My Baby Comes Home*."

Largely deprived of male companionship, Mary and her three girl-friends, nicknamed Cath, Mitt and Wooly, would gather at Wooly's apartment for what they called "hen parties." Here they would practice up on their smoking techniques, trying, between coughs, to appear as sophisticated with their cigarettes as Bette Davis ("waving her cigarette haughtily for emphasis") and Lauren Bacall. And, of course, they discussed the boys who made unavailing demands for sexual favours. "The other night he asked me to do it," Mitt announced one day, speaking about Kenny, a boy she had been seeing. "He said it was my patriotic duty since he was risking his life for me by joining the Navy." But, Mitt indignantly told her friends, Kenny was only stationed downtown, at the barracks on Drummond Street. Yes, Wooly pointed out, but this brave sailor *could* get hit by a streetcar on his way downtown.

In the 1940s, in Montreal, almost all middle-class teenage girls were determinedly virginal, but Mary Peate and her friends were not prudes. In the crowded ski trains coming back from the Laurentians, they happily joined in the raunchy singsongs that featured traditional ditties like "Roll Me Over, Lay Me Down and Do it Again" and "Today Is the Day We Give Babies Away." The war years were the heyday of the singsong, and people at parties would inevitably gather around the piano to sing. Young men joining the army or the navy quickly learned a host of traditional ballads, to be sung while marching or with a bottle of beer in the canteen. In the navy, "The North Atlantic Squadron" was a favourite:

Away, away with fife and drum,
Here we come, full of rum,
Looking for women who peddle their bum
In the North Atlantic Squadron.

The song went on for innumerable verses, each more scurrilous than the last. The same was true of another ancient maritime favourite, "The Good Ship Venus":

We were the good ship Venus,
My God, you should have seen us,
The figurehead was a whore in bed,
The mast an upright penis.

Newer songs, devised for this particular war, breathed patriotic defiance, like this one, sung to the tune of "Colonel Bogey":

Hitler . . . has only got one ball.
Goering . . . has two, but they are small.

Himmler . . . has something sim'lar,
But poor old Goebbels
Has no balls at all.

≈

Although the good life was being lived in Montreal during the war, the city was far from indifferent to the momentous struggle that was going on in Europe. Families that had a son, a husband, a brother serving with the armed forces overseas read newspaper accounts of the fighting with particular anxiety. The official casualty lists published in the papers were scanned apprehensively, readers hoping that they wouldn't see a familiar name among those listed as killed in action, wounded or taken prisoner. The section listing men who had been wounded was particularly disturbing, being unaccountably subdivided into categories like "Dangerously Wounded," "Severely Wounded" and "Seriously Wounded."

Besides reading the newspapers, people listened to CBC war correspondents broadcasting from the war fronts via shortwave radio. For the first time, the actual sounds of battle could be heard in your living room. And there were graphic descriptions of the fighting, like the broadcast from Italy by Matthew Halton in December 1943, when the Canadian Army was attacking the German stronghold of Ortona. "Soaking wet, in a morass of mud," Halton said, "against an enemy fighting harder than he's fought before, the Canadians attack, attack, attack. The enemy is now fighting like the devil to hold us. He brings in more and more guns, more and more troops. The hillsides and farmlands and orchards are a ghastly brew of fire. . . . Sometimes a battlefield looks like a film of a battlefield, but not this. It's too grim."

Another famous war correspondent, Ross Munro, had come to Montreal the year before, in September 1942, to speak to a mass meeting in the Forum, where he gave an eyewitness account of the raid on Dieppe. That raid, which had taken place two weeks earlier, had taken almost five thousand Canadian soldiers from their bases in

England across to the shores of France, the first such large-scale operation of the war. After a fierce battle on the beaches of Dieppe, the
Canadian force – what was left of it – returned the same day to
England. In his account of the raid, before an audience of ten thousand in the Forum, Ross Munro stressed the heroism of the Montreal
soldiers who had fought at Dieppe. He did not say that the raid
had been a disaster, and would come to be known as one of the
war's greatest follies, basically a public relations exercise planned
by incompetent and irresponsible generals. In the action, 907
Canadians had been killed and many more seriously wounded, with
1,946 being taken prisoner.

No one was braver at Dieppe than the men of Les Fusiliers Mont-
Royal, Munro told his audience. He had particular praise for their
commander, the twenty-nine-year-old Lieutenant-Colonel Dollard
Ménard, who led the regiment ashore and up the beach toward its
objective, a concrete pillbox atop a twelve-foot parapet. They were
met by murderous German fire, and Ménard was wounded five times
before he was evacuated to a boat heading back to England. Two
months later, brilliant klieg lights illuminated the old Bonaventure
railway station, on St. James Street, as families and friends awaited
the hospital train bringing home the first group of men who had been
wounded at Dieppe. Volunteer women went aboard the train to serve
the men coffee and doughnuts and were dismayed to find that some
of the disfigured men were too sick to eat. Those who were willing
to talk about the raid were unanimous in saying that for the Germans
the action was not the surprise it was supposed to have been. The
Germans had known the raiders were coming and had been waiting
for them, in great numbers.

In November 1942, Montreal welcomed a hometown boy who
was Canada's most famous war hero, Pilot Officer George Beurling,
fondly known to the public as Buzz Beurling and to his mates in the
air force as Screwball. As a fighter pilot in Europe, he had shot
down twenty-nine German and Italian planes, more than any
other Canadian. When he arrived in a Liberator bomber to start a
tour of Canada, to promote the sale of war bonds, the slim, shy

twenty-year-old ace was greeted by Prime Minister Mackenzie King and top-ranking officers of the air force.

Beurling had made most of his kills in the sky over Malta, the strategic Mediterranean island that was a stepping stone between Europe and Africa. In a book that he later published, Beurling described Malta, as he found it on arrival there: "Bombs were liable to come whistling around your ears any minute. If you looked up you'd see Spits [Spitfires] and ME's [German fighters] split-assing all over the sky and every once in a while some poor devil who hadn't kept his tail clean would come spinning down in flames. Flak went up in flowerbeds and parachutes came drifting down. From the ground the constant din of ack-ack batteries. . . . Up high the clatter of machine-gun and cannon bursts and the roar of full-engined Spitfires, ME's and Macchis [Italian fighters] diving. . . . Erks [ground crew] scurrying about the drome, patching up bomb craters. . . . Engineers detonating time bombs. . . . Rescue launches rushing to sea to pick up floating parachutists. . . . The Maltese population trying to carry on the day's chores between headlong dives for shelter and protection. . . . Cats and dogs fighting in the streets in keeping with the tempo of the place . . . Never a dull moment, day or night."

Beurling threw himself into this melee with gusto, displaying unsurpassed skill with his Spitfire and his guns. On one occasion he managed to shoot down four enemy planes in a single day and was immediately awarded the Distinguished Flying Medal. Several other decorations followed, and by the time he came back to Montreal he was a legend. At the Auditorium in suburban Verdun, where he grew up, he was given an ovation by an adoring crowd. Asked whether he felt any sympathy for the fliers he shot down, he answered that he didn't. "You can't afford to," he said. "There's always someone sitting on your tail. The best way to go into a fight is hard-hearted." Later, addressing students at Verdun High School, where he had never managed to graduate, he went even further, describing the joy of the kill. He told how he had once decapitated an Italian pilot by raking his bullets across the edge of the enemy's cockpit. The

Italian's severed head rolled backwards along his plane's fuselage before dropping down into the sea. It left a trail of blood on the fuselage and, Beurling told the students, the red of the blood, on the white of the plane, made an inspiring sight against the bright blue Mediterranean sky.

After the war, Buzz Beurling, with few interests other than aerial combat, had great difficulty adjusting to civilian life. Finally, in the spring of 1948, there came an opportunity for him to resume his deadly craft: he signed up to fly for the fledgling Israeli Air Force, to fight against the Arab states in Israel's War of Independence. After several troubled years, his spirits were now rekindled as he took off from an airfield near Rome, piloting a small plane and heading for the Middle East. But the plane crashed soon after takeoff, for reasons never ascertained. Buzz Beurling had survived several crashes during the war, but this one killed him, at the age of twenty-six.

~

In 1942 and again in 1944, there was turmoil in Montreal over the issue of conscription. In 1939, on the eve of Canada's declaration of war, Prime Minister Mackenzie King had solemnly pledged that service in the armed forces would be on a purely voluntary basis. His government, he said, would never introduce conscription for overseas service. But after two years of war, although Canada's industrial mobilization had been phenomenal, the rate of enlistment in the services was falling off. The worst of the fighting in Europe still lay ahead and many more men might be needed. And so, in January 1942, King asked the people of Canada to release his government from its no-conscription pledge. There would be a plebiscite in April, when the country would vote on the issue. In words destined to become part of the national folklore, King said that if Canada voted Yes in the plebiscite it would mean "not necessarily conscription, but conscription if necessary."

In Quebec, Ottawa's careful ambiguity failed to have the desired effect. Reaction to the plebiscite plan was immediate and furious. Although French Canadian nationalists knew they would be able to muster a No majority in Quebec, they were equally sure that the rest of Canada, under the spell of Toronto's Committee for Total War, would vote Yes. Conscription would surely come in, and the Mounties would surely descend on Quebec farms, to drag young men away from the plough and ship them off to die on foreign shores. The anti-conscriptionists quickly came up with a song to bolster their cause. It was to be sung to the tune of "God Save the King" and, translated into English, one verse asked:

Why does England
Which is but our stepmother
Wish to have our boys
As cannon-fodder?

To rally support for the No side in the plebiscite, the nationalists quickly formed La Ligue pour la Défense du Canada, its name an assertion of the idea that French Canadians would fight bravely, but only on Canadian soil, if Canada were attacked. Three weeks after the plebiscite was announced, La Ligue held its first mass meeting in the hall of St. James Market, in the east end. The hall was quickly filled and on the street outside hundreds listened to the speeches on loudspeakers. One after another, leading Quebec nationalists mounted the podium to denounce conscription, among them the venerable and revered Henri Bourassa, who predicted that within ten years Canada would be annexed by the United States. The young Jean Drapeau, who would one day be mayor of Montreal, was master of ceremonies at the rally, and in his speech he bitterly attacked foreign domination of French Canadians. He pointed out the irony of the fact that the hall where they were meeting was located on Amherst Street, named after Lord Jeffrey Amherst, who had led the conquering British army into Montreal in 1760.

The fiery oratory, pouring out of the loudspeakers onto Amherst Street, quickly inflamed the overflow crowd, now grown to an estimated thousand people, most of them students looking for a fight. Before long they were stopping streetcars, smashing windows and attacking the few soldiers who were on hand. The police were out in force, but they couldn't stop the rioters, who surged down St. Catherine Street, hurling stones and breaking glass. They rushed into taverns, overturning tables and spilling beer, and they even broke into a brothel on Ontario Street, rousting indignant clients in mid-copulation. The police finally put an end to the frenzy by charging into the crowd on motorcycles. Eighteen of the rioters were arrested and five policemen were taken to hospital.

In the plebiscite, the vote in Montreal was clearly split along linguistic lines, with French ridings like Mercier and Hochelaga voting overwhelmingly No and English ridings like St. Antoine-Westmount and St. Lawrence-St. George voting solidly Yes. In effect, the east end of the city was against conscription and the west end was for it. Quebec as a whole voted 73 percent No, but the rest of Canada voted 80 percent Yes, giving Mackenzie King a clear mandate to conscript young men for overseas service. But he refrained from doing this for more than two years, and conscripts, contemptuously called Zombies, were required to serve only in Canada. In 1944, however, after the Allies invaded France, Canadian casualties mounted quickly and the generals started making urgent requests for reinforcements. In November of that year, after much dissension in the federal cabinet, an order-in-council finally decreed that sixteen thousand Zombies were to be sent overseas. Again in Montreal there was rioting, this time the mob storming down toward St. James and St. Antoine streets, intent on breaking into the offices of the English newspapers. But a large phalanx of policemen blocked the marchers' way, and they had to content themselves with smashing the windows of Le Canada, the morning daily that supported the Liberal Party.

Also in 1944, Montreal saw civil disorder with a different flavour – the zoot-suit riots, where servicemen, mostly sailors, battled in the streets with youths whose clothing they found offensive. The jacket of the zoot suit, inspired by some jazz musicians, had grotesquely wide, padded shoulders and hung down almost to the knees; the baggy pants, which came up well above the waist, almost to the armpit, were extra wide at the knee and tapered to a tight, narrow cuff. Accessories included flashy neckties and heavy key chains that hung down from the belt to the knee. It was, in the hep-talk of the time, "the drape shape with the reet pleat and the stuff cuff."

Men in uniform considered the zoot suit an affront, particularly when the long-haired civilian youths wearing it taunted the servicemen and called them "suckers." On a hot Saturday night in June, the animosity boiled over into riot. At the Verdun Pavilion, a dance hall, sailors who were barred from entry used benches from the nearby boardwalk to batter down the doors. They were looking for zoot suiters and they found them cowering inside, some of them having climbed up into the rafters to escape a beating. The navy came after them, stripped their extravagant clothes off their backs and chased them naked down Wellington Street. On the same night there was a pitched battle between soldiers and civilians in Lafontaine Park, and on St. Catherine Street east of Bleury some four hundred sailors roamed the area, looking for zoot suiters in restaurants and taverns. When they found them, hiding under tables, they hauled them out into the street to be beaten. There were affrays in other parts of the city, and on the South Shore, with many injuries to sailors, civilians and the police who were trying to keep them apart.

The zoot suit was definitely illegal, its grotesque dimensions calling for the use of far too much fabric. In the wake of the riots, the Wartime Prices and Trade Board issued a stern warning to tailors, reminding them of the permissible lengths and widths of men's clothing and stipulating that suits "shall have no belt, bi-swings or pleated backs; shall have no vents either at the back or the sides, no buttons on the sleeves." One tailor was soon fined four hundred dollars for making a zoot suit, and others trembled in fear lest the youths who were being arrested tell the police where they had bought their drape shapes.

In Ottawa, the events in Montreal were causing concern, and questions were being asked in Parliament. Responding to them, the minister of justice, Louis St. Laurent, said that there did not seem to be any sinister significance to the riots and they were not the result of any racial animosities. Instead, he said, they seemed to be "simply spasmodic outbreaks between people who do not agree." One analyst supported the justice minister's theory by pointing out that sailors' pants flared out widely at the bottom of the leg – bell-bottoms – whereas zoot-suit trousers were the opposite – "peg-tops" that tapered in to hug the ankle; this difference, he said, was enough to start red-blooded boys punching each other. But another observer had a more convincing theory: it had all started at a dance, he said, when a zoot-suiter stole away a sailor's girl.

Besides fighting between servicemen and civilians, scrapping between members of the three branches of the armed forces was not unknown. A prominent venue for this was the Music Box, a bar in the basement of the Mount Royal Hotel, where soldiers, sailors and airmen could find lots of girls to dance with – and quarrel over. Don McVicar, in his book *Ferry Command*, describes the scene in the Music Box when he visited it one evening: "Just then the shouts and oaths drowned out the music. A violent disturbance had broken out. The Air Force had decided to exchange blows with their mortal enemy, the Navy, who were responding vigorously. Soon the Army decided this was too good to miss, and the melee became general. Most of the girls tried to get out of harm's way, but a few remained, screaming encouragement to their favourite warriors. Tables and chairs went flying. A few unlucky combatants were lying on the floor."

As Marguerite Preston saw it, apathy was the problem. Montrealers simply weren't involved enough in the war, they weren't doing enough to hasten victory. After brooding about this for several days, she decided to do something about it. She went downtown to Phillips Square one evening, with a box to stand on, and launched into a patriotic speech. She was a twenty-five-year-old stenographer with intense dark eyes, and she had no trouble attracting a crowd of passersby, who stopped to listen patiently as she lashed out at them for their inertia in comfortable Montreal while soldiers were risking their lives overseas. The applause as she finished her discourse encouraged her to come back the following night. On the third night the police arrived to arrest her for disturbing the peace. In court, Judge Aimé Leblanc was lenient. He fined Marguerite $3.50, to cover court costs, and warned her never again to address street crowds without a permit. English Montreal was outraged that a fine, however small, had been imposed on a young patriot who had the courage to speak out. It was the same token penalty that had been imposed, two weeks earlier, on each of fifteen French Canadian youths who had been arrested for rioting in the streets, breaking windows and shouting anti-British slogans.

If Marguerite Preston thought Montrealers were apathetic about the war, she could not have been familiar with the activities of many young women living in the west end, like Barbara Whitley, who was a volunteer with the Red Cross. As such she marched up and down in a drill hall on Monday nights, took home-nursing classes, served as an air-raid warden during blackouts, worked in blood donor clinics, administered first aid in mock disaster drills, worked in an information centre for troops, encouraged shy soldiers to dance at parties, and acted, sang and danced in theatrical benefits for causes like Aid to Russia. Other Red Cross volunteers worked in a plant in Ville LaSalle, packing food parcels for prisoners of war. The Civilian Protection Committee enlisted women to help police and firemen in emergencies, and all over town women in church groups sat by the hour knitting socks and sweaters to send to soldiers.

The most active volunteers were usually women from affluent families, daughters who didn't have to work for a living and wives who had maids to do the housework. The war gave a new dimension to their social life, with more reasons than ever to get together and more parties than ever – all in a good cause. But here on the home front, where everyone was being officially urged to "pull together," there was little blurring of Montreal's well-defined social barriers. In their sincere efforts to help win the war, the French and the English were not being brought any closer together and neither were the blue-blooded rich and the not-so-rich. Irene Kon, working in the

University Tower Building, felt these divisions keenly. She tried to organize the various offices in the building for war work – collecting salvageable silver paper from cigarette packages, knitting, sending cig-arettes to troops overseas – but she found that the bosses didn't want to work with the secretaries and the secretaries didn't want to work with the file clerks. In the 1930s Irene had been an organizer of groups to support left-wing causes, but now, in her office building, she had no success in her efforts to organize discussion groups about the war effort. Non-Marxists, she found, had little appetite for serious palaver.

The biggest contribution to the war effort made by Montreal women was their work in factories, helping make guns and ammu-nition, ships and planes. By the thousands they responded to urgent appeals from industries that wanted to train them as riveters, welders and handlers of high explosives. In the fall of 1944, when the tempo of fighting in Europe was increasing, the government's industrial recruiting service called for more and more women to fill shells for the artillery. In advertisements it reassured the ladies that making these deadly missiles, in the factory, was "actually safer than working in your own home." It was an era when a woman's place was thought to be in the home, but now, in movie theatres, newsreels showed earnest women of all ages, their hair swept up in kerchiefs, hunched over the most complex industrial tasks. "Joan Canuck has forsaken *Vogue* and *Vanity Fair* for blueprints and construction plants," the booming voice of the newsreel narrator intoned. "When victory is won, a great share of the credit will be due to our fair Amazons in overalls."

Meanwhile, housewives were busy responding to the demands of frequent "salvage drives." Household waste of every kind was wanted to help feed the war machine. Old pots and pans could be melted down to make tanks and guns. Old newspapers could be used for packing shells. Old bones could be turned into the glue that was used in the making of airplanes. Even bones that had been chewed by the dog were wanted. On one Saturday in 1941, Boy Scouts visited fifty thousand homes and collected two hundred tons of scrap. Anyone buying a tube of toothpaste or shaving cream was asked to return an empty tube at the drugstore. In January 1944, the Used

Goods Administration announced that in the previous seventeen months empty tubes turned in by Montrealers had helped build engines for 845 bombers. Old fur coats were also in demand, to make vests for merchant seamen shivering on the decks of their ships in the frigid North Atlantic, and women brought their cast-off minks and moutons to the Navy League headquarters on Closse Street. Rubber was particularly valuable. In 1942, after the Japanese had overrun much of Southeast Asia, the source of most of Canada's rubber supply, it became illegal to destroy anything made of rubber, from tires to hot-water bottles. Prolonging the life of rubber household articles was "every woman's patriotic duty," according to an article in the *Gazette*. It went on with lengthy instructions on how to properly dry raincoats and where to store galoshes (avoid bright sunlight).

"*De la poêle à frire jusqu'à la ligne de feu*" – "from the frying pan to the firing line" – a government newspaper ad proclaimed. It showed a huge frying pan being emptied over a German submarine. The fat dripping from the pan was, in mid-air, turning into bombs that were wreaking havoc on the submarine. It was a plea to housewives to save their used cooking fat, which could be turned into glycerine for the making of high explosives. "Imagine the satisfaction it would give you," said another ad, "to pour that hot fat right down the back of Adolf, Tojo or Benito."

Much of the advertising urging Montreal housewives on to greater efforts to help win the war was being placed by large corporations, but as 1944 progressed they realized that women were becoming tired of the endless exhortations to scrimp and save in the kitchen, to scour the cellar for bits of old metal. It now looked as though the war was finally being won, and it was time to take a new tack. The ladies should be cheered up by promises of a better life to come, when the bullets stopped flying. "*Nous faisons des plans pour la cuisine de vos rêves*" – "We are making plans for the kitchen of your dreams" – said a large ad from General Steel Wares Limited. It announced that even while inventing things like better filters for gas masks, GSW technicians could not keep themselves from dreaming of the appliances they would be perfecting for the post-war kitchen, as soon as industry was allowed to produce things other than armaments. The GSW ad showed a happy housewife putting her kettle on a futuristic-looking stove.

A Canadian General Electric ad showed a draftsman at his drawing board and promised new automobiles, new streetcars, new buses, new parks, new arenas, new swimming pools, and a host of other new items. A Royal Bank ad was more personal. It showed an optimistic couple staring into the distance. "He wants a new car," the ad said. "She dreams of real nylon stockings." The ad assured readers they would have these things. With the return of nylon, women who wanted to appear fashionable would no longer have to paint their legs and then draw a line up the back, with an eyebrow pencil, to look like a seam. To pay for all the good things that were going to become available after the war, Montrealers were salting away a substantial part of their earnings. They bought government bonds in great quantities, encouraged by Victory Loan parades, rallies and pep talks by visiting Hollywood celebrities, like Westmount's own Norma Shearer. In the Seventh Victory Loan, in November 1944, Montreal continued to help finance the war effort by buying bonds worth some $300,000,000.

Now, as the Allies chased the retreating German army back to its own frontiers, each week brought new evidence that the war, on the home front at least, was winding down. In October, the bright lights had been allowed to come on again downtown, putting an end to two years of energy conservation and dim-out. Garish neon signs started blinking again outside cabarets and theatres; store windows were flooded with light. St. Catherine Street was becoming her old self, and people paraded up and down to enjoy the spectacle. In November, McGill announced special classes for war veterans, to prepare them for regular university courses. In December, the Aluminum Company of Canada announced that after it converted to peacetime production, it hoped to have jobs for three times as many people as it had employed before the war.

As 1945 got under way, more trains were arriving from Halifax with returning soldiers, some of them having been overseas for more than five years. Many Canadian soldiers had married women in

Britain and Holland, and there were special trains bringing these war brides and their babies to their new homes, trains that gave off a distinctive aroma of oranges and wet diapers. Bonaventure Station was draped in flags, and bands played as happy families and friends greeted the Halifax trains, but the newspaper reports of these scenes only intensified the grief of many who read them. So many husbands, sons, fathers, brothers would never be coming back.

By the end of April it was obvious that Germany had been defeated and victory was at hand. At 9:35 a.m., on May 7, radio station CKAC was the first to break the news: Germany had signed an unconditional surrender. The war in Europe was over. The news went up on the big bulletin board outside the *Montreal Star* offices on St. James Street, in the heart of the financial district, and within minutes stockbrokers and stenographers were running out of their offices to read it. Streetcars coming down the street stopped in front of the bulletin board and passengers jumped out to stare at it. By now horns and whistles could be heard from ships in the harbour, and sirens were sounding. The financial district erupted. From windows high above, ticker tape showered down into the canyon of St. James Street, onto singing, cheering crowds. All work came to an end and people hurried out to the street to join the surging mob. But here and there a few people stood in doorways, silently watching and weeping.

Uptown, stores, offices and schools closed for the day, and thousands headed for the corner of Peel and St. Catherine Streets, the focal point of the pandemonium. The crowds there, and in other parts of the city, were so thick that cars could barely get through. People were waving flags, marching, shouting, dancing and kissing one another. Through it all, thirty squads of the Quebec Liquor Police moved discreetly, making sure that all bars and taverns were closed, and that no restaurants were serving alcohol. Premier Duplessis had decreed that booze must stop flowing the minute the anticipated news came from General Eisenhower's headquarters in Europe; with artificial stimulation, the premier felt, the victory frenzy might get out of hand.

One sober note in the midst of the celebrations was a sign outside an army recruiting depot that said, "Open for business – with

Japan." Germany had been defeated, but war in the Far East was still going on, and it was destined to continue for another three months. But for Montrealers, for all intents and purposes, the war was over. A new era was beginning. A city grown shabby during the Depression and the war years could at last be refurbished. At home, what was rusty and rickety could at last be replaced – soon, it was hoped – with items new and shiny. There would be new furniture, new bicycles for the children and, above all, a new car to replace the current wreck. As always, the kitchen was the symbolic centre of the fondest hopes. The lady of the house desperately wanted a gleaming white electric refrigerator to replace the gloomy wooden ice-box, a stove where all the burners worked, and crisp new aluminum pots and pans to replace the tired, dented relics in use for so long. As it turned out, she didn't have too long to wait. The wartime factories quickly changed gears, beating swords into ploughshares, and by 1948 the National Film Board could produce a documentary asserting that post-war dreams were being realized. The film's joyous title was *Kitchen Come True*.

3
Wide-Open Town:
Girls, Gambling, Graft

In court, Barney Shulkin pleaded guilty. He always pleaded guilty. And, as always, the judge fined him one hundred dollars. Then Barney was free to go. Within the hour he would be back at the busy downtown gambling den where he had been arrested during the raid. Before making this supposedly surprise raid, the police, as usual, had phoned the establishment's proprietor, Harry Feldman, to warn him they were coming. Whereupon Feldman had sent Barney Shulkin upstairs to prepare to be arrested. Barney was a loyal employee whose duties included taking the rap for the boss, who himself was never arrested. Raids on Montreal's many illegal gambling houses, carried out by the well-bribed police, were an elaborate charade, designed to persuade the public that something was being done to combat rampant vice in the city.

At the time – 1946 – Harry Feldman was operating his betting parlour in a commercial building on St. Catherine Street, near the corner of Bleury. Here he occupied the spacious second and third floors. The second floor, in a haze of cigarette and cigar smoke, was crowded with gamblers. It looked like a shabby brokerage office, with a big board stretching across the room, listing horse-racing data from tracks across North America. A row of telephones and a tele-type machine brought in race results from Santa Anita, Hialeah, Saratoga. And, of course, men with books stood by to take bets. All this was on the second floor. But when the police came lumbering up the stairs, they didn't bother looking in at the noisy action on the second floor. Instead they went straight up to the third, where the big room was silent and virtually empty, except for a few broken chairs and a dusty table with a telephone on it. The telephone, which was not connected, was important. It was there in case the police wanted to take it away, so they could write in their report that important gambling equipment had been seized.

And, of course, Barney Shulkin was there, patiently waiting to be arrested. The police would tell the judge that Barney was the proprietor of this den of iniquity. But first there was a door to be attended to. Along one wall, Harry Feldman had set up several dummy doors, giving the place the look of a stage set in a Feydeau farce. With due solemnity, a constable affixed a large black padlock to one of the doors. The raiding party had been ordered to shut down these premises, and now the police could state, truthfully, that they had affixed a padlock at 286 St. Catherine Street West. At this address, the stage-set doors constituted a more elaborate and fanciful facility than was to be found in most of the city's many other illegal premises. Usually the police simply put their padlock on the door to a cupboard, a broom closet or a toilet. The front door, on the street, always remained open to customers.

Having completed the padlock ceremony, the police then took Barney Shulkin into custody. The law stated that if an accused like Barney had been convicted twice in the past, he would have to go to jail the third time, not just pay a fine. Actually, this patient, amiable man had, over the years, been arrested an astonishing ninety-seven times – but he never went to jail once. He always pleaded guilty to the charge of operating a gaming house, and he was always quickly fined and released. The police never informed the various magistrates about prior convictions and the magistrates never asked. Each of Barney Shulkin's ninety-seven offences was treated as a first offence. It was all part of a time-honoured system.

The police raids on the Feldman premises came at irregular intervals, always with a warning first. But visits from "the collector" came punctually once a week. Harry Feldman would have an envelope ready for this man, with twenty-five or thirty dollars in it. At the end of the day, the collector would show up at Harry Davis's headquarters on Stanley Street with a large sheaf of envelopes, gathered from gambling establishments across the city. Davis was the underworld's "edge man," which meant that he was the person who distributed the graft to municipal officials and the police.

In a Canada where virtually all forms of gambling were forbidden, where there were no legal casinos or lotteries, Montreal was an oasis in the desert for men and women who wanted to try their luck. The map of the city was studded with establishments that offered horse betting, sports betting, roulette, blackjack, chemin de fer, baccarat, craps and, of course, barbotte, the hugely popular dice game unique to Montreal. There were all kinds of facilities to choose from. In the west end, Harry Ship's luxurious casino on Côte St. Luc Road offered good whiskey and filet mignon on the house, as well as six blackjack tables, two roulette wheels and two crap tables. Its patrons included politicians, lawyers and even judges. "Name me a prominent citizen who does *not* come here," Ship would boast. By contrast, in the east end, on Rachel Street, George Godin's more modest establishment was in the basement, an adjunct to his funeral parlour. To get to the action, patrons had to wend their way through the showroom, sometimes brushing shoulders with the bereaved, who would be selecting a coffin.

In addition to all this, illegal slot machines could be found all over town, as well as dozens of people prowling the streets with lottery tickets for sale. With its toleration of all these vices, as well as prostitution, Montreal was, as they used to say, a wide-open town, uniquely sinful in strait-laced Canada. In the mid-1940s, it was estimated that there were some two hundred major gambling establishments operating in the city and its suburbs. If each of them contributed twenty-five dollars to the edge man every week, that would mean five thousand dollars for regular payoffs to the police and civic officials. Five thousand 1945 dollars would have the same purchasing power as forty-eight thousand 1995 dollars, a respectable sum to be divided among officials awaiting their weekly payola. And fines like those imposed on Barney Shulkin provided the city's treasury with a substantial flow of income, in effect a sort of tax on illegal activities.

Income from gambling, however, was only part of the scheme.

There was also a substantial contribution coming in from the whore-houses, which existed in great numbers and great variety. For the wealthy, there were the chic uptown bordellos, like the one at 150 Milton Street, said to be frequented by government ministers. For the workingman, there were the shabby, budget-priced *lupanars* of De Bullion Street, where they occupied civic numbers 910, 912, 930, 934, 934A, 936, 948, 956, 958, 964, 966, 1016, 1020, 1020A, 1024, 1024A, 1025, 1027, 1028, 1029, 1033, 1034, 1040, 1044, 1045, 1046, 1047 and 1052. Those were only the brothels located on De Bullion south of Dorchester Street; there were many more on the same street going north, toward St. Catherine Street. And still more on neighbouring streets, all part of the red-light district.

While in the courthouse, taking the rap for his boss, Barney Shulkin might well run into Paulette Déry, whose job it was to render the same service for a whorehouse madam. Paulette was a *femme de paille*, a straw woman, who was arrested no fewer than eighty-five times, over the years, to *prendre le pinch* for her employer, Anna Beauchamp, one of the most celebrated brothel owners of the early 1940s. Mme Beauchamp was a familiar figure in the courthouse, invariably arriving in her chauffeur-driven Cadillac to pay Paulette Déry's fine and that of any other of her straw women who might have been arrested in her various bawdy houses. She owned at least sixteen of them on De Bullion Street, as well as four on Charlotte Street and four on Berger Street.

The flamboyant Mme Beauchamp would stride down the court-house corridors in her mink coat, swinging a large red handbag. She would stop to talk shop with other madams, there on similar missions, and to speak words of encouragement to her employees, while they were waiting to appear before a judge. "*Bonjour, ma petite Marcelle!*" she would exclaim. "*T'es-t-encore icitte à matin, toi?*" "Well, if it isn't Rita! Were you arrested last night? Don't worry, my little ones, I've come to look after everything." On those courthouse mornings, Mme Beauchamp would exchange jokes and gossip with many of the lawyers, clerks and judges that she met in the corridors. But her warmest greetings were reserved for certain police officers who happened by. These were the officers who were frequent guests at her elegant Sherbrooke Street residence, where, amid whiskey aplenty, they would carouse with some of her most attractive ladies of the night. On those evenings, the policemen would often consult Mme Beauchamp in drawing up the list of brothels to be raided during the coming month.

In Montreal there was a long tradition of amiable relations between prostitutes and the police. But no relationship was more amiable than that which existed in 1919 between Emma Boucher and Police Lieutenant Louis de Gonzague Savard. Emma was an important brothelkeeper, one of the *grosses madames*, and Louis was the head of the Morality Squad, the arm of the police that was charged with the suppression of prostitution. They became passionate lovers in an affair that could be the stuff of operatic tragedy. Their downfall was precipitated by a postcard that Emma, who was cheating on her husband, sent to Louis while she was on vacation. On the postcard she conveyed "*mille gros becs*" (a thousand big kisses) to her lover, plus "*un gros bec salé*" (a big salty kiss) and "*un gros bec sucré*" (a big sugary kiss). Unfortunately the postcard fell into the hands of the authorities and became part of the evidence that sent Lieutenant Savard to prison for three years.

But punishment for the police, for lapses of this sort, was extremely rare. Captains and constables alike felt no danger in being seen in public with purveyors of illicit sex. On Berger Street, on a Monday morning, passersby would find nothing peculiar in the sight of a uniformed policeman walking along beside a well-known madam and chatting animatedly with her. People would know that she had phoned the police station and had asked for protection from purse-snatchers as she took the heavy weekend receipts to the bank. In the courts and in newspapers, the euphemism for a whorehouse was "disorderly house," yet the proceedings in these places were generally quite orderly, even decorous, one might say. Customers generally came to assuage an urgent need and not to cause trouble. But sometimes too much booze was involved and fights broke out. In these instances, or when a prostitute was being treated too roughly, the madam would not hesitate to call the police to come and quell the disturbance. As soon as the call came over the police radio, several cars would often race to the scene as fast as they could, the officers knowing that the first men to get there would, after breaking up the fight, be given a nice tip by the grateful madam, either in the form of cash or as a "freebie" with one of the ladies upstairs.

~

Collusion between the police and prostitutes was an old story in Montreal, and it was frequently – and fruitlessly – denounced. "Why have these houses not been raided?" Mr. Justice Henri Taschereau asked, in 1905, after conducting an inquiry into the practices of the police. "Do the authorities ever consider the infamy of such a system?" he wrote, in his angry report. "Montreal is the rottenest city on the continent," Evanston I. Hart wrote, in 1919, in his pamphlet entitled *Wake Up! Montreal!* Hart, who was president of the Canadian Citizenship Association, laid much of the blame for "the social evil," as he called it, at the feet of the police – but not all the blame. The police, he pointed out, only did what they were told to do "by those who are higher up."

Many of the "higher ups" – city officials and leading citizens – believed that prostitution was a necessary evil. Without the facilities offered by the red-light district, men depraved by lust would attack honest women in the streets. Montreal was a major port, visited by ships of many nations, and everybody knew about the desperate needs of men who had been at sea for a long time. Innocent wives and daughters, it was believed, were actually being protected by the sexual safety valve that was provided by De Bullion Street. But many prominent citizens were disgusted with the situation and clamoured for reform. In 1925 Judge Louis Coderre, after a painstaking investigation, issued a long and wrathful report denouncing the police force's laxity "from the top to the bottom." What, he asked, was the source of the "small fortune" that had been accumulated by Captain Roch Sauvé in the four years that he had been in charge of the district where most of the bordellos were located. Chief of Police Pierre Bélanger, the judge said, should be immediately retired, and other officers either demoted or booted out.

Judge Coderre, in his report, painted a vivid picture of Montreal in the 1920s. "Vice stalks through our city," he said, "with a hideousness and insolence that appear sure of impunity. So gigantic is the octopus that it stretches its tentacles everywhere and threatens to strangle [the] population. . . . Prostitution itself, the traffic in human flesh, in its most shameful and degrading form, operates and flourishes in Montreal like a commercial enterprise perfectly organized. I would venture to say that few industrial establishments or businesses possess an organization as perfect, a means of operation as vast, a personnel as well trained and [a] discipline so well and rigorously applied. . . . I know of none which has so quickly enriched such a large number of proprietors."

Judge Coderre noted, with extreme displeasure, that ten-year-old boys were hired to go down to the port with the business cards of whorehouses and hand them out to sailors leaving their ships. He was particularly scathing about the madams who owned the houses of ill-fame. "Scandalously they flaunt their wealth," he wrote. "They ride in luxurious automobiles [and] with the greatest possible effrontery attend certain public gatherings. [They] reside in princely houses in distinguished sections, amid respectable people, while downtown, in a house reeking of misery and shame, ten or fifteen unfortunates, under the iron rule of the 'housekeeper,' purchase with their bodies, their health and too often their lives, the outrageous luxury in which the woman owner is swaddled."

In the 1940s, two decades after Judge Coderre handed down his eloquent report, nothing had changed. Brothelkeepers like Anna Beauchamp, Blanche Allard and Marcel les Dents en Or – Marcel with the Golden Teeth – were as prosperous as ever. And children who happened by, in the notorious streets, were still getting an early education in the business practices of vice. One such child was Alfred Segall, twelve years old. His father was the proprietor of Segall's Flour, Hay and Grain, a store on Ontario Street East, on the fringe of the red-light district, and Alfred was sometimes sent on errands in the neighbourhood. "What took you so long?" his father would ask, when Alfred got back to the store. The boy would mumble an excuse, unable to confess that he had been ogling the prostitutes leaning out of the windows in their tight sweaters, calling out to passing clientele. "Jeune homme, jeune homme!" the women would cry, holding up two fingers to indicate their price – two dollars. This was the atmosphere of "this lovely slum of lust" that was nostalgically recalled by John Glassco in his poem entitled "Montreal":

> Homes of the pink-gartered barrel-bellied whores
> The garlicky laughter and the gramophone
> Smells of a thousand sweaty summer nights. . . .

Glassco was writing about "the long rows / of little houses," small, run-down dwellings that had been built in the previous century to house the families of honest workingmen. In contrast to these anonymous little places, with their eight or ten whores, 312 Ontario Street East stood as a landmark in the red-light district, an imposing three-storey structure where seventy-five to eighty prostitutes were employed, working in shifts around the clock. Some Montrealers took pride in the fact that 312 Ontario, just down the street from No. 4 Police Station, was known across Canada, and perhaps around the world. Among young boys, the mere pronouncing of the words "Three Twelve" would evoke knowing snickers.

"Let's go to Three Twelve," a brave fourth-year high-school boy might suggest to his friends, as a celebration after they finished writing their final exams. Five or six of them might then take a streetcar to a tavern near 312, to take on beer and gather courage enough to ring the bell on the legendary door. Would they, in their youth, be admitted? But yes, even the most baby-faced among them would be welcomed, after he assured the doorman that he had the requisite two dollars. Once they were inside, the madam would ask the boys if they'd like to begin with "a show," and the answer, of course, would be yes. They would then be taken to a back room, where they would stand around a bed and watch two naked women writhing about, making vigorous use of a large dildo. For most of the apprehensive, virginal seventeen-year-old lads this would be their first acquaintance with details of the female anatomy, and what was being done with this anatomy was beyond their most fevered imaginings. After the show, the boys would be asked if they'd like to go upstairs with a girl and personally experience the real thing. But few would have the courage for this, most preferring to hasten back to the tavern, to steady their nerves and discuss the astonishing things they had just witnessed.

The Class of 1943 was the last for quite some time to be able to roam the downtown houses of ill-repute. In February of 1944 almost all the houses suddenly closed their doors. What decades of exhortation by social reformers had failed to achieve was accomplished overnight by the Canadian army. Far too many soldiers were contracting syphilis or gonorrhea during their visits to the red-light district. In Quebec, five times as many servicemen were contracting venereal disease as in British Columbia. The war effort was being endangered. Military authorities confronted civic officials and said that if the houses were not shut down, the entire city of Montreal would be declared out of bounds to all members of the army, navy and air force. Montreal would be disgraced in the eyes of the country.

The cynical city fathers could live with the disgrace – after all, the sinfulness of Montreal was already legendary across Canada – but a military boycott would be an economic disaster, and that was something to reckon with. Without the patronage of thousands of soldiers, sailors and airmen, there would be a sharp decline in the business of hotels, stores, restaurants and especially taverns. The public outcry would be tumultuous, and civic elections were not too far away. Immediately the word went out to the whorehouses: the old games were over, the police told them, and if they didn't close down at once they would face real and severe penalties. And so the *dames de petite vertu* streamed out into the cold, snowy February streets, to see what they could do on a free-lance basis, and behind them the doors swung shut on Clark Street and Mayor Street, Dumarais Street and De Bullion.

But if *les lupanars* were now closed, *les tripots* were going full blast. The army seemed to have no quarrel with Montreal's other main vice – gambling – even though plenty of soldiers were losing their pay at illegal tables all over town. But soldiers' bets were small potatoes in the big joints run by operators like Max Shapiro and Julius

Silverberg. In those places, wagers of many thousands of dollars were common, with big wartime profits bulging in the pockets of many Montreal businessmen in the 1940s, much of it "black market money" that was not known to the income tax department. And it was not only money that was being wagered at the tables; the town was rife with stories about apartment houses and restaurants that had changed hands with a roll of the barbotte dice.

Barbotte, a game of unknown origin, was by far the most popular form of gambling in Montreal. It was played by everybody – businessmen and bus drivers, lawyers and labourers. Some establishments had a "little table" for little bets – as low as a dollar – and a "big table" for bets that could run into the thousands. The game was played at a large, baize-covered table, with players lined up along two sides. The players bet against each other, siding either with or against the man casting the dice. If the caster threw 3-3, 5-5, 6-5 or 6-6, he and his supporters would win. 1-1, 1-2, 2-2 or 4-4 would lose. All other rolls would be neutral, and the dice would be rolled again. As each bet was settled, the house would take its substantial percentage. The game was very fast, and if people played long enough the house could end up with all the money.

~

$75,000 AN HOUR IS PLAYED HERE
DURING 'RUSH' HOURS AT BARBOTTE
Entrance to Gaming Tables Is Free and Unquestioned
Polite Checkroom Attendants Escort You to Play;
$700 Average Throw at 'Big' Table

The story appeared in the *Gazette* on July 21, 1945. The paper's law-abiding readers in Notre Dame de Grâce and Westmount had always known that there was illegal gambling going on in Montreal, but few of them realized its extent. Now, for the first time, here was chapter and verse, and the good burghers were astonished. A seven-hundred-dollar "average throw" was equal to more than four months' wages for an office clerk out in NDG. This ground-breaking story in the

Gazette was by Jacques Francoeur, a brash, ambitious young reporter. July – the dog days of summer – was a traditionally slow month for news, and Francoeur's city editor had asked him if he had any ideas for feature stories. Francoeur suggested a series on illegal gambling and he got the go-ahead. The next day he visited the University Bridge Club and wrote a story telling exactly where it was located – 1222 University Street – and what the hours of business were at this and similar establishments.

"With these houses open 24 hours a day," he wrote, "there are always enough customers to keep two or three tables going all the time, some customers staying eight or 10 hours. To accommodate them, there is in each house a restaurant with four or five attendants bringing sandwiches and soft drinks to the players so they will not lose their places by the table." Francoeur had spent hours at the "bridge club" on University Street, carefully noting the amounts of money being wagered at the four barbotte tables. The total here, combined with the totals being bet at eight or nine other local establishments, would, he estimated, come to about $75,000 per hour – equal to almost $725,000 in 1995 dollars.

Other *Gazette* stories followed, including one with this headline:

BARBOTTE GAME RAIDED AT 9:30 P.M.
BACK IN FULL SWING AT MIDNIGHT

Jacques Francoeur, only nineteen years old, was causing dismay in the gambling industry. Several of the big bosses approached him with sizeable offers of money if only he would stop writing those goddam stories. But Francoeur, who in later life would become the multimillionaire publisher of a large chain of Quebec newspapers, turned down all the offers and kept on writing. The stories soon gave rise to vehement demands for reform. Several city councillors called for a judicial inquiry into the situation, but Joseph Ovila Asselin, chairman of the city's executive committee, would have nothing to do with it. Although Camillien Houde was mayor of Montreal – after four years of internment during the war, he had been quickly reelected in 1944 – it was J.O. Asselin who really ran the city.

Asselin insisted that the city simply didn't have enough money to close down all the gambling dens. It would take five thousand more policemen to do it, he said. But several police officers told journalists, off the record, that they wouldn't need more than twenty-five good men to do the job – if they were ever ordered to do it.

At a city council meeting, Councillor Stanley Allen observed that Montreal was being labelled as "the most lawless city in North America."

"No man who loves his city would make a statement like that," said Chairman Asselin. The executive committee could do something about it, Councillor Allen said, "if its hands weren't tied."

"Our hands are not tied," Asselin retorted.

"Then *use* your hands!" Allen shouted. "Or your fists!"

But making a fist was not J.O. Asselin's style. For him, sitting on his hands was a more congenial approach to the problem of corruption, and, like the chief of police and the judiciary, he remained resolutely immobile. Meanwhile Mayor Houde was saying that perhaps gambling ought to be legalized, but there were few people in authority bold enough to voice such a radical notion. Gambling, many of the churches said, was inherently evil. It was wrong to try to obtain money without working for it, to get something for nothing. Also, children were going hungry when fathers lost all their pay at the barbotte table. Gambling, they said, was part of the alarming collapse of morality that had followed the war.

"Everywhere today there is moral chaos," said a statement by the Montreal Council on Christian Social Order. "Our condition," the council said, "is marked by libertinism and licentiousness, marital infidelity, sexual laxity, dishonesty and untruthfulness. Standards which hitherto have been commonly recognized are ignored and repudiated." The council was asking for an official inquiry into vice and corruption in the city, as was the Citizens' Vigilance League and the Leagues of the Sacred Heart, but all their demands fell on deaf ears. It took a loud explosion on Mansfield Street, early on a July morning in 1946, to start turning things around.

Someone had thrown a hand grenade at the second-floor window of one of the biggest downtown gambling houses. The "pineapple" missed its mark and caused only some small damage to a nearby restaurant. But, as frightened gamblers poured out onto the street, they wondered whether this might not be the beginning of an ominous new era. Up till now, the Montreal underworld had been a reasonably peaceful place, with no bombs or gunfire to interrupt the rolling of the dice. But was Montreal now turning into New York or Chicago? Was there a gang war in the offing? There had been rumours that rival groups were vying for control of the gambling turf, and perhaps this was the opening shot.

Six days later, Louis Bercovitch, a small-time operator in the rackets, walked into the bookmaking parlour operated by Harry Davis on Stanley Street, took out a revolver and killed Davis with three well-aimed shots. Bercovitch wanted to open a bookie operation of his own, but first he would have to obtain permission from Davis who, as edge man for the gambling fraternity, had the last word in matters like this. But Davis felt that the field was already over-crowded, and so he denied Bercovitch the go-ahead that he wanted. And he paid with his life for his decision. Davis was a forty-eight-year-old thug who had spent seven years in prison for drug smuggling, under a sentence that included ten strokes of the lash. When he emerged from prison, he rose quickly in the Montreal underworld and eventually became edge man. With his piercing stare and slicked-back hair, Davis radiated menace, a quality essential to an edge man, who was responsible for much more than just paying off the police. Above all he had to keep the peace within the gambling industry, where tough racketeers were competing with each other. Bercovitch, like others in town, had heard the rumour that Davis was going to import a hit man from New York to have him rubbed out. At his trial, he pleaded guilty to a reduced charge of manslaughter and was sentenced to fifteen years in prison.

At Harry Davis's funeral, police estimated that five thousand people were gathered on St. Urbain Street, outside Paperman's funeral parlour. The police were also there in large numbers, on the alert for any gunplay that might break out. With Davis gone, there was no edge man in control, no enforcer and peacekeeper. This funeral might well be the occasion for the outbreak of the anticipated gang war. The crowd overflowing into the street, on a warm July day, made the funeral look like a pleasant outdoor convention of the underworld. The gambling lords were there, along with family and friends, croupiers and customers, as well as a horde of ordinary citizens, on hand to ogle the legendary big shots. Which one was Charlie the Horse? they wondered. Was Oscar the Hammer here? And how about Albert the Syrian, Moishe the Electrician and the man known simply as The Beast? Detectives circulating among the mourners could overhear a lot of shop talk about the rackets, but they spotted no guns or grenades. The crowd was more festive than funereal, and not at all threatening. If there was to be a gang war, it wasn't going to start here. But for the next several days the city remained on edge. Civic organizations renewed their demands for a judicial inquiry into the gambling situation, and newspaper editorials fulminated, insisting that the authorities do something about it, once and for all.

The chief of police, Fernand Dufresne, hurried back to town from vacation immediately after the Davis shooting. The last thing in the world he wanted, he told associates, was a judicial inquiry. In an effort to appease the reformers, he publicly denounced the head of his Morality Squad, Captain Arthur Taché, and fired him. Taché had been given the job less than a year before, amid trumpetings that illegal gambling would finally be stamped out. Now he was being fired for having accomplished nothing, and was being eased into retirement. It was a time-honoured tactic: whenever the public outcry became too loud, the head of the Morality Squad would be fired and a new man would be brought in, to finally buckle down to this nasty task. In ten years, there had been seven heads of the Morality Squad, each of them fated to be a scapegoat.

～

Shortly after Taché was fired, an obscure lawyer named Pacifique Plante went to see Chief Dufresne and told him that if he was serious about having vice suppressed in Montreal, he, Plante, knew how to do it. For years Plante had worked as a lawyer in Recorder's Court, as the municipal court was then known; he knew all the ins and outs of the byzantine world of the gambling bosses and their protectors; he understood "the whole comedy," as he called it. Now, if Chief Dufresne would put Pacifique Plante in charge of the Morality Squad, he would see some real action.

With some reluctance, Dufresne gave Plante the job, warning him that it was not a pleasant one, that he would be up against sinister forces. "You're going to be dragged through the mud," Dufresne said. "There's nothing they won't do to discourage you. Just don't come back here to complain to me." Plante promised never to cry on Chief Dufresne's shoulder, and he was destined to keep the promise. What the chief did not suspect was that the gambling bosses would finally meet their match in this mild-mannered man he had just appointed, this lawyer with no police experience.

Plante immediately went to work reorganizing the demoralized Morality Squad, giving its members lectures on the intricacies of the law as it applied to their work. After a few weeks, he was ready for his first raid, a big horse-betting enterprise on Bleury Street. For once, there would be no advance warning that the police were coming. Plante went along with the policemen as they burst into the building and, to the astonishment of all, arrested not an *homme de paille* but the actual owner, Julius Silverberg. Although his establishment had been raided many times before, Silverberg himself had never been arrested. Now, as he was being taken down to headquarters, Plante phoned the newspapers and suggested they send reporters and photographers up to the Bleury Street *tripot*. They came in a hurry, and the flashguns popped as the police dismantled the place, carting off a large load of gambling equipment to be used as evidence. As the journalists watched, incredulously, they could not recall anything like this ever happening before in the sacrosanct precincts of a Montreal bookie's domain.

The next day, large spreads in the newspapers showed the general public, for the first time, what the inside of a gambling joint looked like. For Pacifique Plante the raid was also a first – the first time in his life he had ever set foot in a gambling establishment of any kind. In the papers, photos of Plante – who would now become widely known as "Pax" Plante – showed that he bore little resemblance to anyone's idea of a militant gangbuster. A slight thirty-nine-year-old man, he wore heavy, horn-rimmed glasses and had a very unthreatening look about him. As one observer noted, he looked like the prosperous owner of a small beauty salon. After the Silverberg raid, and the publicity it engendered, almost all the city's betting houses quietly closed their doors, biding their time until this new morality crusader could be corrupted like all the others. But Harry Ship, most famous of the city's bookies, defiantly kept on doing business as usual, on St. Catherine Street East. And so Plante was determined to make him his next target, although some police colleagues warned him that he might be biting off more than he could chew. After all, Ship had friends in high places, and was widely believed to be in line to become the next ruler of the underworld, replacing the murdered Harry Davis.

The amiable, soft-spoken Harry Ship was known as the Boy Plunger, a precocious player in the biggest gambling leagues. He had entered the business as an eager apprentice at the age of nineteen, and before he was thirty he owned the luxurious White House casino in Côte St. Luc. Later he opened another casino across the river, in Greenfield Park, and now his most lucrative operation was the big bookmaking establishment on St. Catherine Street. Also, he was wealthy enough to eventually buy the Chez Paree nightclub, which imported entertainers like Frank Sinatra, Dean Martin and Sammy Davis, Jr.

Besides catering to the public's insatiable desire to bet on the horses, Ship was himself an inveterate gambler, and there were days when he would make, on his own account, twenty-five or thirty different bets on horses running on tracks across North America. He could calculate the odds better than anyone, and was said to be a mathematical wizard; he had studied mathematics for two years at Queen's University, an unusual background in a business where many of the big operators were barely literate. The Boy Plunger's bets were enormous: half a million dollars a week was not unusual. "It was crazy," he would recall in later years. "I had no conception of what money meant. I was a millionaire one week, a bum the next. I don't know where I got the nerve. People couldn't figure out how come I stayed alive." But Ship not only stayed alive, he prospered, thanks to a large extent to the profits he made in his St. Catherine Street bookmaking parlour.

Pax Plante and his Morality Squad descended on that establishment on September 16, 1946. They found the front door locked and so they broke it down. They arrested Harry Ship and he spent three days in jail before being released on bail. Leaving the courthouse, Ship was cheerful and confident. "In two weeks," he told reporters, "nobody will remember who that guy Plante was.' But Plante was determined to land this very big fish, and see that he went to jail – an unheard-of fate for a gambling boss. He threw himself into the task of marshalling evidence against Ship, and four months later, when the trial began, Plante was ready to present close to five hundred exhibits and seventeen thousand pages of depositions. To counter all this, Ship mustered a team of four outstanding lawyers, headed by Joseph Cohen, a man renowned for winning acquittals for persons accused of serious crimes. During the year that followed, Ship's lawyers waged an unremitting battle for him, and managed to obtain twenty-two postponements of the case. But in the end, Plante's evidence could not be denied. Harry Ship, the phenomenally lucky Boy Plunger, was found guilty and sentenced to six months in Bordeaux Jail.

With organized gambling now at a standstill, Plante turned his attention to prostitution. After the war, with the army no longer making threats, the bawdy-houses had started to reopen, although there were fewer of them now. Still, there were too many for Plante, and he started to raid them. But what about the elegant bordello at 150 Milton Street, the place with the oriental carpets on the floor? People said Plante would be afraid to disturb that one, known to be a favourite haunt of important politicians. Its madam, Eva Nadeau, boasted about having friends in the highest echelons of the police department, but Plante and his men plunged in, arrested Eva and closed the place down.

Lotteries were next, and they existed in abundance, with names like the Union Four Way and the Royal Five Way. One of the biggest was called the Old Reliable, and when Plante's men burst in on its headquarters, on Bishop Street, they found several young women working at a printing press, turning out tickets to be sold the next day. Emile Pépin, owner of the Old Reliable, protested that he had been printing and selling lottery tickets for twenty years without anybody bothering him. But now Pépin and bushels of his tickets were being carted down to headquarters. Within the next six months, Plante would obtain the convictions of no fewer than forty-five lottery operators.

Even bingo did not escape Plante's crusade. At the time, there were dozens of weekly bingos running regularly in Catholic churches, all of them profitable and all of them illegal. Plante called a press conference and announced that he was declaring war on all church bingos, and that he had the support of Archbishop Charbonneau. Within a week, they all closed down – all except one. The curé of that church was defiant. "Next Saturday night we will have the biggest bingo ever held in this church," he said in his Sunday sermon. "No little lawyer from St. James Street is going to dictate to me." On Saturday night, with that bingo under way, some small boys rushed into the church hall to report what they had just seen on the street outside. Many police cars had arrived, and three large Black Marias. Hundreds of alarmed bingo players immediately poured out onto the street and headed for home, leaving the curé and his priests alone in the church. His bingo never reopened.

For many Montrealers, Plante was going too far, destroying the city's reputation as an easygoing place where people could enjoy themselves. He was a fanatic, a humourless prude, an obnoxious puritan. In an interview, he vigorously denied the accusations. "I'm not interested in personal morals," he said. "I don't want to stop people from having fun. But if we're going to pay taxes to enforce laws, then let's enforce them. If a majority doesn't want the laws, then abolish them. I think honestly that I'm a perfectionist. It sends me crazy to see things in a mess." In less than a year, Pax Plante had achieved what the police force had been unable to do in half a century. The newspapers were full of praise for his efforts, but he received not a single word of encouragement or commendation from City Hall or the chief of police. One could only assume that people in high places were angry at being deprived of their graft.

The underworld made efforts to bribe Plante. One emissary from the big bosses, he said, offered him $250,000 if he would allow a limited number of establishments to reopen. When he turned down these offers, he received threats, and one night, when Plante was entering his house, someone took a potshot at him from the bushes. But Plante had as much to fear from his own colleagues in the police force as from the thugs of the underworld. Their efforts to discredit him, to trip him up, were unceasing. His most determined adversary was Albert Langlois, the new chief of police, who succeeded the man who had originally appointed Plante to the Morality Squad. Langlois was a strict disciplinarian, a policeman who wanted everything done by the book. Plante's flamboyant, impulsive manner was anathema to Langlois, and he detested the enormous amount of publicity Plante was getting.

An incident in the winter of 1948 gave Langlois the opportunity he had been waiting for. It was discovered that three constables of the Morality Squad, in the process of trying to make a case against some prostitutes, had slept with them. When questioned, the constables insisted that they had done this despite Plante's emphatic orders that they must never do anything of the sort. But, in the uproar that followed, Langlois found reason to suspend Plante, for insubordination, and two months later he was fired from the police force. That night there was rejoicing in the Tic Toc and other nightclubs where the gambling bosses congregated. Within two days, sixteen betting and barbotte establishments had reopened. Within weeks, investigators from the Leagues of the Sacred Heart found eight whorehouses in full operation on one short street in the old red-light district. Montreal was returning to normal after the aberration of Pax Plante's eighteen months in office.

Plante's firing was denounced by civic organizations like the Chamber of Commerce and the Retail Merchants' Association, but City Hall ignored them all, and Chief of Police Langlois assured the citizenry that the fight against vice would continue unabated, "without publicity." But after a year, *Time* magazine was able to tell the world that Montreal was once again a wide-open town.

≈

Meanwhile Pax Plante, out of work and brooding about his dismissal, decided to take one more crack at the civic establishment. On leaving the police force, he had taken with him massive files dealing with vice in the city during the past decade. Now he would use them to denounce high officials in the police department and City Hall. *Le Devoir*, the militant daily, agreed to publish a series of articles bearing Plante's name. They would be ghost-written for him by Gérard Pelletier, a young reporter who in later life would become a minister in Pierre Trudeau's cabinet and ambassador to France.

"*Montréal sous le règne de la pègre*" – "Montreal under the Reign of the Underworld" – the front-page headline proclaimed, over the first of the articles, which appeared on November 28, 1949. During the next three months, there would be sixty-two articles, culminating in one entitled "Here Are the Real Guilty Parties." Day by day the articles took law-abiding readers of the paper on a Cook's tour of the Montreal underworld. They learned how barbotte parlours operated and what the daily routine was in a typical whorehouse. It was a vivid picture of the city's sinfulness in the rollicking, wide-open 1940s. Plante told how the authorities had always said that there could be no comprehensive cleanup without a hugely expanded police force and an expenditure far beyond the capacity of the city's budget. Then Plante told how he had shut down almost all the city's vice in eighteen months, with no extra money and no extra personnel – and had been fired for his pains. Among the most interesting articles were those describing the vendetta waged against Plante by Albert Langlois, the chief of police, who at one point went to see the archbishop of Montreal to assert that Plante was a womanizer and the correspondent in a divorce case – an accusation that proved to be a total fabrication.

Plante saved his heaviest artillery for his last article, in which he made specific accusations and named names. At the head of the list was J.O. Asselin, chairman of the city's executive committee, closely followed by four other members of the committee. These men, Plante said, had brazenly tolerated vice throughout the decade. Chief Langlois and former chief Dufresne headed a list of police officers accused of having protected dozens of unconvicted criminals. Then came the list of those who were protected – five owners of whorehouses and forty-one gambling bosses. The gambling roster was headed by Max Shapiro, often referred to as the kingpin of the industry in Montreal, and contained the names of such stalwarts as Sam Cleaver, Frank Petrula, Louis Greco, Abie Noodleman, Magloire Dupuis, Ludger Audet, Benny Cohen, Gordon Dean and Louis Dettner. At *Le Devoir*, the editors sat back and waited for the libel suits. To handle these they had hired Jean Drapeau, a young lawyer who was destined to one day become mayor of Montreal. But neither the civic officials nor the police officers nor the racketeers rose up to defend their reputations. The public could only conclude that Plante's accusations were solidly founded in fact.

The newspaper articles were reprinted as a ninety-six-page booklet, which quickly became a best-seller. Once again there was a public outcry, and citizens of the Public Morality Committee presented a petition demanding a judicial inquiry that would establish, once and for all, who was responsible for the existence of commercialized vice in Montreal in the 1940s. The petition ran to 1,095 pages and contained fifteen thousand specific charges, levelled against members of the city council and the police department. The Superior Court was impressed by the petition and decreed that a probe would go forward, under Mr. Justice François Caron, an energetic jurist known for having cleaned up vice in the city of Hull. His hearings, in the Montreal courthouse, began in September 1950, and it would be four years before his work would be done.

From the start, the expensive lawyers hired by the civic officials and the police threw up every obstacle they could think of to hinder the course of the inquiry. On five occasions they would take issues

to the Quebec Court of Appeal, and each time their appeals were
denied. Groups of defendants, on two occasions, managed to have
writs of prohibition executed, to suspend the probe entirely, and they
carried their fight all the way to the Supreme Court of Canada,
where they were twice defeated. All this made for interruptions of
many months in the course of the inquiry, but Pax Plante and Jean
Drapeau, acting for the petitioners, were not fazed, and were ready to
leap into the fray with renewed vigour after every hiatus. Once,
when the court stenographers threatened to stop working because
they had not been paid, and thus halt the proceedings, Plante
announced that he would pay them out of his own pocket until the
problem was resolved.

To elicit evidence of how the police had been bought off, Plante
and Drapeau subpoenaed a long parade of witnesses from the seamy
side of the city. Testimony from the employees of gambling dens and
brothels provided vivid insights into the business practices of the
purveyors of debauchery. Paulette Déry, a tough, husky woman of
forty-seven, was a star witness. She had started out as a simple prostitute but had risen quickly through the ranks to become a "housekeeper" in one of Anna Beauchamp's De Bullion Street *lupanars*. As
housekeeper, she told the court, it was her job to greet the client at
the door and take him to the salon, where he could choose a "girl."
Paulette would collect the client's payment before the girl took him
off to a bedroom, and she would punch the girl's work card. At the
end of the week, the girl's earnings would be based on the number
of holes punched into her card. In the 1940s, Paulette told the court,
the basic tariff in her house for a simple bout of copulation was three
dollars. The average girl would look after eight or nine clients a night
– or a day, if she was working the day shift – and she would get fifty
percent of what the clients paid. It amounted to a great deal more
than any stenographer or shop clerk could ever dream of earning.

Paulette Déry insisted that, as housekeeper, she ran a clean,
orderly house, although she wistfully admitted that Madame
Beauchamp's many houses were not as chic as Madame Bizanti's,
where the housekeepers were supplied with nice black uniforms,
with white collar and cuffs. Mme Bizanti figured prominently in

Paulette's recollections of life in the red-light district, as did other prominent madams and housekeepers like Madame Manda, Madame Jeanne, Yvette Gilbert, La Grosse Pierrette, La Syrienne, L'Italienne and especially the formidable Simone Burlant, said to weigh 425 pounds.

Questioned by Plante, Paulette Déry willingly told the court about the process Plante called "the comedy of the padlocks." During a raid by the police, they would solemnly affix a court-ordered padlock to the front door. But most brothels were located in rows of small houses, with interconnecting passageways inside. Thus customers could keep coming in through the door to the adjoining house. One witness even told of a padlocked door that had a small, flashing neon sign above it, with an arrow and the words "NEXT DOOR." Sometimes the padlock was put on an inside door, and one witness told of how, on a cold winter day, the housekeeper phoned the police to complain that the janitor couldn't get down to the basement, to tend the furnace, because of the padlock, and the lightly clad girls were shivering. A constable arrived promptly to remove the padlock.

Paulette told of being arrested, over the years, on eighty-five occasions. She would be brought to court where she would plead guilty to being the owner of the brothel, taking the rap for the real owner, Mme Beauchamp, who would pay the fine for her. Paulette showed no resentment to her employer for this imposition; it was all part of a housekeeper's job. Like many other prostitutes and housekeepers, Paulette spoke with respect and affection for her madam. Mme Bizanti came in for special praise for a lavish reception she had given at her Outremont home when one of her girls got married.

But there were sad moments in the courtroom, as ex-prostitutes like Greta and Andrée were made to testify. They were now in their forties, and had lost the good looks that were evident in the photos of them that had been taken by the police ten years earlier and were now being produced in court. They pleaded with the judge not to reveal their surnames. Questioning Mary X, Plante asked her why she had always worked in the sleaziest little houses and never in a big house, like 312 Ontario Street. "I was never pretty enough," was the sad-eyed Mary's response. Spectators who came to Room 24 in the courthouse always hoped to be entertained by the proceedings, and they frequently were. The testimony of Madame Blanche was much appreciated, especially her protests about what a decent house she ran. "We always closed on Good Friday," she said. And there was something touching about the testimony of a young police officer when he said that when he arrested the same woman for the fiftieth time he wondered whether there shouldn't be some small ceremony to mark their "anniversary."

One of the most astonishing witnesses was Dr. Charles Bayard, a close friend of former police chief Dufresne. Dr. Bayard admitted to being the owner of several houses on De Bullion Street, which he rented to brothelkeepers. Prostitutes made good tenants, he said. They kept the houses in good order and occasionally they even effected improvements. By contrast, during the Depression he had rented some of these run-down houses to very poor people, who, during the coldest days of winter, had sometimes ripped up the wood-work to burn in the stove to keep warm. Dr. Bayard did not seem to be unduly bothered by the fact that venereal disease was being trans-mitted in the houses he rented to prostitutes, while at the same time he was being employed by the City of Montreal Health Department as joint superintendent of the contagious disease branch.

Among the gambling bosses who testified, the most important was Max Shapiro, whose word was said to be law in the downtown gam-bling industry. Shapiro admitted that for six years he had operated a fancy establishment on Peel Street, where wealthy people came to play roulette, baccarat and chemin de fer. He had never had any trouble with the police, but he insisted that he had never paid a penny for protection. Harry Ship, the Boy Plunger, was a bit more forthcoming, confirming the fact that he and all the other book-makers could never have operated without the connivance of the police.

Some of the most peculiar testimony heard at the inquiry came from city councillors. Councillor Frank Hanley, very much the man about town, presented a picture of serene ignorance about the tough neighbourhood he represented. "On my oath, Your Honour," Hanley said at one point, "I swear there was never a brothel operated in my district."

"It's your oath," said Judge Caron. "I'm glad it's not mine."

Councillor Dave Rochon said he had complained to the police chief about a brothel on St. Dominique Street that was disturbing neighbours by using a loudspeaker to attract clients, but that nothing had come of this and other complaints. The most damning testimony came from policemen and former policemen, who painted a picture of a department where the most ridiculous orders were never questioned. One retired officer told how he had been fired for putting a padlock on the wrong door. He had locked the main outside door of the bookie's establishment, thus cutting off public access, rather than putting the padlock on a useless inside door, as had been specified. Two hours later he was asked to resign for failing to carry out a court order. When Judge Caron asked Inspector Leo Laviolette why he had done nothing to suppress prostitution in his district, the red-light district, the inspector simply replied that he had been following orders. Captain Horace Thivierge had a more specific excuse when asked why he never collared gamblers or prostitutes. "I was too busy arresting communists," the captain said.

Captain Arthur Taché, whose salary had been about $3,000 a year, was asked how he could account for purchases that included a $3,000 automobile, a $2,990 diamond ring, other items worth $3,500 and a property valued at $10,000. Taché, who had been head of the Morality Squad for nine months, said he had earned extra money by helping people with their housecleaning. Vagueness and ignorance about vice in the city marked the testimony of Police Chief Langlois when it was his turn to take the stand. When Jean Drapeau asked him whether he had not learned anything from the many newspaper articles that gave chapter and verse about gambling in Montreal, the chief replied that it was a tradition in the police department to ignore criticism in the press.

∿

On April 2, 1953, the hearings came to a close. There had been 358 separate sessions and 374 witnesses had been heard. Fifty thousand documents had been filed. It would take Judge Caron eighteen months to sift through all this material and formulate his judgement. Finally, on October 8, 1954, he was ready. When the doors to the courtroom were finally opened that morning, the *Montreal Star* reported, "The crowd surged forward like the surf driven by a hurricane of curiosity. . . . They came to rub shoulders with the ghosts of one of the city's most colorful eras. . . . It was almost as if the historical costume department of a famous museum were to take the renowned old clothes to the laundromat."

The city's dirty linen was in for an unprecedented public airing. Mr. Justice Caron started reading his judgement at 10:30 a.m. and didn't finish until four and a half hours later. He reviewed much of the lurid testimony that had been heard at the hearings and, in effect, gave official confirmation to what everybody in the city by now seemed to know: that the police department could easily have suppressed gambling and prostitution, but instead was organized to permit and protect it. Then came the details everybody had been waiting for. Police Director Albert Langlois was to be fired and fined five hundred dollars. Fines of seven thousand dollars were imposed on former police director Fernand Dufresne and former assistant director Armand Brodeur. Seventeen other police officers, some retired and some still active, were also punished, some of them fired and all of them fined. Although he had scathing criticism for a few city councillors, the judge imposed no penalties on them or on Mayor Houde, who had declined to appear at the inquiry. Instead, the judge left the fate of the politicians in the hands of the voters, with civic elections due in three weeks' time.

Camillien Houde had announced that he would not seek reelection, leaving the race for the mayoralty open to two old political warhorses, Adhémar Raynault and Sarto Fournier. But now there was a new contender on the scene, Jean Drapeau, the lawyer who had been catapulted into fame by his work in the vice probe. Drapeau would be the candidate of the Civic Action League, which had been formed two years earlier with the motto "To serve the public, not ourselves" – a radical notion in Montreal politics. When the ballots were counted on October 28, 1954, Jean Drapeau, the reformer, had twice as many votes as his two opponents together. His wildly cheering supporters were ready to see him go into action on his main election promise – to clean up the city once and for all – and Drapeau would not disappoint them. His mere presence in office was enough to start things moving. Within days of his election, the *Herald* reported, fourteen "shady ladies" were seen departing for New York, presumably to ply their trade in a more tolerant atmosphere.

Drapeau brought Pax Plante back to the police department, and he became its director within a year. The task that faced him was formidable. Montreal's appetite for vice was insatiable, if one was to believe Jean Drapeau when he said that during the heyday of police corruption, clients made 3,800,000 visits a year to illegal establishments. That was three times the population of the city. The gambling industry, one journalist estimated, grossed $100 million a year, a figure that was not challenged. That would make it the city's second largest industry, right behind the manufacture of women's clothing. Plante's objective was to reduce these staggering statistics to as close to zero as possible. He summoned the police department's twenty-one precinct captains and ordered them to visit every bar and nightclub in the city and warn them they would lose their licences if they didn't get rid of the prostitutes who did their soliciting on the premises. Rooming houses would also lose their licences if they rented rooms to streetwalkers and their clients.

There were still a few brothels in town, operating very discreetly, and Plante unleashed a series of vigorous raids on them. He would pay no attention to the advice given to him some years earlier by Monsignor Albert Valois, the director of Catholic Action for the diocese. The cleric had told Plante that no one would fault him if he were to allow a few whorehouses to continue operating, as an outlet for sex fiends who might otherwise be a menace to "honest women." There would now be no toleration of any form of gambling, and even pinball machines were forbidden, thanks to a new bylaw. But perhaps the most sweeping reform concerned the serving of liquor. By law, all bars were supposed to stop providing drinks at

2:00 a.m. on weekdays and midnight on Saturdays, but a great many of them were in the habit of staying open until dawn, with no lack of customers. Now all that had to stop, Drapeau decreed, and those who disobeyed would lose their licences.

As bars and nightclubs reluctantly fell into line, surreptitious "blind pigs" sprang up in many parts of town, mostly private houses where drinks were sold in the living room to revellers who wanted to carouse all night long. Plante responded by ferreting out as many blind pigs as he could, and raiding them. Downtown there were howls of protest. A group of nightclub and restaurant owners issued a statement saying that Drapeau had turned Montreal into a police state. The Bellevue Casino, biggest of the city's nightclubs, claimed that during the first year of this new regime it had twenty-five thousand fewer customers than in the good old days. The union representing waiters and bartenders said that two thousand of its six thousand members had been thrown out of work.

"Tourists used to stay around for a week or two for some fun," said the head of an association of taxi owners. "This summer they got fed up with the early closing and after a couple of days they left." With the sex trade virtually at an end, men from all over the country were no longer coming to Montreal to live out their fantasies. With big-time gambling in limbo, the big bosses were no longer spending their spoils in the nightclubs. "The boys used to come into a club and spend five hundred dollars in a night," one waiter said. "You might get a fifty-dollar tip. Now you get a ladies' bridge club where everybody has one drink and leaves you a dime."

Many Montrealers, the sort who considered themselves worldly, were proud of the fact that their city was famous for being sinful. In the 1940s, they were pleased to read the chapter about Montreal in Bruce Hutchison's book *The Unknown Country*. "There is something here," he wrote, "which for lack of a better name, must be called elegance with a touch of wickedness . . . a certain glittering sinfulness and sophistication, which makes us simple western Canadians feel very young, innocent and gauche." Now, Drapeau and Plante were stifling that wickedness, that glittering sinfulness. Could the elegance and sophistication survive without it? Or would Montreal become as dull and dreary as the rest of the country, where the Bruce Hutchisons came from?

In Montreal, the summer of 1955 was the hottest in fifty years. It was also, in a sense, the most moral summer in fifty years, much to the satisfaction of the Civic Action League and the Leagues of the Sacred Heart. Babylon on the St. Lawrence was changing, and of course there was many a boulevardier who bemoaned the change. Al Palmer, a columnist in the *Herald*, summed up their despair. "The old lady has lost her girlish laughter," he wrote. "Now it's Montreal the Good."

4

Politics:
Houde, Duplessis and la Grande Noirceur

The brothels may have been closed down, but in the summer of 1944 the red-light district was still a lively place, particularly on August 8. That morning Morris Botinsky ventured out of his junk-yard onto De Bullion Street to see what all the fuss was about, and he immediately found himself caught in the crossfire. "A bullet whistled by me," he later told police. "I saw men getting into strategic positions to fire. It looked to me as if we were suddenly transferred to the Normandy front." But it wasn't war; it was just election day in Montreal.

Elections in the city had always been spirited, with candidates hiring thugs to attack rival committee rooms, smash the furniture and destroy voter lists, but in the 1944 provincial contest electoral warfare took on a new dimension: the goon's traditional weapon of choice, the baseball bat, was now being augmented with guns, knives, knuckle-dusters, blackjacks and lead pipes. Rival gangs numbering in the hundreds battled throughout the day in the downtown St. James division, smashing store windows and over-turning cars. Extra-tough plug-uglies were said to have been im-ported from Ontario for the occasion, and in the end seventeen men had been wounded by gunfire, many more injured in other ways, and sixty-eight arrested. But more than mere hooliganism was used to influence the outcome of elections. The art of telegraphy was well developed, a telegrapher being a person hired to impersonate potential voters who had not yet arrived at the poll or, better still, to vote on behalf of dead people whose names had been fraudulently

In the 1939 Royal Tour, King George VI and Queen Elizabeth are driven through Place d'Armes in downtown Montreal. The unstated purpose of their visit was to foster feelings of loyalty to Great Britain on the eve of the war.

Mayor Houde and the king look on as the queen signs the Golden Book at City Hall. A year later Houde was imprisoned for treasonable utterances.

A crowd outside a Peel Street newsstand awaits the arrival of an extra edition of the *Gazette* on September 3, 1939, the day of Britain's declaration of war.

With No from Quebec and Yes from the rest of Canada, Prime Minister Mackenzie King ponders the result of the 1942 plebiscite in which he sought permission to institute conscription "if necessary."

New Year's Eve 1940 at the Montreal Amateur Athletic Association. Although the war in Europe was now four months old, the conflict seemed distant and somehow unreal.

In July, 1939, in the Delormier baseball stadium, 105 French Canadian couples are united in a mass wedding after taking a one-year course in preparation for Christian marriage.

Dancers of the Thumbs Up Revue entertain the troops, 1942. Many citizens tried to provide soldiers with good, clean alternatives to Montreal's many bars and bordellos.

In a munitions factory, technicians examine 25-pounder shell casings. Montreal was Canada's biggest wartime arsenal, producing guns, ammunition, tanks, ships, aircraft.

Author Mavis Gallant, a journalist for the *Montreal Standard* in 1948. She would soon quit her job to devote herself to writing fiction, becoming one of Canada's leading authors.

Mordecai Richler in 1953. His two Montreal novels of the '50s would win international acclaim.

Brian Moore (left) with William Weintraub in 1958. That year Moore was writing his third novel, *The Luck of Ginger Coffey*, about an Irish immigrant in Montreal.

Poets of the Preview Group, circa 1942. Back row, left to right: Kit Shaw, Neufville Shaw, Bruce Ruddick, F. R. Scott. Middle Row: Peggy Anderson, P. K. Page. On floor: Patrick Anderson. The rival First Statement poets considered Preview too intellectual.

inscribed on the electoral list. In the 1954 municipal elections, seventy-nine persons were arrested for telegraphing. On that day, the police reported, calls to deal with disturbances were coming over patrol car radios at the rate of one every twelve seconds. When police answered a call from a Laurier Avenue location, they were confronted by a mob of hoodlums who threw beer bottles at them. These electoral activists were subdued only after the constables drew their revolvers.

In the provincial elections of 1956, musclemen working for Premier Duplessis's Union Nationale Party were especially diligent, and the sound of bricks being hurled through the windows of Liberal committee rooms could be heard well before dawn on polling day. Union Nationale agents were also busy on the telephone, calling opposition scrutineers and threatening to break their bones if they showed up at their assigned polls. As a result, fewer than half of the opposition's representatives were on the job when the polls opened, making it much easier for the telegraphers to do their work. Duplessis's goons were very well paid, as they were working for the party in power which, in the age-old tradition of Quebec politics, had a huge slush fund fed by kickbacks from contractors who did business with the government. The opposition party, which never had that kind of money, could only afford to sponsor a modest amount of thuggery.

Federal elections were just as tumultuous as those at the civic and provincial levels. In the 1957 federal election, in the Laurier riding, a strong-arm man waved a gun at the clerks in Poll No. 121 as he stuffed a handful of fraudulent ballots into the ballot box. This was only one of many incidents described by Dr. Ruben Lévesque, the district returning officer, in his report to the director general of elections in Ottawa. Dr. Lévesque said he had reason to believe that at least half of the polls in his district had been visited by *voleurs d'élection* – election stealers. *Fiers-à-bras, forts-à-bras, personnes louches* and *indésirables* in large numbers, he reported, had barged into polls, grabbed handfuls of blank ballots and made off with them. After putting Xs next to the name of the candidate who had hired them, they would enter other polls and forcibly stuff the ballots into ballot boxes. In his recommendations to Ottawa, Dr. Lévesque suggested that in future all polls have a policeman on hand. At present most polls, often in private houses, were being staffed by women, who did an excellent job, but with a policeman present goons would not be able to take advantage of *la faiblesse musculaire féminine* – feminine muscular weakness.

The municipal election of 1928 was one of the most peaceful in years, but it was one of the most important. There was only one minor street fight and only forty-two telegraphers were arrested, yet that April day would long be remembered as the day when Camillien Houde was first elected mayor of Montreal. He would hold that office, off and on, until 1954 – for eighteen of those twenty-six years – and he would come to be known as Mr. Montreal. No other mayor was ever so adored by the populace, but his flamboyant, theatrical antics were the despair of critics like the *Gazette* which, after one of his many victories, said: "It may be that, having been safely elected, he will settle down to a dignified, balanced and businesslike discharge of his mayoral duties . . . but frankly we see little prospect of it."

Houde was an imposing figure, a short man with a big belly who weighed more than 250 pounds. He had large, bulging eyes and a massive nose. Women, who were among his greatest admirers, said he was so ugly that he was beautiful. He loved fine clothes, and his usual garb consisted of striped trousers, morning coat, pearl-grey vest and ascot tie. Thus attired, with grey spats protecting his glistening shoes, he would often walk the three miles from his home on St. Hubert Street to City Hall, swinging a Malacca cane and occasionally stopping to shake hands with an admiring citizen.

In the eyes of many, Houde was the personification of the Montreal of that era, just as Queen Victoria had been the personification of the England of her time. "No public figure," the novelist Hugh MacLennan wrote, "has ever equalled Houde in his capacity to express Montreal's spirit of wit, tolerance, perversity, cynicism, gaiety, bawdiness, gallantry, delight in living and – make no error here – dignity." MacLennan was writing in 1954, soon after Houde announced that he was retiring from public life. "As the years passed," MacLennan wrote, "his huge personality overflowed the city and province and spread over the whole country. Our national politics were dominated by Mackenzie King's neurotic caution, by his dull, complacent, relentless efficiency. On this drab stage Houde moved with a grotesque *panache*, a bizarre poetry, a colossal appetite for life."

Camillien Houde was born in 1889, in the poorest part of the east end. He was the first of Joséphine and Azade Houde's ten children, but all his brothers and sisters died in childhood, and his father, who had a lowly job in a flour mill, died when Camillien was nine years old. To support herself and her son, Joséphine became a dressmaker. Camillien helped out by working as a butcher's boy, bringing home a dollar a week, plus an occasional piece of meat for dinner. His mother let him keep five cents for pocket money and saved the rest to help pay for the education she was determined he would have. He completed a commercial course when he was sixteen and got a job as a clerk at the Bank of Hochelaga. Rising through the ranks of the bank, he was the manager of a branch by the time he was twenty-six. His first wife died in the influenza epidemic of 1918, and he married again the following year, to a highly ambitious woman who persuaded him to leave the bank and go into business, where his obvious talents could earn him a fortune. He tried his hand as an insurance agent, a biscuit merchant, a candy manufacturer, an importer of wines and a few other ventures – and he failed miserably at all of them. By 1923 he had lost all his money and was broke.

But by now Houde had become interested in politics, and, again encouraged by his wife, he sought the nomination as Conservative candidate in the riding of Ste. Marie for the provincial elections of 1923. In Quebec, the Conservatives were an unpopular opposition party, and so it was not too difficult for Houde to secure the nomination. During the election campaign, as the crowds responded to his oratory, he realized that he had at last found his true vocation. As a youth he had taken part in amateur theatricals, playing Cyrano de Bergerac without benefit of a putty nose, thanks to the protuberance of his own; now, on the hustings, he found that his theatrical talents could quickly arouse his audience to rage and then convulse it with laughter, all within the same minute. Ste. Marie was a work-ing-class riding, and he knew how to talk to the voters in the language they understood. They loved it when he told them that, if elected, he would punch his fist through the shiny top hat of Premier Louis Alexandre Taschereau, the patrician figure who personified French Quebec's moneyed elite. On election day, the labourers and factory workers of Ste. Marie responded by voting him in handily, at once launching his meteoric career and helping him stave off personal bankruptcy, in the nick of time, by putting him onto the payroll of the Quebec Legislative Assembly.

In the legislature, Camillien Houde soon made a name for himself as a furious debater, a master of sarcastic assault and a constant thorn in the side of the smugly entrenched Liberal government. But in the next elections, in 1927, his fickle constituents abandoned him, leaving him defeated, without employment and once again insolvent. Then, on impulse, according to the legend, Houde barged into the office of Lord Atholstan, publisher of the *Montreal Star*, and asked him if he would bankroll his campaign if he were to run for mayor in the forthcoming municipal elections. Atholstan is said to have immediately handed Houde a large cheque because Houde would be trying to unseat Médéric Martin, a man who had been mayor for twelve years and who was detested by His Lordship. Houde entered the fray with his usual zest, and when the ballots were counted he had twenty-two thousand more of them than his opponent. The tenant of a shabby second-floor flat was now mayor of Canada's metropolis.

Elected in 1928, Houde held office for three terms during the Great Depression that followed, when more than a quarter of the city's work force was unemployed. In response to this, Houde initiated the largest program of public works that had ever been seen in Canada. He significantly altered the face of the city with new parks and playgrounds, new police and fire stations, new tunnels under railway tracks. The Botanical Gardens and St. Helen's Island were developed, the handsome Chalet was completed at the Lookout on top of Mount Royal and large new farmers' markets were created – Jean Talon, St. James, Atwater. But what probably endeared Camillien Houde most to the citizenry were his "comfort stations," the handsome public toilets that he installed on city squares in several parts of town. In Paris, blessed refuges like these were called *vespasiennes*, after the Emperor Vespasian, who first caused them to be built in ancient Rome. In Montreal they were, of course, soon dubbed *camilliennes*.

As a man who himself had known poverty for many years, Houde was keenly aware of the plight of the city's poor who, during the Depression years, were often on the verge of starvation. At home, he and his wife tried to set an example by handing out food and clothing to the needy. At City Hall, delegations of the destitute often reduced him to tears. One day he received a group of down-cast women who told him they had no money to feed their children and were about to be evicted from their homes. The mayor told them it would take the City some time to deal with their problem but, for the interim, he might be able to help in a small way. He had just cashed his monthly paycheque, and now he reached into his pocket and emptied it. "Divide this among yourselves," he said, handing some eight hundred dollars to the leader of the delegation. Later that evening he phoned a friend from the Traymore Restaurant. "I've just had dinner," he said, "and I find I don't have any money to pay for it. Could you come down and fish me out?"

The humble Traymore was just up the street from the Windsor Hotel, where Houde would soon be dining on more sumptuous fare with the king and queen of England. His performance during that Royal Tour of 1939 added considerably to the ever-growing legend that he was creating. A favourite story among Montrealers concerned what Camillien had done at the state banquet that caused the shy, reserved monarch to erupt into sudden laughter. It seems that the mayor was not eating his *sorbet au curaçao* but instead was intently studying a sheet of paper. "What are you reading?" the king finally asked him. "Forgive me, Your Majesty," Houde said, "but I have been trying to memorize this list, which was given to me by my advisers, who do not trust my judgement. It is a list of forbidden topics, things that I must under no circumstances bring up when speaking to the king." Houde then handed the list to the king, who startled the banqueters with his loud laughter. After the royal couple got back to England, the queen was reported to have told friends that the mayor of Montreal was by far the most interesting person she had met in all of Canada.

~

Montreal never looked better than it did during that sunny day of the Royal Visit of 1939, but it was a city whose government was heading toward financial ruin. Houde had spent huge sums on public works during the past decade, and large amounts were still being doled out for the relief of the indigent. The civic debt was now $110,000,000, twenty times that of Toronto, and it was growing four times as fast as property evaluations. Finally, on May 15, 1940, the city found itself unable to redeem maturing bonds. Montreal was, in effect, bankrupt. Called upon to answer for this disastrous state of affairs, Houde made an eloquent defence of his policies. He admitted that the banks and other creditors had all along been advising him to be more economical, but what they were really asking him to do was to deny bread to the starving. He found it easier to bear the humiliation of bankruptcy than to witness the agonies of destitute families. Also, he had done everything he could to ward off the disaster. He had brought in a 2-percent sales tax, and that had led to his defeat in the 1936 municipal election and had kept him out of office for two years. He had approached Ottawa and Quebec City with many proposals for remedies, but all of them had been rejected.

In Quebec, Premier Godbout listened politely to Houde's explanation and then promptly put the City of Montreal under trusteeship. From now on, appointees of the Quebec Municipal Commission would, in effect, be making all the decisions, with the mayor and the city council serving in a largely advisory capacity. Furthermore, the entire structure of the council would be revamped. There would now be ninety-nine councillors, with thirty-three being elected by property owners and thirty-three by tenants. The remaining thirty-three would be sent to City Hall by the Board of Trade, the Chamber of Commerce, the Trades and Labour Council,

McGill University and sundry other institutions and organizations. In this profoundly undemocratic system, which would be in force for the next twenty-two years, a man who owned property in each of the city's eleven districts would be able to vote eleven times. As for the one-third of the council that was elected by tenants, only the person who signed the lease could vote. As this was generally the husband, most wives would thus be disfranchised, as well as any adult children who might be living at home and any boarders.

In this new setup, Camillien Houde found himself reduced to being little more than a figurehead. Once he had hired thousands of men to dig tunnels and pave streets, but now he could not even engage a charwoman to clean his office without the approval of the Quebec Municipal Commission. But although he was now virtually powerless, his voice still commanded attention. On August 2, 1940, he made an utterance that would send shock waves across Canada. That was the day when, speaking informally to a group of reporters, he said that he would refuse to obey the law, later that month, when all Canadians over the age of sixteen would be required to register for possible war service. This, Houde said, was the first step toward conscription for overseas service, and not only would he personally refuse to register but he would advise all Montrealers to follow his example.

One of the City Hall reporters who heard the mayor say this was Campbell Carroll of the *Gazette*, who immediately phoned his city editor, Tracy Ludington, and told him about it. Ludington told Carroll to type up Houde's statement, take it in to him and ask him to sign it. Carroll doubted that Houde would agree to go on record with these rash, highly seditious remarks, but as instructed he typed them up as a statement and presented it to the mayor, who surprised him by signing it with a cheerful flourish. That evening the early edition of the *Gazette* was on the street with the story splashed across the front page. Within the hour, the government censor was on the phone to Tracy Ludington, ordering him to drop this story, with its incitement to civil disobedience, from all later editions of the paper. Like all publications, newspapers were subject to censorship during the war, and Ludington had no choice but to do as he was told. But he was determined that the story should not die. He called Robert Hanson, leader of the opposition in Ottawa, and told him about it, and the next day an angry Hanson brought the matter up in the House of Commons. The story was now public property and could appear not only in the *Gazette* but in newspapers across the country. The outcry that followed could not be ignored by the government, and on August 5 the RCMP came to City Hall to arrest Camillien Houde. His utterance had breached the Defence of Canada Regulations. There would be no trial, but he would spend the next four years in internment camps, with other potential enemies of the state.

Why had Houde done this reckless thing? Had he been stupid, with no inkling of what the consequences might be? Or was it all carefully calculated? Political observers in Montreal debated the question at length, with most agreeing that Houde never suspected that his remarks would lead to his being locked up. Perhaps, as some said, he felt that his defiance would further endear him to French Canadian voters and thus assure him victory in the upcoming municipal elections. Or, as others said, now that the mayoralty of Montreal had been reduced to impotence, perhaps he had his eye on bigger spoils – like the premiership of Quebec. For the moment, of course, all this was out of the question, but once the shock of his arrest wore off, and Houde became accustomed to his existence behind the fence of the internment camp, he must have realized that there was no reason for his ambitions to wither. In fact, his incarceration might ultimately work to his advantage. In later years, Tracy Ludington, the man who started Houde on his road to internment, would recount how every year, at Christmas, Camillien Houde would send him a Christmas present. "He realized," Ludington said, "that I had made him a martyr."

During his internment, Houde's political skills stood him in good stead. He was, by all accounts, the most popular man in the camp, and a friend to all, although he said he preferred the communists to the fascists, whom he found too rigid and humourless. He was, of course, elected mayor of his hut, but he did not shirk his share of menial everyday tasks. The internees had to chop their own firewood to heat their huts in winter, and Houde, although he was now in his fifties, became the champion wood-chopper of the Petawawa camp. Later, at the Fredericton camp, he became the Chinese checkers champion and the long-distance skating champion. "It was the only holiday I ever had," he would later say, after his release, after the four long years behind the fence.

Ultimately, they were bitter years. It was fully sixteen months before the authorities allowed his wife and their eldest daughter to make their first visit to him, and then they could only stay for thirty minutes, with a guard close by. Subsequently only one short visit a month was permitted, and the only mail Houde was allowed to send out was one postcard a month, and that was censored. Over the years his supporters kept sending petitions to Ottawa, clamouring for his release, but they were all refused. On at least one occasion, the authorities intimated that he might be set free if he were willing to publicly recant, admit his error and promise not to further hinder the war effort. But he declined, realizing, no doubt, that an abject apology would destroy his credibility among all those voters who adored his impudence.

With the coming of summer, in 1944, Ottawa was besieged with renewed demands from Montreal for Houde's release. By now he had amply paid for his sins and, with the war going well in Europe, there was nothing he could do by way of sabotage. The matter was important enough to come before the cabinet, and finally Mackenzie King and his ministers agreed that the time had come to release Prisoner No. 694. He was set free, at the Fredericton internment camp, on August 16, 1944, in time to catch the train to Montreal. But his first destination was not Montreal. It would not do to arrive too quickly, not giving the city enough time to prepare a proper welcome. And so he got off the train at Sherbrooke, Quebec, and spent the night there. The next morning Montreal newspapers, in large headlines, announced that Camillien Houde would be arriving at Central Station at 6:55 p.m.

The crowd welcoming him was so large – more than ten thousand people, some estimates said – that he had great difficulty making his way through the station to the street. There, on Dorchester

Street, a platform had been erected and a public-address system installed. "I was lonesome for you, in the concentration camp," he told the crowd. "And it looks as though you were lonesome for me, too." He touched his eyes with a handkerchief, and many women in the crowd wept with him. Others threw flowers and everybody sang "Il a gagné ses épaulettes" (He has won his spurs). Then Houde got down to business. "I am ready to accept my mandate from the people who are crying for me," he said. "Your spontaneous ovation should be a warning to all political leaders."

Four months later, to no one's surprise, the former prisoner declared himself a candidate for the mayoralty in the upcoming municipal elections. He launched his campaign before an overflow audience at the St. James Market and drew cheers as he denounced Mackenzie King, whose government had interned him. "Is there no more justice in my country?" Houde asked. Then, getting down to municipal matters, he raised the spectre of mass unemployment in the years ahead, when the war would be over and factory workers would lose their jobs. He reminded his audience that during the Depression of the 1930s he had spent many millions of dollars to create jobs through public works, and he would do it again, if necessary. "No one will starve as long as I am mayor," he said.

Houde's opponent was Adhémar Raynault, the colourless insurance executive who had been mayor for the past four years. "He has not changed," Raynault said, attacking Houde. "He hasn't learned anything." Other critics of Houde brought up the familiar epithets, charging that he was nothing more than a frivolous Falstaff, a demagogue, an incompetent. In supporting Raynault, the *Star* told its readers that the position of chief magistrate called for "dignity, tact, discretion and savoir faire." Raynault, the *Star* said, had these qualities in abundance, but they were obviously lacking in Houde. The voters, however, refused to heed this cautious counsel, and they returned their rollicking Camillien to office with a whopping majority.

But if Houde was immensely popular with the electorate, he was still virtually powerless when it came to the administration of the city. Montreal was no longer under trusteeship, but the mayor remained little more than a figurehead. He presided over the city council, but could only vote to break a tie. The real power resided in J.O. Asselin, chairman of the executive committee, and George Marler, the vice-chairman. These were two remote, austere figures, known to the public as names but not as faces. What the Montreal public craved in a mayor, at least the French-speaking public, was warmth, colour and the occasional surprise. Camillien Houde was the man to give them all of this.

In his ceremonial capacity, he plunged into a brisk round of activities soon after he was elected. He inaugurated *la Semaine des Mères* – Mothers' Week – and Parks and Playgrounds Week and Air Cadets' Week. He led fund-raisers for cancer research and addressed the Chamber of Commerce, several historical societies and a convention of shoe manufacturers. His presence as an after-dinner speaker assured the success of any event. His explanation for this was simple: "Crowds respond to me," he said, "because I love them." One of the things his audiences cherished most was his unpredictability: what he praised yesterday he might well denounce tonight. And he had original ideas, like calling for the abolition of the speed limit on the roads north of Montreal, because driving slowly was so boring. As an orator, he was unsurpassed. Harold Dingman, one of Canada's leading newspapermen, told of sitting rapt through one of Houde's impassioned political speeches, despite the fact that it was in French, a language Dingman didn't speak. "I didn't understand a word the guy said," Dingman told friends, "but he sure convinced me."

~

The French had voted massively for Houde's post-internment election, but the western part of Montreal, the English part, voted just as solidly against him. This was the man who, in 1939, had said that if Italy were to go to war with Britain, Quebec would support Mussolini. This was the man who had tried to sabotage the war effort, and had had to be locked up. Indignation over Houde's attitude, in 1944, was so strong that Anglos in hospitals demanded to be taken to the polls on stretchers so they could vote against this fat, ugly traitor. Yet within a year, English Montreal was ready to forgive. After considerable debate among its executive, the St. Andrew's Society decided to invite the mayor to the first post-war St. Andrew's Ball, the most important event on the social calendar of Montreal's Anglo elite. Houde showed up at the ball in top form, and charmed the kilted guests by informing them that, like them, he was also a Scot, that Houde was actually French for Howe.

"On a score of occasions it would have been a pleasure to throt-tle him," the journalist Leslie Roberts once wrote, "but let him trundle his huge bulk into a room and the political dislike van-ishes . . . to be replaced by a warm glow." When Houde was due to visit the McGill Faculty of Law, on a cold winter's morning, the first-year students were waiting for him outside, with a supply of frozen horse droppings they had picked up from the street. When his lim-ousine pulled up, they pelted it vigorously with the horseballs. Unfazed, the mayor stepped out of the car, smiled broadly, doffed his Homburg hat and bowed to the students. They were immedi-ately won over and burst into applause. For Anglos, part of the Houdian legend derived from the way he spoke English. He had not learned any English until he was in his twenties, and his misuse of the language – perhaps deliberate – added to his appeal. Once, when he was asked if he planned to build more public urinals, he said he would not only build urinals, he would also build arsenals. For some Anglos, he was nothing more than a hulking buffoon, but Hugh MacLennan saw it differently. "In the course of time," MacLennan wrote, "we came to realize that his most endearing quality is his honesty, not the kind best understood in Ontario, but the deeper sort known to Shakespeare's clowns, who are infallibly the most intelli-gent characters in the plays."

Now that Houde had been forgiven by the English-speaking com-munity, Charles Peters, editor of the *Gazette*, wondered whether the mayor was ready to forgive the newspaper that had brought him so much grief. After all, the *Gazette* had been instrumental in having him interned, and after the recent election, an editorial in the paper had accused him of "vindictive personal abuse, tricky resort to agitation of prejudice, and flamboyant parading of personal and political grievances with no bearing whatever on civic affairs." After some hesitation, Charles Peters phoned the man his paper had so frequently denounced and invited him to lunch. Houde immediately accepted, but with one stipulation: they must occupy a table in the centre of the main dining room of the Windsor Hotel, so that there would be many important witnesses to their reconciliation. The lunch was a great success, and now Camillien Houde, more than ever, was living up to the accolade bestowed on him by Robert Rumilly, the historian. Houde, Rumilly said, was *le chum de tout le monde* – everybody's pal.

Outside Quebec, Houde's rehabilitation took longer. In much of the rest of the country, he was still a traitor. Photographers for the *Toronto Star* were instructed to catch him in the most unflattering poses possible, accentuating his fatness and his homely features. But gradually Canada came to appreciate him. When Ontario delegates to a convention being held in Montreal learned that Houde would be addressing their banquet, they sat down to dinner expecting to loathe him, but after listening to him they came away charmed, as did all his audiences. National magazines soon learned that this eccentric mayor made a very good story. He was so colourful that in describing him writers seemed to have to reach for their thesauruses. In *Maclean's*, Eva-Lis Wuorio said he was "irascible, ebullient, indiscreet, sentimental, arch, profound, roaring, intense, raucous, sagacious, excessive, witty, charming, difficult." In *Saturday Night*, Hugh MacLennan said Houde's weapon was his smile and went on to describe the smile as being "ferocious, amiable, seraphic, bawdy, gentle, mocking, threatening, cunning, approving, jolly and invariably surprising." *Time* magazine, after advising its readers that Camillien Houde rhymed with "comedian good," simply described the famous smile as being a "batrachian grin," apparently without fear that the adjective batrachian might be offensive to French Canadians. Articles like that in *Time* spread Houde's renown across the continent, and Montrealers travelling in the United States were often asked if they personally knew "that fat guy, Hood, the mayor."

Camillien Houde, it seemed, was the only Canadian, with the exception of a few hockey players, whose name was known to Americans.

~

It was all very well to thrill a convention of shoe manufacturers with a lively after-dinner speech, but for Houde the ultimate oratorical joy was to be found on the hustings, where he could harangue the electorate and calumniate, with orotund flourishes, the miserable wretches who had the temerity to oppose him politically. And so in April 1945, barely four months after his reelection as mayor, he astonished the city by announcing that he would be a candidate in the forthcoming federal elections. He would become a member of Parliament and would make things hot for Mackenzie King and the dastardly Liberals who had sent him to the internment camp. The voters of Ste. Marie, his old working-class riding, would now have an opportunity to tell Ottawa how wrong it had been to lock away their favourite son for those four long years. The Liberals, however, unleashed their biggest guns against Houde, with their apparently limitless election fund, and in the voting of June 11 the mayor went down to a humiliating defeat.

It was far from being the only defeat Houde had known. He had a tremendous appetite for elections, and in the course of his long career he was a candidate in eighteen of them – municipal, provincial and federal. Of these, he won eleven and lost seven. In the provincial elections of 1931, he was actually a candidate in two different ridings at the same time – Ste. Marie and St. Jacques – and he lost in both of them. Nobody could recall any precedent for a double candidacy of that sort, but apparently it was permissible. When the 1947 municipal elections in Montreal came around, Houde had a much easier time of it. No one was rash enough to challenge him, and he was elected by acclamation, the first acclamation of a Montreal mayor in half a century. In 1949 Houde made another effort to get to Ottawa, in the federal elections of that year, and this time he succeeded, by a very slim majority, and became member of Parliament for Montreal-Papineau.

The year before, Houde had mended the last of his torn fences by making peace with the premier of Quebec, Maurice Duplessis, whom Houde had despised since 1932, when Duplessis had been instrumental in ousting him as leader of the Quebec Conservative Party. Duplessis, for his part, had no great love for Houde. But now, brought together at Duplessis's home at Trois-Rivières by an intermediary, the two giants of Quebec politics were ready for a reconciliation, thanks largely to their shared loathing of the Ottawa Liberals. After several hours alone they emerged laughing, friends forever. Houde had been particularly tickled by Duplessis's retailing of the old joke about the traveller who had been given the privilege of sleeping in the bed once occupied by the late great Sir Wilfrid Laurier. In the morning, the traveller, vigorously scratching himself where the bedbugs had bitten him, said to his host, "It was an honour to sleep in the prime minister's bed, but you didn't tell me that I would be sleeping with the whole Liberal Party."

Now Houde, elected as a member of Parliament, was in a position to confront and harass those Liberals in Ottawa. Great interest was being shown, across the country, in the news that a special chair was being installed for him in the House of Commons, one wide enough to accommodate the massive Houdian bottom. But Houde made few appearances in the House and never made a speech. Ultimately, federal politics seemed of little interest to him – to have won the seat was enough.

In 1950 he was again elected mayor, this time with twice as many votes as his opponent, and he embarked on his seventh and last term in office. Some of the old powers of the Montreal mayoralty had been reinstated by Houde's new friend Premier Duplessis, in return for Houde's vigorous support of Duplessis in the 1948 provincial election. But although he now enjoyed being able to make trouble for his enemies on city council, Houde seemed less interested in the details of civic administration than in his ceremonial role. He was at his best during the 1951 visit of the future queen, Princess Elizabeth, and her husband, the Duke of Edinburgh. He ushered them through the city with the same verve he had displayed when the young princess's parents had visited a dozen years earlier. A royal visit was once again the occasion for more stories to be added to Houde's legend. Montrealers particularly appreciated one remark their mayor was alleged to have made to the princess. "I am very pleased, Your Royal Highness," he supposedly said, "to be your host at dinner this evening. As you may have heard, I was the guest of your father for four years until recently." Having been interned without trial, under the Defence of Canada Regulations, Houde had been technically imprisoned "at His Majesty's pleasure."

Soon Houde's health began to fail, and in September 1954 he announced his retirement. Chronically short of funds, he tried his hand at a few business ventures, but nothing came of them. His loyal and patient wife had suffered brain damage and could now remember nothing of their glory days together at royal banquets. With her he walked silently through the spacious parks he had founded in decades past. To help raise money for her care, he sold their house on St. Hubert Street and moved to more modest quarters. He put many of their household furnishings up for auction by Fraser Brothers, but the sum realized was disappointing. The auctioneer got a laugh when he pointed out that the next item on his list, an outsize rocking chair, had obviously been built for an outsize person, but the bidding was sluggish and the famous man's chair finally went for only ten dollars.

Just before the auction, Houde gave Bill Bantey, a *Gazette* reporter, what proved to be his last interview. People were urging him to run for mayor again, Houde said, but he hadn't decided whether or not to do so. "I've got one good speech on my chest," he said. "I don't know where or when I'll give it, but I'll definitely give it." But he was not destined to give it. He died in his sleep on September 11, 1958. His funeral was the largest and most elaborate Montreal had ever seen. Police said there may have been as many as 100,000 people lining the streets between City Hall, where he had lain in state, and Notre Dame Church, where the service was held. The cortege, marching to a dirge played by the firemen's band, included leading citizens and almost all of the ninety-nine city councillors. Premier Duplessis and half of his cabinet walked in the procession, as well as two great hockey players, Maurice Richard and Butch

Bouchard. It took thirty cars to carry the flowers that citizens had sent. At Côte des Neiges Cemetery, Houde's elaborate tomb was waiting for him. He had designed it himself, three years earlier, modelling it after Napoleon's tomb at the Hôtel des Invalides in Paris.

Among Camillien Houde's mourners were thousands of men and women who remembered how he had helped them survive the Great Depression, when so many were without work for so long. In those years, when there was no unemployment insurance and only the most meagre handouts by way of dole, hunger and malnutrition were widespread. Houde attacked the problem with compassion, imagination and energy. His program of public works created jobs, and his persistence in petitioning the federal and provincial governments, which often seemed so indifferent to the plight of the cities, eventually resulted in more funds being made available, grudgingly, for public welfare. Thus the 1930s were the years of greatest practical achievement for Mayor Houde. In the 1940s and 1950s his contribution had a different dimension, emanating entirely from his eccentric, flamboyant personality. He was, everyone agreed, Mr. Montreal. He set the tone, a unique mayor for a unique city.

If Montreal's colour and gaiety, in those years, were personified by Camillien Houde, the city's overtones of darkness emanated largely from the premier of Quebec, Maurice Duplessis. During his eighteen years in office, Duplessis seemed to be striving for outright dictatorship, what with the restrictions he placed on freedom of speech and other authoritarian measures that he instituted. Graft, patronage and electoral malfeasance had always been prevalent in Quebec politics, but under Duplessis these practices reached new, astonishing heights – or depths. And in a post-war world where democratic governments everywhere were starting to construct the edifices of social security, Maurice Duplessis was able to prevent any significant movement by Quebec in that direction. State-sponsored social security, he insisted, was basically "communist," and as such was a menace to law, order and the primacy of the Catholic Church.

Duplessis's most vigorous efforts were directed toward attracting industry to the province. To do this, he promised foreign entrepreneurs that he would keep wages in Quebec lower than almost anywhere in North America, and he achieved this by waging an unremitting battle against organized labour. In gratitude, the owners of factories, mines and paper mills rewarded him with munificent contributions to his party's election funds, thus enabling him to buy the votes that would help perpetuate his reign. For all these reasons, the Duplessis era would come to be known as *la Grande Noirceur*, the Great Darkness. In his memoirs, Gérard Pelletier says that thanks to Duplessis, Quebec's entire post-war generation was "undereducated, underpaid, and deprived of the most elementary social welfare structures: in a word, sacrificed." Pelletier, who was active in the labour movement at the time and later became a minister in Pierre Trudeau's cabinet, wrote: "We must remember that this man and his regime held back for a quarter of a century Quebec's entry into the modern world."

In rural and small-town Quebec, where Duplessis had his greatest support, there was little disapproval of what the sociologist Marcel Rioux called "that long return to the Middle Ages." Farmers with little education could easily be won over by Duplessis's oratory about the menace of godless communism and the hated "centralizers" of Ottawa. But in Montreal, young intellectuals like Gérard Pelletier were repelled by "the greyness, the boredom and suffocation of a society ruled by too many martinets." In 1950, Pelletier, Pierre Trudeau and others founded a courageous, dissenting magazine to give voice to their frustrations. Its title, *Cité Libre* – Free City – epitomized the aspirations of an enlightened minority in the metropolis, struggling for fresh air in the choking backwardness of the province that surrounded it.

Saturday Night, appalled by "the corruption of democracy" in Quebec, once pointed out to its readers that Duplessis had been born on the same day as Adolf Hitler – April 20, 1890. The magazine was right about the April 20 birthday but wrong about the year; Hitler was actually born in 1889, exactly one year before Maurice LeNoblet

Duplessis came into the world in Yamachiche, a village near Trois-Rivières. The son of a prominent lawyer, Maurice also became a lawyer. He shared his father's passion for politics and, like his father, he was eventually elected to the Quebec legislature as a Conservative. He became leader of the opposition in 1933, and three years later, heading a coalition of Conservatives and disaffected Liberals, he defeated the Liberal government, which had been in power for thirty-nine years. Duplessis's victory was noticed in England, where one newspaper, the *Herald*, announced that the British Empire's first fascist government had just been elected in Canada.

From the start, as premier, Duplessis fought every progressive initiative emanating from Ottawa, including the St. Lawrence Seaway project and a plan for a national system of unemployment insurance. These, he said, were federal incursions into the sacred realm of provincial autonomy. Duplessis had fashioned his coalition into a new party, the Union Nationale, and the protection of Quebec's autonomy was the principal article of the party's credo. But Duplessis's most memorable achievement during his first term in office was the passage of An Act Respecting Communistic Propaganda, commonly known as the Padlock Law. Under its provisions, no one was allowed to distribute any printed matter that might "propagate Communism or Bolshevism," or use his or her house for the dissemination of these doctrines. Besides making the occupant of the house liable to imprisonment, the act stated that the house itself could be padlocked for a period of up to a year, thus throwing the occupant and his family out onto the street. The act contained no definition of what constituted Communism or Bolshevism. That would be decided by the attorney-general, who happened to be Duplessis himself, and soon after the act was passed his provincial police started evicting Montrealers from their premises and padlocking their front doors.

In September 1939, Duplessis suddenly called an election, a move that proved to be the biggest mistake of his long political career. Canada had gone to war only two weeks earlier, and now Duplessis wanted a mandate to oppose any infringement of Quebec's autonomy that the federal government might attempt in its effort to mobilize the national war effort. But the Liberals were able to persuade the electorate that they alone could protect Quebeckers against the possibility of conscription, and in the October voting Duplessis went down to defeat. Voicing his delight at this outcome, Prime Minister Mackenzie King said, "A victory for Mr. Duplessis would have been received with rejoicing in Nazi Germany."

Now, as leader of the opposition in the legislature, Duplessis pursued a line consistent with one of his speeches, in which he asserted that the French Revolution's principles of liberty, equality and fraternity were "false and futile." When the new Liberal government of Premier Adélard Godbout introduced a bill that would give women the right to vote, Duplessis opposed it vehemently. But the bill passed and Quebec women were finally on an equal footing with the women of other provinces, who had had the vote for the past twenty years. Another bill that Duplessis heatedly denounced before it was passed called for compulsory education for all Quebec children between the ages of six and fourteen.

The Maurice Duplessis who campaigned in the next election, in 1944, was a very different man from the hard-drinking Duplessis who had held office in the late 1930s. After a serious illness, he had been advised by his doctors to give up alcohol, and from now on he would drink no gin, but instead would down orange juice by the gallon. No longer would he lurch into the Liberals' Reform Club and astonish the members by urinating into the fireplace, and no longer would his womanizing be so indiscreet. A lifelong bachelor, Duplessis was fond of saying that he was married to his province. He lived in a suite in the Château Frontenac Hotel, in Quebec City, but on weekends he usually came to Montreal, to see his mistress and occasionally attend a hockey game. Montrealers who saw him in restaurants, or striding across the lobby of the Ritz-Carlton Hotel, could sense the air of power and authority that emanated from him. It was easy to see why he was known to insiders as *Le Chef* – the Chief. Always immaculately dressed in a dark, double-breasted suit, he was a man of medium height, erect bearing and – except for his eyes and a long, beaky nose – generally undistinguished features. The nose was the delight of cartoonists, but it was Duplessis's eyes that fascinated his biographers. Conrad Black spoke of "the famous brown eyes that laughed, sparkled, burned, pierced, and darted with vivid and decisive authority." Pierre Laporte wrote of eyes that had "real magnetism," but he also saw menace in them. When UN party members who had decided to criticize some policy of *Le Chef* finally confronted him, they found themselves, Laporte said, "without voice to express their grievance. They could not meet the eye of this leader of men."

The 1944 elections brought Duplessis back to power, with his Union Nationale winning forty-eight seats in the legislature as against the Liberals' thirty-seven. Yet the Liberals got a greater share of the popular vote, 40 percent, as against the UN's 38.2 percent. This anomaly was a reflection of the grotesquely distorted electoral map of Quebec, which gave far more representation to thinly populated rural ridings than to large urban centres. Montreal, with more than a third of the population of the province, had only one-sixth of the seats in the legislature. The English-speaking sections of Montreal voted overwhelmingly against Duplessis, but the voices of the representatives they sent to Quebec City would count for little against those of the farmers' advocates from the hinterland.

In office again, Duplessis launched what he called his "war without mercy" against the Witnesses of Jehovah, a sect whose efforts to convert French Canadians were anathema to the Church. In his capacity of attorney-general, he ordered the police to arrest Witnesses for handing out tracts on street corners, charging them with offences ranging from disturbing the peace to sedition. In the summer of 1946, more than 260 Witnesses were arrested in Montreal, and when Duplessis learned that Frank Roncarelli, the wealthy owner of a popular downtown restaurant, was posting bail for them, he cancelled the restaurant's liquor licence, a move that eventually led to Roncarelli's financial ruin. During the next seven years, Duplessis would instigate 1,665 prosecutions against individual Witnesses, for offences like distributing a pamphlet entitled *Quebec's Burning Hate*. Part of that hate referred to mobs attacking meetings of Witnesses while the police stood by idly. Also, the police, looking for people to arrest, were given to raiding the homes of Witnesses where four or five people might be gathered for prayer. In the course of these raids, in order to emphasize the government's disapproval of this religion, the constables might take time to smash some of the Witnesses' furniture.

But for Duplessis, the most important function of his provincial police was to help break strikes called by unions seeking higher wages for their members. The arrival of the provincials in strikebound towns like Valleyfield or Louiseville was an ominous event. They would come in a procession of cars, many of them thugs in jackboots with beer-bellies that bulged out over the tops of their khaki breeches. Gripping their truncheons in black-gloved hands, they would roam the streets, ostensibly to quell trouble caused by the strikers. But if the strike was peaceful, and there was no trouble to be found, the police – often called Duplessis's private army – would oblige the factory owners by themselves creating enough disorder to discredit the strikers. In the 1946 strike at Montreal Cottons Limited, in Valleyfield, Duplessis said he was sending in his police to protect workers who wanted to cross the picket lines and go back to their jobs. When none of the workers sought to cross the picket lines, and none asked for protection, the police happily supplied the requisite disturbance by moving in on the picketers and manhandling them. Duplessis promptly announced that these scuffles were riots, and were the work of communists.

"The bitterly fought strikes in Quebec in the forties and fifties were reminiscent of the 1890s in other parts of North America," according to historian Ramsay Cook. The provincial police, who played such a large part in these conflicts, usually came to the scene of a strike not because they were called in by worried municipal authorities – who seldom welcomed them – but because the management of the factory or the mine that was involved wanted them to usher strikebreakers through picket lines. By making his police available to break heads where necessary, and by branding most strikes as being illegal and communist-inspired, Duplessis quickly endeared himself to Montreal's business leaders. The St. James Street tycoons also remembered with fondness how energetically he had fought, when he was leader of the opposition, against the Liberal government's legislation that would begin the nationalization of the province's privately owned hydro-electric resources. Duplessis, of course, failed to block this legislation, which laid the foundation for Hydro-Quebec, but his persistent opposition to it firmly established him as the champion *par excellence* of private enterprise. As such, Montreal's English-language newspapers would give him their unwavering support, although most of their readers, middle-class Anglos who detested his dictatorial attitudes, would never vote for him.

As the 1948 provincial elections approached, the Anglo captains of industry were prepared to pour large sums into Duplessis's campaign coffers, something that could easily be done in an era when campaign contributions were not limited by law or open to public scrutiny. These were contributions from the very *trustards anglais* that Duplessis would denounce, in French, of course, in his election orations to the farmers and villagers of the province. Duplessis was without doubt the greatest political genius Quebec had ever seen, and there was no aspect of that genius that was more impressive than his ability to convince French voters that he was protecting them against the rapacity of those *maudits* English capitalists, while at the same time he was doing everything he could to further the interests of those same factory owners, especially by keeping French wages at a minimum.

As those Anglo gentlemen continued to dominate the economy of the province, Duplessis was, in the words of the Quebec nationalist André Laurendeau, a "Negro king," akin to a tribal ruler in one of Britain's African colonies. The British would let this potentate do as he pleased, as long as he kept the natives down and didn't interfere with the colonialists' interests. "They dominate the Negro king," Laurendeau wrote in *Le Devoir*, "but they allow him fantasies. On occasion they allow him to cut off a few heads. . . . One thing never comes to their minds, and that is to demand that the Negro king conform to the high moral and political standards of the British."

~

Patronage was an old tradition in Quebec politics. Duplessis's pre-
decessor, Premier Taschereau, at one point had no fewer than forty-
five of his relatives on his Liberal government's payroll. But Duplessis
brought the practice into new and more imaginative realms. Early
on, he did away with the calling for tenders in the awarding of public
contracts. "Tenders are hypocritical," he said. "A government always
gives business to its friends, never to its enemies." Needless to say,
before a contract was signed the contractor was told exactly how
much was expected of him by way of kickback. This sum would be
added to the price being charged for the work to be done and thus,
through this diversion of public funds, the taxpayer enriched the war
chest of the Union Nationale Party, or perhaps helped one of its
officers to build himself a nice summer cottage.

Practices of this sort were not unknown in other provinces, but
what distinguished Duplessis among his fellow Canadian leaders was
the breathtaking openness and candour with which he operated.
When the town of Cap de la Madeleine found itself in grave financial
difficulties, he told its citizens, in an election speech, how they could
solve their problem. "Elect my man," he said, "and the day after the
election your mayor will have a cheque for thirty thousand dollars.
Otherwise, not a cent." In their wisdom, the townspeople elected
the right candidate. At election meetings Duplessis didn't beat
around the bush but told voters in no uncertain terms that if they
wanted a new school, a hospital or a bridge for their community they
had better vote Union Nationale. Motorists driving through the
province could tell how a region had voted by the quality of its roads.
The good pavement of a highway going through a Union Nationale
county might end abruptly when it reached the border of a Liberal
county, where it would suddenly turn into an unimproved dirt road.
The South Shore highway between Montreal and Quebec City was
a notorious example, its disrepair making it known as a death-trap
as it passed St. Hyacinthe, which persistently voted Liberal.

In rural communities, people saw government expenditures not
as their right as taxpayers but as gifts to be received with gratitude.
In his reverent biography of Duplessis, Conrad Black describes
him as "an all-seeing father, severe but benign [who] rewarded the

deserving, punished the unworthy and ruled vigilantly over his brood. . . . The Duplessis government endured not because it suppressed democracy but because it embodied it. . . . Everything and everyone in French Quebec . . . rose or fell according to the credit they had with Maurice Duplessis. It was gratifying for him and simple for everyone else."

Besides the practicality of offering bribes, Duplessis's election oratory always had ideological content, always involving his three Cs – the Church, the communists and the centralizers. The first of these had to be protected from the onslaught of the second; the third, the hated centralizers of Ottawa, must be kept at bay, their proposals for joint federal-provincial enterprises being nothing more than sinister manoeuvres designed to rob Quebec of its cherished autonomy. These themes echoed through the election campaign of 1948, bolstered by what was believed to be the largest election fund in Quebec history, probably five times what the Liberals were able to spend. In rural ridings this money allowed Union Nationale organizers to go from door to door, offering, among other things, to pay a voter's unpaid bills in exchange for his ballot. In Montreal, the fund paid for skulduggery on a lavish scale – the wrecking of Liberal committee rooms by goons, the seizure and destruction of Liberal pamphlets, the arrest of Liberal canvassers by the provincial police on the flimsiest of pretexts, and the hiring of platoons of telegraphers to vote fraudulently on election day. The Union Nationale operatives were wise enough to attempt relatively little of this kind of activity in middle- and upper-class ridings like Outremont, Westmount-St. George and Jacques Cartier, and Duplessis's candidates lost in those ridings, as they had in the previous election. But in working-class ridings the thuggery knew no bounds, and it helped the Union Nationale snatch four seats from the opposition. In all, the election was a tremendous victory for Duplessis. With 51 percent of the popular vote, he won eighty-two of the ninety-two seats in the legislature.

Among those who were delighted with the Union Nationale's victory were the *Montreal Star* and the *Gazette*, which, in an editorial, praised Duplessis's adherence to the principle of free enterprise as opposed to the Liberals' promises of "state security payments." The *Gazette* disdained the assertion by Adélard Godbout, the Liberal leader, that the present social order was one that tended mainly to make a very few people rich. More to the paper's liking was the Duplessis credo that "the individual will do better to stand on his own feet than on any government's back." The relationship between Duplessis and the *Gazette* was close and affectionate. He and John Bassett, the paper's publisher, were great friends, and it was said that Bassett was the man who first introduced the premier to the executives of St. James Street as the force that could keep labour in its place. In return, Duplessis saw to it that the Gazette Printing Company got a good share of the government's printing contracts. Duplessis was also a close personal friend of the *Gazette*'s chief correspondent in Quebec City, Abel Vineberg, whose stories always showed *Le Chef* in the best possible light. And the paper's news editor, Tracy Ludington, was for several years employed by Duplessis to look after his English-language public relations, which included writing campaign literature and even making speeches. Far from seeing this relationship as a conflict of interest, John Bassett approved heartily and saw it as an asset for his paper.

J.W. McConnell, who by now had succeeded Lord Atholstan as publisher of the *Star*, also became a good friend of Duplessis, frequently sending him gifts of cigars. At election times the gifts were more substantial – cartons containing up to $100,000 in fresh banknotes. Like Bassett, McConnell had spies in his newsroom who kept him posted on efforts by his poorly paid journalists to form a union, and Duplessis would be an invaluable ally in thwarting the formation of that union or fighting it if it ever came into existence. Also, the two publishers were indebted to Duplessis for using his power to keep down the price of newsprint. Whenever the big Quebec paper companies threatened to raise their prices, Duplessis reminded them that the province controlled their timber-cutting rights; he could curtail those rights or he could impose price controls if St. Lawrence Paper or Consolidated Paper proceeded to make supplies more expensive for Quebec publishers. This ability to help assure the profitability of newspapers helped Duplessis keep almost all the Quebec press docile and uncritical of his policies. In Montreal, *La Presse* and *Montréal-Matin* were just as subservient as the *Gazette*, the *Star* and the *Herald*, another McConnell paper. Only *Le Canada*, the morning paper owned by the Liberal Party, and *Le Devoir* spoke out against Duplessis. *Le Devoir* was particularly biting in its criticisms and exposés, and this infuriated *Le Chef* to the point where he once had his police throw a *Devoir* reporter out of a press conference; the man, who had not even opened his mouth to ask a question, had offended Duplessis by his mere presence. In his campaign against *Le Devoir*, Duplessis would send his agents to visit businessmen who advertised in the paper, offering them lucrative government contracts if they would withdraw their ads and thus help drive the paper, which was always on the financial brink, into final bankruptcy.

Le Devoir was a newspaper favoured by intellectuals, a class of people held in the utmost contempt by Duplessis, who boasted that he had not read a book since leaving college. "Any opponent of Mr. Duplessis," Gérard Pelletier wrote, "unless he was an illiterate or a travelling salesman, became by the very fact of his opposition an intellectual and a communist. According to this usage, one might have thought the two terms were synonymous." Duplessis had good reason to fear intellectuals. During the decade that followed his 1948 election victory, French Canadian intellectuals, most of them in Montreal, would mount increasingly telling attacks on his policies. It was also a decade in which he would have to face important legal challenges to his Padlock Law and in the Roncarelli affair. And the momentous asbestos strike of 1949, a turning point in Quebec labour history, lay ahead. These struggles, with the opposition to Duplessis mainly emanating from Montreal, will be described in a later chapter, dealing with a period when a few shafts of light would start penetrating *la Grande Noirceur*. But what Ramsay Cook called "the Ice Age in Quebec politics" would not be over until after the death of Maurice Duplessis, in 1959, and until then its chill winds would continue to be felt in Montreal.

5

Show Business:
Lili St. Cyr's Town – and Al's and Oscar's

From the start, Tommy Conway, the theatre manager, knew that this new stripper was going to be different. Unlike the other girls, she wasn't just going to peel off her clothes, while the drums rolled, and thrust her pelvis out at the old lechers in the audience. No, this lady was making weird demands, for special props.

"For my first number," she told Conway, "I'll need a Chinese temple, with a little altar. And a statue of Buddha in front of the altar." After some thought, Conway told Kenny, the set designer, to get her what she wanted, including two incense burners. Kenny had to scramble to find this strange stuff, but he managed to get it all together before midnight on Sunday. By law in Montreal, the Gayety and other theatres like it had to stay closed on Sunday, but at five minutes after midnight it was Monday, and that's when the first show of the week began. And tonight, there was a full house for the midnight show, anxious to see this new artiste – Lili St. Cyr.

As the curtain went up to reveal the Chinese temple, the music from Len Howard's orchestra was languorous and melancholy, quite unlike the usual raucous striptease overture. After the music and the incense set the scene, Lili came drifting out onto the stage, a tall blonde in a flowing oriental costume. Her slow dance conveyed sadness and despair, and she hoped the audience would understand what her problem was – that her husband, a rich noble, had gone off to the wars, leaving her locked into a chastity belt. Bowing down before the Buddha, her pantomime implored him to free her from this accursed belt, so that she could properly entertain her lover. The thought of this ecstasy made her writhe with desire and as the music quickened she allowed her clothes to slowly fall away, revealing what was perhaps the most voluptuous body ever displayed on the stage of the Gayety. Now, as the music approached its climax, her naked undulations became more and more frenzied. Then, suddenly, a dazzling flash of light lit the shadowy stage. The Buddha, liking what he had seen, had answered her prayer. Triumphant, Lili held aloft a large key and ended her dance by unlocking the wretched chastity belt and hurling it away. As the curtain came down, the applause was thunderous. The patrons of the Gayety had seen them all – Gypsy Rose Lee, Georgia Sothern, Noel Toy, Rosita Royce – but nothing like this new performer. This was not the coarse bump-and-grind of a Peaches or an Ann Corio, this was art – and it spoke to Montreal's well-known craving for the sublime.

This mid-winter night in 1944 was the beginning of Lili St. Cyr's seven-year reign as Montreal's most famous woman, the city's femme fatale, a person whose name invoked sophistication, mystery, sin and – for many males – instant arousal. Her fame soon spread beyond Montreal, and gentlemen from Toronto and Winnipeg were known to schedule their business trips to the city at times when Lili was going to be on the bill at the Gayety. They and local fans, including many women, sat patiently through the preliminary acts – comedians, ventriloquists, jugglers, knife throwers – waiting to see what Lili had come up with this time. Her act always had a little story, although the story was sometimes a bit hard to follow, as in a number called "Jungle Goddess," in which she seemed to be making love to a large parrot. More popular was a piece entitled "Suicide," in which she was in the depths of despair after being jilted by her lover. Clutching his photograph, she slowly divested herself of her clothes, hoping that the sight of her body might bring him back. When it failed to do so, her grief was such that she clambered up on a window sill, and stood poised, ready to destroy herself. At this point, the audience invariably shouted, "No, Lili! No! Don't jump!"

If Montreal loved Lili, the sentiment was more than reciprocated. She danced in New York, Los Angeles, Miami, San Francisco and Las Vegas, but she always said that Montreal, where she frequently performed, was her favourite city. "*Montréal a été une ville enchantée pour moi*," she wrote in her autobiography. "*C'était l'endroit où mes rêves devenaient réalité*." ("Montreal was an enchanted city for me. It was the place where my dreams became reality.") Her book, *Ma vie de stripteaseuse*, was written for her by Matthew Tombers. It was aimed at the Quebec market, and was thus written in French, a language Lili didn't speak. Because of her stage name, French Canadians tended to think that Lili St. Cyr was one of them, but actually she had been born Marie Klarquist, in Minneapolis, of Swedish-Dutch parentage. She was twenty-seven years old when she first performed in Montreal.

What Lili liked best about the city, besides the adoration she got from her audiences, was the revelry that awaited her every night after her last show. She loved the bars and the nightclubs, the Algiers, the Samovar, Slitkin's and Slotkin's, and the roisterers she would meet there – newspapermen like Al Palmer, hockey players like Boom-Boom Geoffrion, boxers like Rocky Marciano, promoters like Eddie Quinn, wrestlers like Yvon Robert, gamblers like Harry Ship. After the bars closed, she and her entourage would repair to one of the town's many blind pigs. "Every night in Montreal was like New Year's Eve in New York," she said in her book.

At the El Morocco, Lili met Jimmy Orlando, the hockey idol who, she said, became the love of her life. But whenever she left town, to strip in another city, Jimmy tended to cheat a bit with various chorus girls, and eventually Lili ditched him, tearfully. But over the years, Montreal was still able to supply her with some of her favourite lovers, between – and during – her six marriages. She particularly liked rich businessmen and gangsters with lots of money to spend on gifts of jewels, mink coats and trips to Europe on transatlantic liners. "I broke hearts and emptied pocketbooks," she said. "What's the use of being beautiful if you can't profit from it?" And she was, indisputably, beautiful, with her regal bearing, her perfect dimensions, her high cheekbones, her extravagantly arched eyebrows.

Not everyone in Montreal was an admirer. There were dissenters like Marie-Joseph d'Anjou, the well-known Jesuit priest. In the spring of 1951, Father d'Anjou wrote a lengthy denunciation of Lili

St. Cyr in *Le Devoir*, calling on the city authorities to run her out of town, once and for all. Whenever she danced, he wrote, *"un relent de frénésie sexuelle empeste le théâtre"* ("the theatre is made to stink with the foul odour of sexual frenzy"). It was a menace to the morals of the young. And as Quebec's national holiday, la Fête Saint-Jean-Baptiste, approached, the event would be soiled by the presence in the city of this woman who danced the story of Salome. After all, Salome was the biblical slut who had asked for – and had been given – the severed head of John the Baptist on a platter. As John was the patron saint of Quebec, Lili's choice of this dance, at this time of year, was not exactly tactful.

Father d'Anjou's outcry was echoed by the Public Morality Committee, and a week later Lili was arrested and charged with behaviour that was "immoral, obscene or indecent." At her trial, Chief Judge Edouard Archambault was irritated by the fact that the prosecution's most vocal witnesses had never personally seen Lili dance. Moreover, three housewives who had been at the Gayety the night she was arrested testified that they had seen nothing that was morally wrong. In her number called "Eve," they observed, Lili had retained her bra and panties as she danced around the huge apple. Testimony like this convinced Judge Archambault, and he found Lili innocent of all charges.

Among those who rejoiced in her acquittal was an unlikely body, La Chambre de Commerce de Montréal, the French counterpart of the Board of Trade. Blazoned across the front page of its newsletter were the words "BRAVO LILI!" This dancer, said the newsletter, was a national treasure. "She awakens the adolescent," the article said. "She stimulates the young man, gives comfort to the mature man and sweet memories to the elderly." The article burbled with praise for Lili, calling her the Goddess of Love incarnate, and it denounced the puritans who wanted suppress her. More soberly, it warned its businessmen members that if the puritans prevailed, Montreal would cease to be Canada's capital of night life, and millions of tourist dollars would be lost. But Lili's years in Montreal had now come to an end. Las Vegas, the new resort in the desert, was starting to bloom, and there were new worlds to conquer out there. Besides, the arrival of television was keeping people at home, and burlesque and vaude-ville were everywhere on the decline. In Montreal, within a few years, the splendid old Gayety Theatre would close its doors forever.

As a girl, Marie Klarquist, who would become Lili St. Cyr, shared none of her schoolmates' housewifely ambitions. Enchanted by the movies, by Garbo and Dietrich, she wanted to grow up to be mys-terious and seductive, to be, in her words, "an adventuress." She suc-ceeded brilliantly. Still in her twenties, she dined not only with boxers and gamblers in Montreal but also with Franchot Tone, in his Hollywood mansion. She slept not only with hockey players and barbotte operators in Montreal, but also with Orson Welles, in his bungalow at the Garden of Allah Hotel, off Sunset Strip. But as the 1950s wound down, the adventuress, as a type, was on her way out in North America. Like the millionaire playboy of the supper clubs, the flamboyant seductress, in pursuit of the best luxury money could buy, was becoming extinct as a species. In Montreal, the likes of Lili St. Cyr would never again be seen.

~

The middle-aged man who was causing the disturbance was obvi-ously drunk and, even more obviously, was an out-of-towner, proba-bly from some strange foreign place like Toronto. The Montrealers in the room watched indulgently as he lurched toward the stage, where the chorus girls were doing one of their high-kick numbers. "Would you girls like a little drinkee?" he was calling out as the headwaiter took him firmly by the arm and led him back to his table, where his fellow businessman-bumpkins, all similarly sloshed, were applaud-ing his wit.

It was almost always the out-of-towners who were the rowdy ones in nightclubs like the El Morocco. They were, Montrealers knew, simply busting loose after being confined to the parched prison that constituted the rest of the Dominion of Canada. In most provinces, in the 1940s, you couldn't legally consume hard liquor in public, except in a few private clubs. There was no booze to be had in restau-rants, no wine with meals. For a night out on the town, you would buy a twenty-six-ouncer of rye at the gloomy government liquor store (where the act of purchase was somehow made to feel sinful) and take it to the restaurant or the dance hall, where you'd keep it under the table, in its brown paper bag. Men and women could not be trusted to drink together, and so the drab, sour-smelling beer parlours were for men only, with separate "beverage rooms" for the ladies. And, needless to say, there was nothing vaguely resembling the elegant, glamorous nightclubs that Canadians saw in Hollywood movies.

But Montreal had nightclubs aplenty – fifteen of them in 1948, all with elaborate floor shows, plus about twenty-five smaller "lounges," with more modest entertainment. These flourished despite ecclesiastical disapproval. "We are ashamed," Cardinal Léger said, a few years later, "that our city has more nightclubs and drinking places than churches." This in a Montreal that now had even more churches than it did in the 1880s, when Mark Twain said, "This is the first time I was ever in a city where you can't throw a brick without breaking a church window." But there had always been plenty to drink in Montreal. Back in 1720, there were nineteen taverns in the city, one for every 105 inhabitants, and this despite the bishop's having ordered his priests to deny absolution to the operators of these Sodoms, where, he had heard, dancing was permitted and immorality was commonplace.

Two centuries later the Church in Quebec still had serious doubts about dancing. In 1936, Canon Cyrille Labrecque issued a warning. "*Les danses lascives sont interdites,*" he wrote. And, he added, even non-lascivious dances were to be avoided. He listed the forbidden lascivious ones as "*le tango, le turkey-trot, le fox-trot et le cheek-to-cheek.*" But in Montreal the fox- and turkey-trotting never let up, not even in the dark days of the 1930s Depression. These dances had come north a decade earlier, along with hordes of tourists avid for the liquor and the nightlife that was being denied to them by Prohibition in the United States. Montreal was famous across the continent for its enlightened attitude toward having a good time, and visitors found the drinking and dancing they were looking for at the Venetian Gardens, the Pagoda, the Jardin de Danse, the Palais de Danse, the Brass Rail on Drummond Street and the Frolics on St. Lawrence Main. At the Frolics, as patrons came through the door, they would be greeted by a brassy blonde hostess called Texas Guinan, who would shout, "Hello, suckers!"

The nightclubs, often owned by sports promoters, gamblers and gangsters, were forever closing down, changing ownership, being redecorated, changing their names and opening up again. But most of them always stayed in the same locations along the city's main commercial artery, St. Catherine Street, or just north or south of it on cross streets like Stanley or Mountain. By the 1940s all the old names had disappeared and had been replaced by a new roster that included establishments like the Latin Quarter, the Esquire, the Maroon Club, the Samovar, the Copacabana, the Top Hat ("the largest bar in town"), the Tic Toc ("a show every hour on the hour") and the Normandie Roof ("Canada's most beautiful room"). And, of course, the El Morocco, by all accounts the best club in town. "The El," according to Al Palmer, nightclub critic of the *Herald*, had "the prettiest chorus girls, the funniest comics, the thickest steaks and the strongest drinks." It was to the El that you came if you wanted to meet celebrities like boxing champions Jack Dempsey and Jack Sharkey, or the legendary Lili St. Cyr. After a hard night's stripping, Lili would often relax with a few drinks at the El, which, she said, was "the point of departure for my greatest romantic adventures."

Clubs like the El Morocco had long bars, many small tables, a stage and a small dance floor. There was much chrome in evidence, red leather or velvet upholstery and subdued lighting. Patrons, while they sipped their Singapore Slings and sliced into their filets mignons, would watch floor shows with music by the resident band and dancing by the girls of the chorus line, plus a procession of imported performers which, besides the featured *chanteuse*, might include Apache dancers, jugglers, magicians, mind readers, knife throwers and Borscht Belt comedians. Most of these were little-known performers, booked from New York, but there were also "headliners" like Milton Berle, Sophie Tucker, Dorothy Lamour. Red

Skelton appeared at the Tic Toc, Dean Martin and Jerry Lewis at the Esquire, Sammy Davis, Jr., at the Chez Paree. Mistinguett, at the age of eighty, bravely came to the Montmartre, and the El Morocco proudly presented Christine Jorgenson, who had been propelled to stardom by being the first person to undergo a sex-change operation. Harry Ship, the gambling czar who owned the Chez Paree, vowed to bring in the biggest name of them all, Frank Sinatra, but Sinatra refused to come to Montreal unless Ship gave him an advance of ten thousand dollars, an enormous sum at the time. After agonizing over this demand for days, Ship finally gave Sinatra what he wanted, and was amply repaid by the crowds that lined up to get in, in sub-zero weather, all the way down Stanley Street.

Advertising for the clubs often boasted that acts were "direct from New York," but down the hill, on St. Antoine Street, the acts were billed as being "direct from Harlem," black musicians and entertainers who attracted large white audiences to Rockhead's Paradise. Its owner, Rufus Rockhead, an immigrant from Jamaica, was one of the city's most adroit impresarios. During the 1920s he had worked as a railway porter, on the Montreal–Chicago run, a job that allowed him to make a good deal of money smuggling liquor into the United States, then in the grip of Prohibition. He saved enough to go into business, opening a tavern and a small hotel, and by the 1940s he was operating one of Montreal's largest and most popular clubs, importing Harlem stars like Mable Smith – "300 pounds of jump and jive and song and mirth." Besides the crowds of uptown white patrons that Rockhead's attracted, it was a favourite destination, in summertime, for black tourists from the United States, among them celebrities like Louis Armstrong and Joe Louis.

Rockhead's competition was another black club, just around the corner on Mountain Street, the Café St. Michel, whose fame derived largely from the presence of Louis Metcalf's International Band. Metcalf, a trumpeter who had once played with Duke Ellington's orchestra, was the man who first brought bebop to Montreal, the new kind of jazz that was being pioneered in the United States by avant-garde musicians like Charlie Parker. The seven musicians of

Metcalf's band called themselves Canada's greatest jazz band, and the critics agreed with this boast. Montrealers adored Metcalf's music. Often, after a hard night's partying elsewhere, they would arrive at the St. Michel at 3:00 a.m. on Sunday morning for the club's "breakfast dance." It might be 9:00 a.m. before Metcalf and his men could go home to bed, but they would be back on deck at the St. Michel less than seven hours later, for the Sunday afternoon jam session.

Besides New York, entertainers came from the music halls of Paris for the city's French audiences. Edith Piaf sang at the Sans Souci, Charles Trenet and Lady Patachou at the Café de l'Est. The Faisan Doré on St. Lawrence Main brought in Dédé Pastor, Jean Rafa, Charles Aznavour. Nearby, a new club called the St. Germain des Prés took its name from Paris but encouraged new homegrown talent like Raymond Lévesque, Paul Berval and Clémence Desrochers. Stars-to-be like Monique Leyrac, Dominique Michel and Denise Filiatrault got their start at places like the Café St. Jacques and the Bal Tabarin, but although English Montreal produced many show-business entrepreneurs, it gave birth to no night-club singers or comedians destined for fame.

One of the most successful of the entrepreneurs was Harry Holmok, who for years had dreamed of operating "the biggest damn club in Canada." He finally opened it in 1949, on Ontario Street near Bleury, and called it the Bellevue Casino. On its main floor and its balcony, the Bellevue could seat seven hundred people, far more than any other club, and it was an overnight success, with seldom an empty table. Its shows were the most elaborate in town, with a new production every month. These were mounted by George and Natalia Komorov, who had staged shows for the Latin Quarter on Broadway and the Folies Bergères in Paris. The Komorovs always had a theme for the show – Old Vienna, Old Spain, Old Whatever – and Bix Belair's orchestra produced appropriate waltzes or *paso dobles* for the dances of the eight elaborately costumed chorus girls. And, of course, there was the usual roster of featured singers, "specialty dancers," acrobats and musical novelty numbers, all whipped into perfection by the dictatorial Komorovs. But it was not only the spectacle on stage that made for the Bellevue's phenomenal success; it was also Harry Holmok's policy of making his club the cheapest as well as the biggest in town. "Fifty cents to get in, and fifty cents for a beer," Holmok would say. "How can you beat that – for the best show in town?"

While the cavernous Bellevue Casino could provide a bargain night out for the hoi polloi, smaller, more intimate clubs could be dauntingly expensive. But in Montreal, in the post-war years, there was lots of money in circulation: businessmen had safety deposit boxes full of black-market cash they had accumulated by circumventing wartime rationing and price controls, and young war veterans had reestablishment credits the government had given them to help them in their return to civilian life, money some of them would choose to spend carousing until dawn with hookers at Aldo's.

By law, closing time for drinking places was 2:00 a.m., but at most clubs the owners stayed open as long as there were any big spenders in the room who wanted to keep on spending. Waiters spoke fondly of the millionaire who, one night, kept announcing that he would buy drinks for everybody in the house. It was a slow night, with few patrons on hand, and so the waiters kept trotting out onto St. Catherine Street to bring in relays of passersby to consume free champagne. By the early morning hours their tipsy benefactor had run up a tab of over a thousand dollars.

One of the big spenders most cherished by nightclub managers was Allen McMartin, the mining engineer who had struck it rich in the goldfields of Northern Ontario. McMartin was particularly fond of the music of the Peter Barry Trio, especially its rendition of his favourite tune, "Pagan Love Song." One night, at the Tic Toc, McMartin kept insisting that Barry play the song over and over, each time sending a large tip to the bandstand. Finally, as the last customer in the house, McMartin was persuaded to go home. "But Peter and the boys have got to come with me," McMartin said, and so the trio went home with him, to his apartment in Haddon Hall. Here they watched as his valet helped him into his pyjamas and, as the happily sozzled mining magnate slid between his satin sheets, Peter and the boys stood around the bed and softly played his last request of the evening, "Pagan Love Song," until he fell asleep. The next day McMartin's chauffeur arrived at the Tic Toc with a hundred-dollar tip for Peter Barry.

Barry was one of the most successful musicians of the era, with his Havana Rhumba Band playing, at one time or another, almost everywhere – at the El Morocco, the Chez Maurice Danceland, the Maroon Club, the Black Sheep Room at Ruby Foo's and even at the plebeian Dagwood's. He knew the favourite songs of all the very big spenders, and as soon as one of these worthies entered a club with his entourage the Peter Barry band would burst into the appropriate tune. Tips would flow to the bandstand and invitations would come for the band to play at important social functions, like Bronfman weddings and Shapiro bar mitzvahs.

But Peter Barry's biggest hit was a song of his own composition, perhaps the only song of the era to make a political statement. It was called "Margie Margarine," and patrons of the Copacabana loudly applauded its implicit criticism of Quebec's Premier Duplessis. The premier's Union Nationale government, much despised in English Montreal, had banned the sale of margarine in Quebec, at the instigation of dairy farmers who wanted no competition for their butter. The province's distorted electoral map gave the farmers' rural ridings lots of seats in the legislature and comparatively few to Montreal, to poor folks who couldn't afford much butter. Hence Peter Barry's lament, sung to a calypso beat:

> My mother go to the grocery store,
> To buy a pound of butter or more
> But the butter price is much too high
> So mother sit at home and cry . . .
> This is democracy, I am told,
> So why can't margarine be sold?

～

The hard edge of "Margie Margarine" was a rare exception in the usual nightclub repertoire of song, where almost all lyrics were deeply sentimental. At the Baronet Room Colleen Enright sang "You Belong to My Heart," while at the Clover Café Eve Brien sang "Love for Sale." Vic Damone's offering at El Morocco was "Tangerine," Patricia Windsor's at the Normandie Roof was "Night and Day." At the Tic Toc, gentile patrons thought they could detect professions of love in Kathryn Chang's renditions of Chinese songs with Yiddish lyrics. At the Ritz Café, in Montreal's most posh hotel, the vocal fare was, according to one critic, "sophisticated, seductive and invariably low-key." The café's bistro decor – blue-and-white checked tablecloths and little gold lamps – helped make this the city's most elegant supper club. With Johnny Gallant accompanying them at the piano, singers like Suzy Solidor, Celeste Holm and Jane Morgan held forth, and among the patrons who had come to hear them you might see visitors to town like Marlene Dietrich, Charles Boyer, Maurice Chevalier, Charles Laughton, and Tyrone Power.

While the middle-aged businessman and his wife were dining and drinking at the Ritz, their teenage sons and daughters were down the street, a few blocks away, jitterbugging at the Chez Maurice Danceland. There was no floor show here, no tables, no dinner, no alcohol – just dancing to the music of the greatest of the big bands: Glenn Miller, Tommy Dorsey, Woody Herman, Cab Calloway, Stan Kenton. The era of the big band was at its height in the 1940s, and you could dance to the new swing music at a dozen venues in Montreal and the suburbs, places like the Palais d'Or, the Auditorium, and the Verdun Pavilion. But the greatest of them all was the Chez Maurice Danceland, above Dinty Moore's restaurant on St. Catherine Street.

Among the enthusiastic patrons of Danceland, on a Friday or a Saturday night, was Maureen Forrester, who would some day embark on an international career as one of the world's great contraltos. She was fourteen years old in 1945, growing up in the east end of Montreal, singing in a church choir and, for the purposes of her visits to dance halls downtown, trying to look ten years older than she was. "I would dress up in my imitation wool plaid skirt," she wrote in her autobiography, "and the oversized sweaters that were all the fashion, then I would borrow a little detachable white Peter Pan collar and pearls from my sister. . . . I would dare a little lipstick, stuff my bra with socks and stick my comb in the peroxide bottle to see if bleached blondes had more fun." But Maureen declined invitations to dance; what she had come for was to listen to the music, to study the inner workings of the orchestra. "When they would lower the lights for the slow dances," she wrote, "and the big mirrored silver ball in the centre of the ceiling would throw its rainbow reflections wildly over the crowd, I would press myself up against the stage and close my eyes, swaying to the music. I would dream I was a singer with the band. That was the height of my musical ambitions then: I wanted desperately to be a band singer at Danceland."

In addition to the big bands on tour from the U.S., the Swing Era in Montreal saw the formation of a number of local bands, both professional and semi-professional. The most successful of these was the Johnny Holmes Orchestra, which provided the music for the Saturday night dance at Victoria Hall, in Westmount. Thanks to the original arrangements of hit tunes made by Johnny Holmes, his fifteen-man band produced a distinctive sound, quite different from the familiar stock arrangements played by other local orchestras. It was a sound that pulled in large crowds, week after week, for almost a decade. One of Holmes's admirers was Maureen Forrester, and when she heard that his vocalist had left town, she approached him and asked if she could audition for him. "But he said he had decided not to use a girl singer that year," she wrote in her book. "I was crushed." Forrester would never realize her ambition to sing with a swinging band of that sort, but would go on to share the stage with maestros like Zubin Mehta, Bruno Walter and Sir Malcolm Sargent.

Other promising young artists did manage to play with the Johnny Holmes Orchestra. One of them was Maynard Ferguson, a young trumpeter from Verdun, who was only sixteen years old when he moved on from Victoria Hall to form his own orchestra at the Verdun Pavilion. His high-note trumpet was a sensation, and in later years he would play in the bands of Charlie Barnett and Stan Kenton. But the most distinguished alumnus of the Johnny Holmes group was a shy young pianist named Oscar Peterson, who one day would elicit ovations at Carnegie Hall.

Peterson was born in St. Henri, the shabby, working-class district that was home to much of Montreal's small black community. His father, like most black men at the time, worked for the railroad, as a sleeping-car porter. But he was determined that his children achieve more out of life, and he decided that music would be their best route out of St. Henri. Oscar and his four brothers and sisters started playing their instruments at the earliest possible age, and by the time he was five Oscar was showing promise on both the piano and the trumpet. His father, himself an accomplished amateur musician, was his tutor, punishing him with a strap if he failed to master the assigned Liszt or Chopin. But Oscar's preference was for jazz, despite his father's disapproval, and by the time he was in high school he was being called the Brown Bomber of Boogie Woogie. He was the star of the Montreal High School Victory Serenaders, and in 1942 won a nationwide CBC amateur piano contest.

Later that year, at the age of seventeen, he joined the Johnny Holmes Orchestra, and the Canadian Pacific Railway, suddenly proud of the fact that one of its sleeping-car porters was the father of this musical prodigy, issued a press release that was redolent of the era's white condescension toward blacks. Referring to Daniel Peterson's musical children as his "sepia brood," the press release predicted a "stellar career at the piano keyboard" for Oscar. "Built like a piano himself," it said, "genial, mahogany-stained Oscar is close to six feet tall and measures about four octaves wide at the shoulders. His broad smile displays a set of ivories fit to make the ivories on any piano keyboard yellow with envy. . . ." But Peterson, like all black musicians, was subject to discrimination that went well beyond simple condescension. He was the only black member of the Johnny Holmes band, and once when the band had been booked to play for a dance at the Ritz-Carlton Hotel, the manager phoned Holmes and told him that he didn't want "that nigger" in the hotel. If that was the case, Holmes said, he would put ads in the city's three English newspapers announcing that his band would never again play at the Ritz, because of the hotel's racist policy. Angrily, the manager relented and Peterson played at the dance, with Holmes making a point of featuring him on every third number.

In 1945 Peterson made his first recording – "I Got Rhythm" – in the Montreal studio of RCA Victor. In the next few years he would record twenty-nine more titles in this studio. Meanwhile, he had left the Johnny Holmes band and had formed the Oscar Peterson Trio, to play at the Alberta Lounge, across the street from Windsor Station. His renown was spreading, and when they were in town jazz greats like Coleman Hawkins, Woody Herman and Ella Fitzgerald dropped in at the small, smoky lounge to hear him. Count Basie raved about him and Jimmie Lunceford and others offered him big money if he would join their bands in the U.S. But, for the moment, Peterson chose to remain in Canada, close to his family, where he felt secure. Finally, in 1949, he was persuaded to go to New York to be an unheralded "surprise guest" at one of the prestigious Jazz at the Philharmonic concerts at Carnegie Hall. Peterson was a sensation, having "stopped the concert dead cold in its tracks," according to *Down Beat*, the authoritative, hard-to-please music magazine.

Now about to embark on an international career, Peterson knew that the road to success would never be easy for a black musician in a white world. To face the challenge, he decided that he would have to become the very best. What he would have to do, he said, was "frighten the life out of everybody pianistically." Over the years Peterson would engender more admiration than fear, winning the *Down Beat* readers' poll as the world's best jazz pianist fourteen times. At home, in Canada, nine universities would award him honorary degrees, accolades that would have been considered utterly impossible in the 1940s, when Peterson's career began and when the establishment looked down on jazz as low-brow and subversive, fit only for disreputable bars and dubious dance halls.

～

Besides bars and nightclubs, restaurants were very much a part of the good life in Montreal in the 1940s and '50s. For many would-be bon vivants, "atmosphere" was just as important as cuisine, and American tourists sought atmosphere at places like Au Lutin Qui

Bouffe. They'd heard all about it, but the name was hard to remember and even harder to pronounce. But they'd been told that all they had to do was tell the taxi driver to take them to the restaurant with the little pig. The driver would immediately head up St. Denis Street, leaving the downtown tourist area far behind, and turn into a nondescript street called St. Gregoire. The restaurant – you might translate its name as the Gorging Gremlin – was located in a rambling old house where its owner, Bert McAbee, had been born. After you had been seated, and had ordered your cocktails, a waiter would scoop up the little pig that had been grunting about underfoot and hand it to you. It was pink, powdered and perfumed, and the house photographer was standing by, ready to take your picture as you fed the piglet milk from a baby's bottle. These frequent feedings made the little porker grow quickly, and after about a month it would be too big for easy handling and would have to be replaced by a new, three-day-old piglet. When asked what happened to those lovable little pigs after they reached retirement age, Bert McAbee dodged the question. The food at Au Lutin was nothing to write home about, but the photograph made a wonderful souvenir and that, essentially, was what the tourists came for.

Another place at which to be photographed was just out of town, on Ile Bizard, at Le Petit Robinson. Here you ate on platforms in the trees, and the waiters climbed ladders to bring you your onion soup. But for non-tourists, the serious eating in the 1940s and '50s was far from places like these. It was downtown that the gourmets were to be found, at restaurants like Chez Son Père. Behind its unprepossessing facade, on St. Lawrence near Craig, Chez Son Père offered memorable cuisine under the direction of its chef-owner François Bouyeux, who had trained in the great restaurants of Paris and had cooked for Leopold, King of the Belgians. Bouyeux was much praised for two of his specialties, *la mousse de foie d'oie* and *le suprême de volaille truffée*. Chez Pierre, on Labelle Street, was another celebrated eating place. To assure a supply of the freshest vegetables, Chez Pierre's owner, Louise Leroy, grew them on her own farm, not far from the city. And to prepare her son Jean to be the best of wine stewards, she sent him, as a teenager, to hotel school in Paris. On her menu she was particularly proud of her goose with chestnuts, her bear steak, her saddle of hare and her sorrel soup made with sorrel from her own garden.

Café Martin, on Mountain Street just south of the Ritz, was the resort of what the gossip columnists called the bluebloods. In view of the average blueblood's appetite for drink, Café Martin's head bartender, Jos Pouliot, was considered as important as its chef, especially in an era when women patrons might ask for drinks like brandy alexanders, pink ladies, stingers, sidecars and grasshoppers. In view of the complexity of these potions, bartenders like Pouliot were treated reverently in the gossip columns, where they were called mixologists. As for food, the pre-dinner booze often emboldened the predominantly English-speaking clientele to try the frogs' legs, and Café Martin's chef, Roger Delfour, was proud to tell you that in an average year he would order four thousand pounds of frogs' legs from his suppliers.

A few blocks to the west, on Mackay Street, there was Chez Stien, one of the oldest and most elegant of the city's restaurants. Here dinner was served with all the ceremonial of *le grand service à la française*, which meant that the *pièce de résistance* would be brought out on a large silver platter and the waitresses, in black satin uniforms, would distribute it to the diners' plates with spoon-and-fork legerdemain. The plates were of porcelain, the tablecloths of snowy Irish linen, and the cutlery of silver that was forever being polished. As for the menu, popular items included *bouillabaisse*, pheasant and partridge. At lunchtime, Chez Stien was less formal, and among the politicians who favoured it you might see Pierre Trudeau and René Lévesque lunching together, in the latter's pre-separatist days.

Politicians also liked The 400, nearby, where the three-hour, three-martini lunch was considered conducive to making the wisest decisions for the public good. As for The 400's food, its proprietor was famous for his slogan, "*Je mange chez moi.*" At the many eateries, as the gossip columnists called them, along St. Catherine Street, between Peel and Guy, birds of a feather often lunched together. You'd find advertising executives at the Indian Room and radio announcers at Dinty Moore's, where corned beef and cabbage was the great attraction. Nightclub musicians and chorus girls favoured the Chic-n-Coop, while dance studio instructors and more admen chose Drake's. Young salesmen and shipping clerks perched on the soda-fountain stools at Macy's or at Bryson's Drug Store, because that's where they could ogle the fashion models eating their bacon-and-tomato sandwiches. At Aux Délices, it was the pastries that were being ogled, the ne plus ultra of pastrydom, so tempting to women shoppers, resting up from their assault on the department stores.

For late-night dining, after the hockey game, there was Slitkin's and Slotkin's, run by two boxing promoters and a favourite with newspapermen. It was at Slitkin's that Morley Callaghan, in town from Toronto, would sit for hours, drinking with his pal Dink Carroll, sports editor of the *Gazette*, and avidly absorbing local colour for use in the novel he was writing about Montreal. Even later at night, there was Bens Delicatessen, at Mansfield and Burnside, open twenty-three hours a day, one hour being reserved for cleaning. Founded in 1908 by Benjamin and Fanny Kravitz, Bens (it never had an apostrophe) was a pioneer in the field of fast food. Its smoked meat sandwiches were much appreciated by show-business people, after the show, and some of them would even take briskets of Bens smoked meat back to New York, to show pastrami eaters down there what the real thing tasted like.

People who liked to dine in the privacy of their automobiles found curb service up north, on Decarie Boulevard, at Miss Montreal or at Piazza Tomasso, where, in 1953, the carhops were outfitted with roller skates. Inside Tomasso's, every Thursday night was Kiddies' Cabaret Night, with a magician named Tom Auburn going from table to table and amazing the children by making things disappear and by plucking eggs from their mothers' hairdos. Tomasso's spaghetti palace was a pioneer in the area, just out of town in the wide-open spaces off Decarie, near the Blue Bonnets Racetrack. In his 1952 paperback thriller, *Murder over Dorval*, David Montrose takes his detective hero, Russell Teed, on a perilous mission to the Decarie Strip (in aid of a damsel in distress, naturally) and in the process gives a somewhat exaggerated but perceptive description of the area's new restaurants, which opened after the war. "Most of them," Montrose wrote, "had the same basic architectural style – Recent American Roadhouse, long and low with peaked roofs and widespread wings. They were overlaid with trappings that disguised them into everything from Ann Hathaway cottages to villas from the Riviera to Burmese pagodas. They varied just as much inside. You could spend anything from a dime to a century-note, depending on which wide parking lot you rested your machine on."

In real life, in the 1940s, the most important pagoda on the Decarie Strip was Chinese, not Burmese. Its parking lot was the largest in the area, harbouring more Cadillacs than any other lot in town, and your expenditure inside would be much closer to that century-note than to the dime. It was called Ruby Foo's and it claimed to be the finest restaurant in Canada, as well as being the largest, with room for seven hundred diners. For decades, Montrealers had been used to Chinese food, down in Chinatown, but here were garlic spareribs and egg foo yung of a new gourmet dimension. There was an occidental menu, too, with the roast beef and Yorkshire pudding considered by authorities to be the equal of London's finest, at Simpson's in the Strand. Besides the food, every amenity was offered. There were, of course, several bars to calm the impatience of people waiting for their table, as well as a trio to play for them and often a comedian to tell them jokes. In the gentlemen's washroom, there was an attendant to hand you your towel or lend you a comb. And there was Frances Lim, the attractive cigarette girl, whose only task was to circulate with her tray, ready to supply you with your favourite brand, or a Havana cigar, if you ran out of smokes.

"Preferred by the town's most interesting people," Ruby Foo's newspaper ads said. If they were not the most interesting, they were certainly among the wealthiest. In the restaurant's several dining rooms on a Thursday night – maid's night out – you would see, with their wives or their mistresses, gobbling their moo goo guy pan, the elites of Montreal's three mainstreams – the Jewish clothing manufacturers, the Anglo insurance company executives, the French

Canadian real-estate men and notaries. It was important to sit at the right table, and politicians particularly wanted the booths on the right, just past the entrance, where they could see and be seen, and make contact with potential purveyors of graft. A banknote, discreetly "slipped" to Frank Goral, the maitre d', would not harm one's chances of getting a choice table. The presence of important persons, at the choice tables, was often noted in the gossip columns of the English newspapers, or in the scandal sheet *Montreal Midnight*.

Ruby Foo's was the creation, in 1945, of four wealthy businessmen, men who liked to stand in the foyer of this new showplace and "meet and greet." Ten years later they were growing old and ready to retire, and when one of them, Max Shapiro, suggested that the management of the restaurant be turned over to his two very capable young sons, his partners agreed. Harold and Bernard Shapiro, twins, had just graduated with great distinction from McGill. They ran the restaurant successfully for a few years and then, after their father died, they allowed themselves to be bought out, so they could do what they'd always wanted to do – go back to university, earn their doctorates and pursue academic careers. The administrative experience they gained in running a big restaurant stood these twins in good stead, as became evident many years later, when Harold Shapiro became president of Princeton University and Bernard Shapiro became principal of McGill.

~

Marion Steele was "a vocalulu." Alys Robi was "the Habitant chantootsie." Other singers were seldom singers – they were canaries, thrushes or songals. The words were those of Al Palmer, the poet laureate of Montreal nightlife. As the writer of the column "Cabaret Circuit" in the *Herald*, Palmer produced a constant stream of vivid neologisms that should have caught the attention of lexicographers. In pronouncing judgement on the artistry of visiting entertainers, Palmer seldom called dancers dancers; they were glamorines, hoofers or female tapperettes. They "pitched their curves around" in nightclubs that were "upholstered playpens" and where liquor was "stagger syrup." At the Copacabana, Pierrette Doré was a thrush who "curls her tonsils around *Mon Homme* in such a manner as to cause goose pimples among the taxpayers." Palmer was fond of referring to the customers in the upholstered playpens as the taxpayers.

A handsome, dapper man about town, Al Palmer, with his fedora firmly on his head and his press pass in his pocket, was – or strove to be – a hard-drinking reporter out of a Hollywood movie. He knew everything and hobnobbed with everybody – gamblers, gangsters and the proprietors of drinking places. In many ways, he personified the Montreal-New York connection. His lingo and his breezy, slangy style was much influenced by the Broadwayese of columnists like Walter Winchell and Leonard Lyons and, above all, by the guys and dolls in the tales of Damon Runyon. Dollops of this kind of parlance could also be found in the writings of the town's two gossip columnists, Fitz (pen name of Gerald FitzGerald) in the *Gazette* and Sean Edwin (pen name of Ted McCormick) in the *Herald*. The appropriation of vocabulary was only one aspect of the Montreal-New York connection. Most of the entertainers who appeared in Montreal nightclubs were booked through New York agencies, and they brought with them an aura of Broadway – clothes, manners, attitudes – that was eagerly aped by local showbiz people. The underworld, too, derived much of its style, and some of its personnel, from New York. Back in the 1920s, when Prohibition was in force in the U.S., emissaries of gangsters like Al Capone were frequent visitors to Montreal, to engage in rum-running. In the 1950s, when the heat was turned on by the U.S. Senate's Kefauver Crime Commission, Mafia hoodlums from New York like Carmine Galante fled north, to set up shop in a colder but more tolerant climate.

In 1950, when Al Palmer published his book *Montreal Confidential*, the influence of New York was again in evidence, as only two years earlier Jack Lait and Lee Mortimer had come out with *New York: Confidential!* These New York newspapermen were enthusiastic boosters of their city, which they described as "this wacky world of fancy, flesh, piracy, pruriency and pure poesy." Al Palmer believed his Montreal world was just as wacky as theirs, and his book – a twenty-five-cent paperback – set out to prove it, as promised by the words on its cover – "The Low Down on the Big Town."

Like Lait and Mortimer, Palmer had copious advice for yokels from the sticks on how to comport themselves amid the sophistication of the big town and how to avoid its pitfalls. He told them how to deal with taxi drivers and how to tip head waiters. "If it is at all possible," he advised, "don't go out on Saturday night. That is the night when all the niteries are jampacked by those of the lesser income brackets. . . . Saturday night is the one night when the shoe clerks can go out and howl." Palmer seemed very concerned lest the visitor from Saskatoon cause a disturbance. "Don't whistle your appreciation of the floor show," he warned. "Don't hammer your glass with a swizzle stick." And for the amorously inclined, he had practical suggestions. "Don't try to smuggle a doll up to your hotel room without first making a deal with the staff," he wrote. "Montreal house detectives are a competent lot. They know all the answers, they've heard all the questions. A fin [five dollars] proffered in a discreet manner may get you under the wire, but don't count on it."

For Al Palmer, 1950 was a banner year. He published not only his vade mecum for the yokels but also a novel, *Sugar-Puss on Dorchester Street,* another twenty-five-cent paperback. In its description of the Montreal of the time, the book presents a stylishly cynical picture. Dorchester Street (in later years to become Dorchester Boulevard and, still later, Boulevard René Lévesque) is described from one end to the other, beginning in the east-end slums. "Her spawning ground," he writes, "is wedged solidly between vermin-ridden tenements where French and English meet – but do not blend – and the greasy waters of the St. Lawrence River. . . . Heading westward, she bisects the one-time world-famous Red Light district which pollutes the air just east of St. Lawrence Main; hurriedly skirts the Jewish ghetto at Clarke [sic] Street and pauses only after passing the sordid commercialism of Bleury. . . ." Moving past Peel Street, Palmer still finds little to commend Dorchester Street, and he bemoans the vulgar tourist lodge signs that now adorn the old houses where the best families once lived. "Leaving her bitter-sweet memories," he writes, "she travels west, past Guy Street, and slowly wends her way past Victorian mansions now reeking of shabby gentility until she reaches Atwater. Once west of the city limits she loses herself in middle-class squalor. This is Dorchester Street. For this Gisèle Lépine traded the cool cleanliness of a Laurentian village."

Gisèle Lépine is Palmer's heroine, his much-abused innocent abroad in the big town. As the book begins, she is an eighteen-year-old "farmerette" living in the village of St. Christophe sur Lac, bored with life in the hinterland and determined to seek something better. After working in a nearby hotel, so she can meet tourists and learn English, she sets out for Montreal, to the dismay of her parents. In the big city, Palmer hints, Gisèle will not fail to be appreciated, as he notes that "her breasts were large and firm, a legacy of her Norman ancestry. . . . Her feet were small and beautiful, as were those of most French-Canadian women. . . ." The former farmerette soon finds work, as a dancer in the chorus line at the Coq d'Or nightclub, despite the fact that she has no training or experience as a dancer. But she does well at it and soon meets and falls in love with Jimmy Holden, a dashing, smartly attired newspaper reporter who was always on the lookout for a story. In this and in several other ways, Jimmy Holden resembled author Al Palmer.

The romance between Jimmy and Gisèle is a tempestuous one, especially when she has reason to doubt his love for her. "You are in love with a newspaper," she wails, on one occasion. "That I do not wish to compete with." But by the final pages of *Sugar-Puss* all misunderstandings are cleared up, and, after a passionate embrace, the young lovers "disappear into the brilliant sunshine of Dorchester Street," the now-luminous street that was so sombre at the beginning of the book.

If the fictional Jimmy Holden was in love with newspapering, that was also true of many a real-life young reporter, twirling his spaghetti and drinking his quart of Black Horse Ale at Slitkin's and Slotkin's. In the mid-1940s, this restaurant was the city's unofficial press club, as well as being the real-life model for the fictional café that Al Palmer called The Breakers. It was here that newspapermen met and mingled with what Palmer called "characters, characters – never any normal people." Being a newspaperman gave you an entree to a raffish world beyond the reach of ordinary "civilians," a world where you could come to know the people who had served as models for characters in *Sugar-Puss*, like Palmer's fictional Diane, the chorine with the platinum hair and the heart of gold; Gaston Courtney, the suave but sinister racketeer; and Jim Schultz, owner of The Breakers, "who mangled expensive cigars and the King's English."

In the sin-ridden Montreal of the time, many newspapermen found nothing more stimulating than being on a first-name basis with the gamblers and the gangsters, who were often also the owners of the nightclubs and the restaurants. For Al Palmer, his encounter, on a July afternoon in 1946, with a gangster named Louis Bercovitch was perhaps the most memorable event of his career. Earlier that day, Bercovitch had shot and killed Harry Davis, the city's gambling kingpin. After doing the deed, Bercovitch fled to a friend's apart ment, from where he phoned Ted McCormick, managing editor of the *Herald*, to tell him that he wanted to surrender, but to McCormick and not to the police. McCormick would then hand Bercovitch over to the police who, Bercovitch reasoned, would be more gentle with him if they knew that a newspaper was witnessing his being taken into custody. For Ted McCormick this was a gift from heaven. His paper, a breezy tabloid, was the smallest of the city's three English dailies, but it was the only paper with any real com-petitive spirit, in contrast with the stodgy, somnolent *Star* and *Gazette*. The Bercovitch surrender would be the scoop of the century.

But there was a problem. The *Star*, an afternoon paper, was already on the street, but it was still six hours before the *Gazette*'s deadline. Bercovitch had to be kept under wraps until the *Gazette* was put to bed, so that it wouldn't have the story first. The city was crawling with detectives and reporters, from the French as well as the English papers, looking for Bercovitch the killer. And there were rumours that the *Herald* knew something that nobody else did. A safe house had to be found for Bercovitch, and it was Al Palmer who came up with the solution – his sister's place in Verdun. With photographer Buster Arless at the wheel, Palmer, McCormick and Bercovitch made the nervous trip to Verdun in Arless's car, with the murderer on the floor in the back, covered with a coat. In Verdun, Palmer and

McCormick took turns at a portable typewriter, taking down Bercovitch's rambling, ten-page confession, the gist of which was that he had shot Davis in self-defence. With the confession complete, and the murder weapon duly photographed, Bercovitch was spirited back to the *Herald* building, where he had to be hidden for another few hours, until the presses rolled at the *Gazette*, only a few streets away, with its last edition. But there were several policemen in the *Herald* now, looking everywhere except in the one place where Bercovitch was being hidden – the ladies' room. And so Ted McCormick and Al Palmer had their scoop, emblazoned on the front page in big, black letters: "DAVIS SLAYER SURRENDERS TO HERALD."

It was adventures such as this, and Oscar's music, and Lili's dancing, and Chef Bouyeux's *suprême de volaille truffée*, and the warm, boozy camaraderie of the dimly lit little bars that made for Al Palmer's lifelong love affair with Montreal. "It is not so much a city as a state of mind," he wrote. "To live there is to love it. Those of us who were fortunate enough to be born there consider it the nearest approach to Heaven we know of without leaving the ground."

6

English Spoken Here:
Above the Tracks, Below the Tracks

The mournful sound of the bells rolled out from the steeple and across Dominion Square. Arthur Burgess, the campanologist, was outdoing himself this chilly September afternoon, in 1941, ringing no fewer than five hundred changes on the mighty chimes of St. George's Church. It was a fittingly opulent clangour for the funeral of the richest man in all of Canada, Sir Herbert Holt, a titan who symbolized the fact that although Montreal was largely French, the money was English.

The prospect of Holt's funeral posed a cruel dilemma for the city's Anglo-Scottish business elite. He had died early on a Sunday morning, but another extremely affluent pillar of the community, Senator Lorne Webster, had died only a few hours earlier, on Saturday night. Now, through some incomprehensible lack of coordination, both funerals had been scheduled for Tuesday afternoon, within ninety minutes of each other. Even with their chauffeurs standing by and motors idling, the St. James Street tycoons realized that it was highly unlikely that one could manage to make it a double-header this afternoon. One church was downtown, the other far away in Westmount. The services would be long and the hymns numerous. And so, how should one choose, with the whole world looking on? As always in Montreal, when a very rich man was being sent to his eternal reward, reporters from the *Gazette* and the *Star* would be out in force, on the steps of the church, taking the names of the mourners as they entered. The next day, the papers would carry long lists of names, and everybody would know exactly who had paid their respects and who had not. Now, with the Holt-Webster dilemma, the agonizing choice that had to be made by every club-man in town would be subject to close scrutiny on Wednesday, and talk of disloyalty and betrayal would be inevitable.

As it happened, the Holt funeral attracted what was by far the larger crowd, with dignitaries, functionaries and businessmen overflowing the church. This was quite understandable, as Holt was considerably richer and more powerful than Webster. Webster was a giant in the coal business and director of a dozen major Canadian corporations, but Holt – ah, Holt! – he was the colossus. Once pres-ident of the Royal Bank, his portrait was in the pockets of thou-sands of Canadians, engraved on the five-dollar bills issued by the bank. In his time, he was president of twenty-seven major corpora-tions and, it was believed, a director of some three hundred other companies. Once, when an inquiry in Ottawa asked him exactly how many companies he was involved with, he said he didn't know, that he had never kept any record of them. But his interests included pulp and paper, textiles, tobacco, mines, railroads, shipyards, insurance companies, flour mills, streetcars, hotels and theatres. In Montreal it was said that one got up in the morning and turned on lights powered by Holt's electricity, cooked breakfast on a stove that burned Holt's gas, smoked one of Holt's cigarettes, read a newspaper printed on Holt's paper, rode to work in one of Holt's streetcars, sat in an office heated by Holt's coal, and then, in the evening, went to see a movie in one of Holt's theatres. And during the war, fighter pilots flew Holt's airplanes, as he had bought the air force the gift of a squadron of Spitfires.

No Canadian had ever amassed as much wealth and power as Sir Herbert Holt, a man who had risen from humble beginnings, having immigrated from Ireland as a young civil engineer in 1873. He had laid the foundations of his fortune at a time when there was no income tax and little government regulation of business. Now, with his death at the age of eighty-five, observers sensed the end of an era. Sydney Dobson, general manager of the Royal Bank, summed it up in his tribute to Holt when he said, "He belonged to an era of individual effort and initiative now unfortunately fast becoming extinct." But if bankers found this unfortunate, others could only cheer, as Sir Herbert Holt had become, for many Canadians, the exemplar of unrestrained capitalist rapacity and greed. Although people who knew him said he was painfully shy, the public saw only arrogance. During strikes against his companies, when his life was frequently threatened, he refused to give up his daily habit of walking to work, and would march through downtown Montreal surrounded by four armed guards, with rifles over their shoulders.

It was French Canadians who most detested Holt, remembering him as the president of Montreal Light, Heat and Power Consolidated which, during the Depression, did not hesitate to cut off electricity to the unemployed when they couldn't pay their bills. "*La compagnie était impitoyable*," said the writer Hertel LaRoque. "The company was without pity. Even if a woman was in the process of giving birth, even if children were dying in the house, the service was cut off." For many French Canadians, Sir Herbert Holt was the man who was happy to see them freeze in the dark, the man who symbolized the worst of *les Anglais*, always ready to rob and humiliate them. It was no wonder, Hertel LaRoque wrote, that they "applauded frenetically" at the news of his death, unaware, apparently, of the English newspapers' listing of his many contributions to charity over the years.

Among the chief mourners at Holt's funeral that September afternoon was Sir Edward Beatty, president of the Canadian Pacific Railway. For Beatty it was a particularly sad occasion. Here was another luncheon companion gone. Beatty, Holt and Sir Charles Gordon, president of the Bank of Montreal, used to lunch together at the Mount Royal Club, and Gordon had died two years earlier. They had been an odd trio over lunch – Gordon the reputed womanizer, Beatty probably a homosexual and Holt, sometimes known as Old Stone Face, austere and puritanical. But if their proclivities differed, they had one distinctive thing in common: all had been knighted and bore coveted British titles, ornaments long cherished in the city's high society. Now, with the death of his two friends, Beatty was one of the last surviving businessman-knights, and there would be no new ones in the future. In 1935, Prime Minister

Mackenzie King, always anxious for Canada to shed vestiges of its colonial past, had told Britain that it must no longer bestow titles on Canadians. In this detail, as in others, English Montreal would henceforth become somewhat less British.

Sir Edward Beatty was not quite as rich as Sir Herbert Holt, but he might have challenged him in terms of power. As president of the CPR, with its worldwide steamship routes as well as its railway, he had what one American newspaper called "the biggest business job in the world." It was by far the biggest corporation in Canada, and Beatty's decisions probably had more effect on the lives of ordinary citizens than did those of the prime minister. In Montreal, especially after the death of Holt, he might well have been called Head of Everything, including the two keystone institutions of the Anglo establishment – the Royal Victoria Hospital, of which he was president, and McGill University, of which he was chancellor. A lifelong bachelor, he was president or a director of a dozen charitable or cultural institutions. He was particularly concerned about the welfare of young boys and served as president of the Boy Scouts of Canada and of the Boys' Farm and Training School at Shawbridge, a facility for juvenile delinquents. One of his favourite outings was to go up to Shawbridge to meet young offenders from the slums. He would make the short trip north from Montreal in his private railway car, having had a special siding built from the main line so that the car could be hauled right up to the farm.

When Beatty died, in 1943, his obsequies could have been seen as symbolic of the economic grandeur that was once Montreal's, and the decline that lay in the future. After the funeral service, in the Church of St. Andrew and St. Paul, in the heart of the old Square Mile, his mahogany and bronze casket was borne in a cortege along Sherbrooke Street and down Drummond, to Windsor Station, with thousands of people lining the rainy streets to see it go by. At the station, that cavernous Victorian temple of the Railway Age, the coffin was placed on a baggage cart, draped in purple velvet, and drawn across the concourse toward the departure gates. A company of the Victoria Rifles of Canada formed a guard of honour, recalling the fact that this regiment had supplied the guard for the first transcontinental passenger train to depart from Montreal, in 1886. Beatty's coffin was placed aboard a special train, to be taken to St. Catharines, Ontario, where he was to be buried in the family plot. This mighty railway that was taking him on his last voyage, the railway so central to the history of Canada, had been built through the enterprise of Montrealers, but now the old vigour of the city's Anglo-Scottish business elite was becoming much diminished and, in the years to come, the engines of finance, like the funeral train, would be moving in the direction of Toronto.

Toronto's economy was growing more quickly than Montreal's, a situation that could not have been predicted in earlier decades. At the beginning of the twentieth century, members of Montreal's Anglo-Scottish elite controlled three-quarters of the wealth of Canada. These men, often rough-and-ready adventurers with little education, were innovators and expansionists. As they made their fortunes, they sent their sons to the best private schools, where they learned to be little English gentlemen, and the hallmark of an English gentleman was to excel at sports and disdain the grubbiness of trade. And so, in the 1940s and 1950s, the sons and grandsons of the old robber barons displayed little commercial ambition or drive, seemingly content to maintain their inherited wealth rather than make it grow. They were, for the most part, caretakers rather than builders, not looking for new worlds to conquer, not partial to long hours in the office. Promptly at five in the afternoon, Charles Fleetford Sise, president of the Bell Telephone Company, would be off to the Mount Royal Club to play bridge with other magnates. As for Herbert Molson, scion of the beer dynasty, if he wasn't at the afternoon bridge table it was because he was off fishing or playing golf.

Although the process of Montreal's gradual economic decline was already under way in the 1940s, its effects were not easily perceptible. In 1947, Watt Hugh McCollum* published a booklet entitled

---

*Only a few friends knew that Watt Hugh McCollum was the pen name (said quickly it's "What you m'call'em") of Louis Rosenberg, statistician of the Canadian Jewish Congress. Rosenberg did not want his employers to know that he was moonlighting for Woodsworth House, a left-leaning publisher.

Who Owns Canada?, which concluded that most of the owners still resided in Montreal. McCollum counted the number of company directorships held by "Canada's Fifty Big Shots," as he irreverently called them, and the amount of corporate capital each man's directorships represented. Of the fifty names in the list, twenty-seven were from Montreal, only six from Toronto, and seventeen from the rest of the country. And nine of the ten very biggest of the big shots were Montrealers.

~

In his *Montreal Confidential* the versatile Al Palmer departed briefly from the fleshpots to give tourists a quick sketch of Montreal history, and in it he rightfully emphasized the importance of the earliest immigrants from Scotland. He quoted a prayer attributed to the first Scots fur traders, in which they said, "O Lord, we do not ask you to give us wealth, but show us where it is." Whether or not through divine intervention, the French Canadian voyageurs who paddled the Scotsmen's canoes showed them where it was, as they travelled the continent, trading with the Indians and laying the foundations of their fortunes. It was these men who became the first big shots of the nineteenth century – the McGills, the McTavishes, the McGillivrays. Later in the century, Scots like R.B. Angus, Sir Hugh Allan, Lord Strathcona and Lord Mount Stephen amassed tremendous wealth with their banks, factories, railroads and steamship lines. Although never more than a fifth of the city's population, the Scots would dominate the commerce of Montreal well into the twentieth century. In his book, Al Palmer quotes the French author André Siegfried who, in 1937, wrote: "In the telephone directory here are six pages of Macs. Tear them out and Montreal is no longer a financial capital but an immense French village with a little English garrison."

Every year, at the end of November, the city was reminded of the dominance of the Scots when they staged their St. Andrew's Ball, the season's most lavish social event, a frolic for the rich that flowed with Scotch whiskey and champagne. Among the elite, every mother wanted her daughters to "come out" at this event, rather than have to make their debuts at one of the city's lesser balls. As Al Palmer noted, "Any deb with social aspirations who lacks a bid to this affair will find her career set back no end." The St. Andrew's Ball had been suspended for most of the war years, but in 1945, with the war over, it was revived with more splendour than ever and dubbed the Victory Ball. Once again the ladies could wear their ball gowns, with their escorts in kilts, white tie and tails, or military uniforms. Once again, in the Windsor Hotel, Peacock Alley and the ballroom were ablaze with flags, chrysanthemums and tartan shields of the clans. This would be the biggest edition of the event's seventy-two-year history, with more than 2,200 guests and with the Earl of Athlone, Governor General of Canada, and his wife, the Princess Alice, as guests of honour.

There were 183 debutantes this year, more than ever before, all dressed in white. They formed a long line in front of the flower-bedecked dais, where Their Excellencies were enthroned, the shortest girls at the front, the tallest at the back. Then, when her name was called, a girl would step forward and curtsey. That was all it took, in this most simple of tribal rites, for a young woman to formally enter society and become available for marriage. Of course, before the ball, there were weeks of intense activity with dressmakers, hairdressers and photographers. After the debutantes were presented, there was dancing to the music of Eddie Alexander's orchestra, supper after midnight and, amid the skirl of the pipes, the stabbing of the haggis and the guzzling of whiskey and Drambuie. In the elegant marble washrooms of the Windsor, a few young blades, not yet accustomed to ingesting so much hooch, would rush in to throw up before returning to the dance, which went on until seven in the morning. It was, in the words of Al Palmer, "quite a clambake."

The *Star* and the *Gazette* were entranced by the St. Andrew's Ball. Almost every day, in the month leading up to the event, their social pages would carry two or three large photo portraits of girls who would be making their debuts. There would be endless little paragraphs announcing dinner parties to be held for them before the ball. And on the day after the ball, the papers would carry column after column of unrelieved grey type detailing what hundreds of girls and ladies had been wearing. At the 1945 ball, Miss Gloria Just, the shortest debutante and thus the first to make her curtsey, wore "a hoop-skirted gown of white satin having an off-shoulder decolletage and trimmed with butterflies of silver sequins." All this publicity gave rise to great curiosity among the unwashed masses, and at the hotel detectives in dinner jackets patrolled the hallways to repel gate-crashers. One year a poor young Greek girl was found standing on a box in an alley behind the hotel, trying without success to peer in at the gaiety inside. This melted the hearts of the ball's organizers, and the following year the girl was given a pass so she could sit in the balcony and watch the rich at play.

The St. Andrew's Ball sprang back as soon as the war was out of the way, but another pleasure of the Anglo elite, the Montreal Hunt, took longer to reactivate itself. It was not until 1948 that its scarlet-coated members, on their spirited steeds, were again following the hounds in pursuit of the fox, across the green fields of Ste. Scholastique. During the next few years, the foxes became more plentiful than ever, and the spectacle of them being torn to bits by the dogs could be enjoyed on the weekend by huntsmen with upper-crusty names like Beaufort Lewis, Tupper Porter and Storrs McCall, to say nothing of the much-admired Mrs. Oscar de Lall, astride her thoroughbred chestnut, Espinchal.

The upper crust revered everything British, and its members, from Westmount or the Square Mile, usually felt very much at home when visiting England or Scotland. They knew in which hands to hold knife and fork and they knew the difference between sitting above the salt and below the salt. And, generally, they were quickly accepted by the gentry. As Elsie Jean Gordon, a young Montreal woman, wrote in her diary, in 1945, "Lady Ryder arranged for me to spend two days with Lord and Lady Raglan at their 15th century estate in Wales. They were delightful, even though like many of their kind they had no servants." Elsie Jean had been serving as a Red Cross volunteer in wartime London. Here, amid the explosions of German buzz bombs, she met the Right People – Lord Soulbury, Sir Raymond Evershed and people like Peggy and Toby who lived in

Evelyn Waugh-sounding places like Eggington House. All this is recounted in her book *E.J. Looking Back*, which gives many glimpses of the affinities between the mother country and its admirers from Montreal.

When she got back to Montreal, after the war, Elsie Jean Gordon got a job as assistant to Irene Cains, the much-feared dragon lady who was society editor of the *Gazette*. "My working clothes," Elsie Jean writes, "became ball gowns and long white gloves: the uniform of the evening." She was everywhere during the social season, at the Royal Victoria Hospital Charity Ball, at the Hunt Club Ball, at the extravagant parties aboard the Atlantic steamship *Homeric* and at the St. Mary's Hospital Ball, where in 1953 the guests of honour were Senator John F. Kennedy and Jackie. And there were society weddings to be covered in great detail, with Miss Cains sitting in harsh judgement over which supplicants were of sufficiently good family to get their weddings into the paper and which upstarts had to be turned away. The social whirl, for the upper crust, was all-consuming. "There's no way I can go to university or take a job," one debutante told Elsie Jean Gordon. "There's just too much going on."

The journalist Peter Desbarats called them the Anglostocracy, and they did indeed think of themselves as aristocrats. But in chronicling their decline, in her excellent book *Remembrance of Grandeur*, Margaret Westley points out the weaknesses in their pretensions. "They lacked," she writes, "a rootedness in the land and its traditions, and the acceptance by the majority of native inhabitants of their right to power and privilege. These are the supports on which an aristocracy depends."

The wealth of the Anglocrats usually went back two or three generations, but now in the prosperous post-war years new aristocracies were arising, based on new money. Lady Allan, wife of Sir Montagu Allan, must have sensed this when Elsie Jean Gordon phoned her one day to see if she had any society news to impart. "No, I won't give you any news," Lady Allan said. "Too many common people are getting into the *Gazette* these days." But non-Anglocrats were doing interesting things. What stuffy society wedding could compare with the splendiferous nuptials that united Phyllis Bronfman and Jean Lambert in 1949? The bride's father, Samuel Bronfman, had fourteen thousand lilac blooms picked in Ontario the day before the wedding and had them flown to Montreal in a chartered plane. The city had never seen anything like it. And what shindig in the stodgy confines of the Mount Royal Club could compare with the rollicking parties and the great Greek food at the home of Phrixos Papachristidis, on Forden Avenue, where you might meet celebrities like the Lord Mayor of Dublin and Harry Belafonte? Slowly but surely, in the 1950s, the centre of social gravity was shifting away from the old guard, the Anglostocracy, in the direction of what its members would probably consider the lesser breeds.

Frederick Molson's house was one of several mansions owned by the Molson family in the Square Mile. It was a massive structure, built in 1901 in a mixture of Tudor and Jacobean styles. It met its fate in 1957, when the wrecker's ball attacked its brick facade and brought it down, to make it possible for McGregor Street to be pushed through, eastward past Drummond Street. That same year, down the hill on Drummond, the splendid Angus house was also demolished, to make way for an ungainly apartment building. Its big conservatory, where orchids once grew, came down with it. Across the street, the year before, another apartment building had gone up, replacing Sir Robert Reid's mansion, an outstanding example of Victorian architecture. One by one, in the 1940s and '50s, the Anglostocracy's great houses in the Square Mile were either coming down or being abandoned as dwellings and converted to other uses. Sir Herbert Holt's house, with its fourteen bedrooms, was demolished after his death. On Pine Avenue, Sir Edward Beatty's bachelor pad, four storeys high, was turned over to McGill University and became Beatty Hall.

The Square Mile covered an area somewhat less than a square mile, with University Street on the east, Guy-Côte des Neiges on the west, Dorchester on the south and Pine Avenue on the north. Leading Anglo businessmen started building their mansions here in the middle of the nineteenth century, on leafy streets lined with great elms and maples. For the next seven or eight decades the richest men in Canada lived here, with platoons of servants to look after them and their families. But a number of residents of the Square Mile suffered devastating losses in the stock market crash of 1929, and during the Depression that followed they began to leave their great houses for more modest quarters.

The Second World War accelerated the area's decline, with servants joining the armed forces or going to work in munitions factories. In the prosperous era after the war, few wanted to return to the long hours and drudgery of domestic service, and it was impossible to maintain these huge houses without large numbers of trained servants. And so families moved away, leaving these monuments to Montreal's Golden Age either to be demolished or to find new uses. At the end of the 1950s, some fifty of them were still standing, their architectural diversity – Italianate, Gothic Revival, Scottish Baronial, Second Empire, Beaux Arts – reflecting the strong individuality of the robber barons who originally built them. But now they had been turned into facilities for McGill or the Royal Victoria Hospital, or they housed consulates, private clubs or company offices.

The gradual migration away from the Square Mile was under way as early as the 1920s, with the younger members of the old families making the courageous trek westward, to Westmount. Geographically it was only a mile or two away, but socially it was a world away, beyond the pale, devoid of prestige. "To think that I should live to see a daughter of mine married to a man from Westmount," a Square Mile matron was heard to complain. By the mid-1950s, the resettlement of the refugee rich from downtown was virtually complete and, with the exception of a few who had fled to the tax-friendly Bahamas, most found themselves ensconced on the upper reaches of Westmount mountain. It was a comfortable ensconcement, as Westmount was even more of an enclave than the Square Mile, with its own police force and fire department. As Miriam Chapin put it, in her 1955 book *Quebec Now*, "Westmount is a city within Montreal like a kangaroo's baby."

The lower level of Westmount – "on the flat" – was a fairly modest preserve, site of the homes of small businessmen, academics and young professionals. The big money was to be found up the hill. Here, although their corps of servants was much reduced in size, the transplanted Anglocrats lived lives that were not greatly changed. On Belvedere Road, The Boulevard and Sunnyside their houses were grand, although not quite as grand as their Square Mile mansions of yore. And there were advantages: for the children, the private schools – Selwyn House, Miss Edgar's and Miss Cramp's – now were often within walking distance, making life easier for the chauffeurs. There were no taverns, no bars, no hotels, and commerce was not encroaching, as it was downtown. There were more trees here, creating canopies over the streets, and more space for lawns. In a magazine article he wrote decades later, Ron Graham recalled his childhood in Upper Westmount. "It was not extraordinary," he wrote, "to see pheasants, rabbits, and even a fox crossing the lawn in the evening from the dense woods that clung to the hillside below us. At night we felt we were in the country, Montreal a glowing hum in the distance."

As for routines and attitudes, little was changed. As Miriam Chapin wrote: "*Les dames de Westmount*, as their charwomen call them, lead busy lives. Their charity boards relieve any itch of discomfort they may feel about the contrast between their circumstances and that of their [poor] neighbors in St. Henri, so near below the tracks. . . . The Red Cross, I.O.D.E., the Grenfell Mission, the hairdresser . . . all these obligations leave little time to think. . . . A woman can live her whole life there and come in contact with no French Canadian except janitor, tram conductor, store clerk." But there *was* a new element. In the Square Mile, virtually everyone had been of British descent, their money old and inherited. But up on the heights of Westmount, they were living cheek-by-jowl with the *nouveaux riches*, often affluent newcomers with strange surnames, and even the occasional moneyed French Canadian. In school, the children of different elements were getting to know each other. Perhaps some day old money would fraternize with new. Perhaps the old aristocracy would be absorbed into something else, a plutocracy, which would give rise to snobbery with a different flavour.

But not yet. Recalling the six houses on the small street of his childhood, in the 1950s, Ron Graham related how they were occupied by a French Canadian professional, two prominent Anglo families, a McGill professor, a Jewish factory owner and his own family. "We all knew everything about one another, yet I can't recall myself or my parents ever visiting, or being visited." He spoke of this in his article entitled "Above All, Westmount."

~

I guess what was important
As we all grew up down there
Was the sense of being equal
When all our cupboards were bare.

Donna Gosse Francis, a housewife poet, was celebrating her beloved Point St. Charles, an area very much down the hill from Westmount, as socially remote as could be. This was where the working-class English and Irish lived, and the poor. Down here, front doors were unlocked, in contrast to the tightly shut gates on the silent streets of Westmount. Here the streets were alive, life was convivial. In 1945, when the soldiers came home from the war, their families threw open their doors on streets like Liverpool and Hibernia, the beer flowed freely and everybody walking by was urged to come in. Saturday night was a continuous party, and outside the Bucket of Blood Tavern on Wellington Street disputes were settled with fistfights that could develop into glorious, block-long melees. People from uptown Montreal seldom set foot in Point St. Charles, where young men revelled in their reputation for being tough and dangerous.

If "the Point" was tough, the Griff was tougher and the Village tougher still. The Griff was Griffintown, a district just east of Point St. Charles, across the Lachine Canal, and the Village was Goose

Village, to the south, close to the river, near the entrance to Victoria Bridge. Goose Village – also known as Victoriatown – was just half a dozen streets, wedged in between the coal yards and the abattoirs, where many of the residents worked. The uptown pheasants and rabbits never ventured down to this latitude, but wildlife was occasionally seen – rats from the river. People in cars driving past the Village, on their way to the bridge, wondered how anyone could live amid the foul stench of the animal wastes being burned at the slaughter houses, but the Villagers were used to it, and to the coal dust that sometimes blew across from the coal yards to begrime the washing that was drying on clotheslines.

In decades to come, Goose Village would disappear, to make room for an expressway and an industrial park, but former residents would remember it with affection. All would speak of the neighbourliness, the unlocked front doors of their run-down houses, the festivities and dances on Britannia Street and Conway Street. There was pride in how well residents of Irish, Italian and Ukrainian descent got along. But "outsiders" from other districts were not welcome, and a good punch in the nose might await a man from uptown who was caught going out with a Goose Village girl. For the children, the abattoirs and the coal yards provided playgrounds: boys would sneak into the stockyards and try to ride the cows and, in winter, the huge piles of coal near Bickerdike Pier would be covered with snow and would make excellent slides. In the autumn, in the early '40s, wagons laden with produce from South Shore farms would come lumbering across Victoria Bridge on their way to Montreal markets, and Village lads would be lying in wait, ready to jump up and swipe watermelons.

Like Goose Village, Griffintown was also living out its last years in the 1950s, many of its shabby, century-old houses having already come down to make way for street widenings and railway viaducts. Here, too, there was a fierce pride in the community. In 1954, St. Ann's Church, the spiritual heart of the Griff, celebrated its centenary, and many former residents who had moved "over the hill" to more prosperous districts came back for the occasion. "We remember the men of the past," Father James Dwyer told them, in his sermon, "who climbed ashore from ships, without much of this world's goods, but with no fear of work." They were immigrants from Ireland, in the nineteenth century, fleeing their country's desperate poverty. In Montreal, many of them settled in Griffintown, living close to the industries along the Lachine Canal – brickyards, foundries, sugar refineries, breweries. As labourers, they helped build much that was important in Montreal, like the Victoria Bridge which, in its time, was the eighth wonder of the world. But they lived in a slum, in wretched housing where four children might share a bed in a tiny room. Streets were prone to flooding, and diphtheria and typhoid were frequent. In the 1940s, many of the descendants of the original immigrants, more affluent now, moved away from the Griff, often to the adjacent Point St. Charles, which also had many Irish residents and was one rung up in the social ladder.

There were good blue-collar jobs available in the Point, at factories that were within walking distance – Northern Electric, Continental Can, Dominion Glass. Some young women, after graduating from O'Sullivan's Business College, found jobs as stenographers in offices "uptown." (What was uptown to the Point was downtown to Westmount and NDG.) Beverley Boyle of Paris Street got her first job as a secretary/steno in 1950, starting at $130 a month. She found this a handsome stipend at a time when a quart of milk cost eleven cents, or thirteen cents for Jersey milk with the cream on top. She had money enough for a good lunch every day at Woolworth's lunch counter, on St. Catherine Street, and occasionally would pick up one of Woolworth's renowned chocolate layer cakes to take home with her, on the No. 58 streetcar, back to the Point. Before going to work uptown, Beverley Boyle knew little of the Montreal that lay beyond her own neighbourhood. And she didn't realize that Point St. Charles was a "disadvantaged" area until she read that contention in the newspapers.

The Sherwin-Williams paint factory was an important employer in the Point, and after the war, Frank Conlon left the navy and went back to his old job there as a filler and capper of paint cans. The job paid sixty-five cents an hour, an income that gave him confidence enough to get married, to a fellow worker at the factory. Wedding gifts, from his family and hers, included a new stove and a shed full of coal. Recalling that ton of coal, half a century later, Conlon said that it helped make for "a very good start in life." The Point offered every convenience for the newlyweds, especially little corner stores that sold good take-out food like savoury meat pies from Muir's and crisp, golden fish and chips from Taylor's, wrapped in yesterday's newspaper. Also, to wash it down, there was spruce beer from Barabe's or Jumbo, the big economy soda. When the Conlons made one of their rare visits to the more prosperous part of Montreal, uptown, Frank was always conscious of coming from a working-class area. Although he didn't feel inferior or intimidated by that fact, he knew that many other people from the Point did not share his confidence. With the Point's bad reputation uptown, some men from the area, looking for jobs, lied in their applications by saying that they came from elsewhere.

Frank Conlon felt Point St. Charles was a good place to live. Neighbours were friendly, and in time of trouble people helped each other. When a woman was sick, the woman next door would without question look after her children. On Paris Street, Beverley Boyle's mother became known as a healer and unofficial nurse, ministering to anyone who needed help. Once she even washed the body of a woman who had died, in preparation for burial. In those days, with funeral homes expensive, the dead were often laid out in the front parlour of the house. The front door would be draped in black, causing awe and excitement among the children of the street.

After school, the streets were alive with the games of children. In the winter, it was hockey, with frozen horse droppings serving as pucks. When the snow disappeared it was Kick the Can, Stando and Run Sheep Run. Or, when the boys were a little older and girls were in the offing, C.C.K. – Chase, Catch, Kiss. On the night of the 24th of May, Point St. Charles would glow with the light of bonfires, lit in the streets. The birthday of the long-dead Queen Victoria was being celebrated in the traditional fashion, and police on motorcycles buzzed through the streets, trying to stop the roving gangs of youths that were tearing up fences to feed the flames. Oddly enough the bonfires honouring the old queen were often lit by boys of Irish descent, whose forefathers had little love for anything British. For the fire department, many of whose members were also Irish, it was a trying time.

Besides the entertainment that arose spontaneously in the streets, there was a good deal of organized diversion, like evening singsongs and band concerts in Marguerite Bourgeoys Park. Many of these were organized by Frank Hanley, who represented the area on the Montreal city council. In the summer, Councillor Hanley would say, he organized streets dances and festivals to keep people's minds off the fact that the rich were vacationing in the country. "I keep them busy," Hanley would say, of his constituents, "so they won't have time to start an uprising." Hanley's jokes, and his benefactions, were so popular that no one would run against him in elections for the city council, and he was elected by acclamation through the 1940s and '50s. Potential opponents knew, Hanley would say, that if they dared to run against him he would simply use his well-oiled political machine to steal the election. In 1948 he used that machine, which included very persuasive strong-arm men with baseball bats, to win election – this time a contested election – to the Quebec Legislative Assembly, as an independent. In his first speech in the legislature, Hanley called for the legalization of gambling, a preposterously radical idea at the time.

In many ways, the diminutive Frank Hanley, once a flyweight boxing champion, personified the spunk and the spirit of the Point. In the Irish tradition, he could spin a great yarn in the tavern. One that he liked best was about how, in the thin years of the Depression, when so many people were on the dole and shivering through the winter, he and his mates would steal coal for the stoves of the unemployed. He was working for a coal company at the time and, he said, "Me and my boys used to put only eighty pounds in the hundred-pound bags. We'd charge the Westmounters the full price and deliver the rest to the poor." They called him the Robin Hood of the Point, and after he became a city councillor he could usually find a bit of money, somewhere or other, for constituents who came to him in desperate need. He had the skills of an old-style ward heeler, listening patiently to tales of woe and offering solutions to every kind of problem. He attended every funeral and many christenings, and he used his influence with the police to get drunks out of jail. People would say that, if, in the course of his largesse, the odd dubious dollar found its way into Frank Hanley's own pocket, nobody would have any objections. People of the Point were always proud of one of their number who could better himself.

Those who did manage to better themselves often moved away, often to Verdun, the adjacent municipality that was considerably above the Point on the social scale; besides its working-class majority, Verdun had, in its west end, white-collar residents who could be defined as middle class. Like Westmount, Verdun was a small enclave with its own mayor and its own police force – and no taverns. And like Westmount, its English-speaking residents had a high regard for all things British. Verdunites didn't ride to the hounds, but in school their children sang "Rule Britannia" and studied British history in considerable detail. The chewing gum they bought came not only with baseball and hockey cards, but also with cards carrying pictures of historic kings and queens of England. Many young men in Verdun grew up reading the *Magnet* and the *Gem*, the twopenny weeklies that were the British alternative to comic books. Here, in papers denounced by George Orwell for their snobbery, they followed the adventures of boys like Billy Bunter and Harry Wharton in exclusive English public schools.

In reality, working-class boys in Verdun had nothing remotely in common with the young toffs of Greyfriars and St. Jim's, in their Eton jackets. They often left school at thirteen or fourteen to get jobs and help their families pay the rent. Jobs were easy to get during the war, and in December agents from the big downtown department stores sometimes went out onto the streets to approach likely looking young men and women and offer them part-time work during the Christmas rush. Doug and Betty Whyte both left school in their early teens and after they married, in 1952, Betty left her well-paying office job to raise their family. They brought up their children in much the same way that they themselves had been brought up, with discipline and churchgoing as cornerstones in their development. Morality was defined as honesty, monogamy and good manners. The mildest profanity was considered offensive, and sex was never discussed in any way. Even diapers were changed behind closed doors. But none of that meant that young married people couldn't enjoy themselves. For Doug and Betty, as for many Verdunites, there was a constant round of house parties, in the 1950s, with lots to eat and drink, singing around the piano, big-band music on the hi-fi and the carpet rolled back for jitterbugging.

Amid the prosperity of the '50s, other kinds of partying could be much less welcome, as far as women were concerned. In dozens of dingy taverns, where only men were admitted, their blue-collar husbands often sat drinking their beer well into the night, having forgotten to go home for supper. In 1956, Father Patrick Ambrose, director of the Catholic Welfare Bureau, said that during the previous three years there had been a 400-percent increase in the placement of children in foster homes "due to broken marital relationships caused by . . . exaggerated use of alcohol."

⁓

For working-class Anglos, it was the happy hiss from the beer bottle as its cap was being pried off; for middle-class Anglos, it was the chuckle of the ice cubes in the cocktail shaker. During blue-collar revelry in the tavern, the furniture might occasionally get damaged, but it would be wrong to think that white collars were always more subdued in their merrymaking. Long after the event, a prominent physician recalled a stag party held during the war years by interns in their residence at the Montreal General Hospital. "Frank Zahallan, the pharmacist," he wrote, "was inveigled into mixing up his famous Purple Passion and Tiger's Milk – by the bucketful. The party was riotous and long. The fire screen made a convenient toboggan down the long stairway. A fight with fire hose versus fire extinguishers seemed to be a logical activity, resulting in four inches of water on the billiards-room floor. . . . It was an inspiring sight to see three naked interns (now all respectable practitioners) lolling on the floor, tossing firewood at the chandeliers."

Before the war, among much of the middle class, drinking had been a discreet, even furtive, activity. But during the war, young men of a new generation experienced the conviviality of the officers' mess or the wet canteen, and developed a taste for whiskey and beer; in France and Italy, they discovered wine. Back home, after the war, they fell in heartily with a new way to socialize – the cocktail party. Before the war, the middle class generally looked with disfavour on women who "took a drink," but now, in Notre Dame de Grâce, women like Alison Annesley, Helen Henry and Audrey Corrigan were frequently invited to cocktail parties in the houses of friends, or were hostesses in their own houses. Mixed drinks were in vogue, and there was much scholarly debate about what the proportions of gin and vermouth should be in the perfect martini. In Montreal West, Charles Baerman was an enthusiastic attender of cocktail parties, but he was on his guard when visiting one particular host who always served his guests triple shots on arrival "to get them started."

Although their drinking habits might differ, middle-class and working-class Anglos were alike in a number of ways. In both groups, adult children who didn't marry often continued to live with their parents, rather than move into apartments of their own. Most members of both groups went to church regularly and put on their best clothes for the occasion. The whole family frequently turned out for events like picnics that were organized by the churches. In both groups, parents expected to be obeyed by their children, who were given many rules to be followed. Miscreants were punished, and use of the strap was not unknown.

For English-speaking Montrealers, the decade after the war was an era of migration and social mobility. The dispossessed of Griffintown sought refuge in Point St. Charles, and when they could afford it, many people from the Point moved to Verdun. From Verdun, for the better-educated children of blue-collar fathers, the next move up the ladder was to Notre Dame de Grâce, the largest of the traditional habitats of the middle class. But in NDG there was many an insurance company executive or department manager who wanted something different. The solid, dark, boxy English-style houses that had been so comfortable before the war would no longer do. What they wanted now was in the new American mode – the two-storey, split-level ranch house with picture windows and a two-car garage. These were going up, at a great rate, in the Town of Mount Royal, where the railway tunnel emerged from under the mountain. For company executives, it was easy commuting to offices downtown. But others were prepared for much longer commutes, and, in the old Montreal tradition, they set sail westward, this time to the burgeoning exurbs on the Lakeshore, where there was space for bigger front lawns and backyards.

On the Lakeshore, later to be called the West Island, the countryside was being devoured by developers. In Pointe Claire, Farmer Legault, after refusing to do anything about the smell emanating from his huge chicken house, was persuaded to close it down and move away. At the end of the war, the population of Pointe Claire was 5,500; by 1953 it had almost doubled. In the great construction boom of the later '50s, new schools, new churches and new shopping centres went up in Pointe Claire, and the population almost doubled again, to just under 20,000, by 1958. Here was another largely English enclave on the French island of Montreal, and British immigrants who settled there often said that it reminded them of home. The story was similar down the road, in Beaconsfield, and in Baie d'Urfé, still farther out of town, the last of the big family farms had disappeared by the end of the 1950s, a decade in which the town's population increased fivefold. Although the early settlers of Baie d'Urfé had names like Bonneau, Lajeunesse and Lemoyne, and some of their descendants were still living in the area, the town's new streets of the 1950s were given names that were defiantly English, like Westchester and Coventry. Essex Drive ran from Churchill Road to St. Andrew's Road.

Among the people considering a move out to the Lakeshore was Mary Peate, whose book *Girl in a Sloppy Joe Sweater* described her life as a teenager growing up in NDG in the war years. Now with a husband and two children, Mary had a weekly talk-and-music program on CBC radio, entitled *Tea and Trumpets*, and she entertained her listeners by describing her quandary – whether or not to move out to the suburbs. She told of weekend forays to the hinterland with her husband Bob, to examine houses and calculate commuting time. She read the latest American authorities on the subject and quoted from John Keats's new book *The Crack in the Picture Window* in which he described the new suburbs as "the fresh-air slums we're building around the edges of America's cities." These big developments, Keats said, were "conceived in error and nurtured in greed, corroding everything they touch." In *The Exurbanites*, A.C. Spectorsky was equally scathing about wealthier areas, farther from town. The comic novelist Max Shulman shuddered at the social life of the suburbs, with parties "where you ate cubes of cheese on toothpicks and talked about plywood, mortgages, mulches and children." Finally, Mary Peate told her listeners about an article in *Chatelaine* magazine entitled "The Sickness of Our Suburbs," by Dr. Alastair MacLeod, a Montreal psychiatrist. "Clinical experience," Dr. MacLeod wrote, "has led to the conviction that many of the personality problems of our age – the feeling of something missing in life, the fear of failure, the lack of vivid identity – are often made more acute by suburban living."

Having carefully considered all these warnings, Bob and Mary Peate finally made up their minds, and, in the spring of 1959, they joined the thousands of English-speaking Montrealers who were moving to the outer reaches of the island – to a brand-new split-level in Baie d'Urfé.

7

The French:
From a Grain of Mustard Seed

On the afternoon of May 18, 1942, a procession of sixteen horse-drawn carriages set out from City Hall and made its way westward along Notre Dame Street. In the first carriage, Mayor Adhémar Raynault sat beside Monsignor Conrad Chaumont, auxiliary bishop of Montreal. In each of the carriages that followed there were three or four civic or religious dignitaries, the churchmen in their black soutanes, the politicians in cutaway coats and shiny top hats. The procession was part of the observance of the tercentenary of the founding of Montreal, for it was on this day in 1642 that Paul de Chomedey, Sieur de Maisonneuve, came ashore with his small band of settlers. Their purpose, in making the hazardous voyage from distant France, was to convert the heathen Indians to Christianity. Today's procession, three hundred years later, was in recognition of the city's deeply religious past – and present.

The procession made six stops. The first was at Hôtel-Dieu, on Pine Avenue, the hospital founded by one of Maisonneuve's settlers, Jeanne Mance. Here the dignitaries presented the nuns who operated the hospital with a commemorative parchment thanking them for all they had done to further the development of the city. The procession then moved on to visit members of five other religious institutions: the nuns of the Congregation of Notre Dame at Sherbrooke and Atwater, the Franscican fathers at their monastery on Dorchester near Fort, the Grey Nuns at Dorchester and Guy, the Jesuits at their Collège Sainte-Marie at Dorchester and Bleury and, finally, the Gentlemen of St. Sulpice at Place d'Armes. These were but a small fraction of the city's Roman Catholic institutions, but they were the most historic, aptly recalling the first Mass celebrated for the colonists that day in May 1642, by their priest, Father Vimont. "You are a grain of mustard seed that shall rise and grow until its branches overshadow the earth," Vimont told them. "Your children shall fill the land." Three hundred years later, the city's religious underpinning seemed as strong as ever, and Montrealers liked to boast that the grain of mustard seed had grown into the world's second largest French city.

The tercentenary year resounded with oratory, but almost none of the speeches were in English, despite the fact that more than a third of the city's population was of non-French origin and spoke mainly English. But the anniversary's official three-hundred-page souvenir book did permit five pages to be *en Anglais*. In these pages, Henry G. Birks, the jewellery tycoon, wrote, among other things, that "English Montrealers are proud (and justly so) of their great business houses." T. Taggart Smyth, president of the Civic Improvement League, contributed an essay entitled "The Last Rampart of Freedom," in which he contended that Montrealers had "the broadest freedom of speech, creed and association." He overlooked the Padlock Law, which gave the police the power to arbitrarily lock you out of your house if they thought you were spreading communist ideas, and he did not foresee the return of Maurice Duplessis to power, two years hence, when it would be open season for the arrest of heretical Witnesses of Jehovah. Smyth also neglected to mention that the city's faithful were forbidden to read Voltaire, Rousseau, Anatole France, Flaubert, Zola and the works of hundreds of other authors listed in the Vatican's *Index Librorum Prohibitorum*.

But, as everyone acknowledged, it was the Church and its discipline that had to be thanked for the survival of the French language in this corner of North America. And so it was understandable that all the sermons and oratory of the tercentenary year should have religious or nationalist themes. In January, eleven mayors of Montreal island communities joined the congregation of Notre Dame du Rosaire Church, on St. Hubert Street, for ceremonies lauding the sanctity of the Christian family, with a sermon in which Father

Emile Bouvier denounced divorce, birth control and masturbation. In his prescription for a happy marriage, he advised wives to show "respect, obedience, sweetness and the patience to endure his faults and bad moods." In June, on Saint-Jean-Baptiste Day, Father Joseph Ledit delivered a keynote sermon in which he told French Canadians not to worry if outsiders pitied them for being poor and for living in a backward province. Instead, he told them (perhaps harking back to Henry Birks's boast about the commercial success of the Anglos), the French should thank God for not giving them "the souls of traders." In September, the celebrations included an exhibition of missionary work at St. Joseph's Oratory. Here crowds came to hear about the battle against "the cruel spiritual poverty of [the world's] pagan people" which was being waged by priests and nuns from Montreal in sixteen countries, from Basutoland to Palestine.

The Church attempted to influence or govern almost every aspect of life in French Montreal, and it was usually successful. Persons who defied its edicts, or disregarded its advice, usually did so in secret; open defiance could lead to social ostracism. The priest, the nun or the lay brother was everywhere: administering and staffing hospitals, teaching in schools, colleges and the university; overseeing charitable organizations and youth groups; watching vigilantly over cultural activities and trade unions. The Women's Jail on Fullum Street was run by the Sisters of Our Lady of Charity, while the Sisters of Providence ran the notorious St. Jean de Dieu, one of the two Montreal institutions then known as insane asylums. In 1941, when the population of the Island of Montreal was little more than one million, one estimate put the number of priests, nuns and members of religious communities in the city at ten thousand.

Children, from their first day in school onward, were immersed in religion. They learned to read from stories about angels and saints, they learned arithmetic by calculating the dimensions of church buildings. Geography and history paid little attention to Canada but concentrated on Quebec and on the voyages of missionaries. Spelling tests featured words like *choeur* (choir) and *tabernacle*, and much time was spent in prayer. At the Collège de Montréal, an elite residential secondary school, students arose at five in the morning to pray, meditate and attend Mass, all before breakfast. After the morning's studies, they went back to the chapel for more prayers before lunch. When afternoon classes were over, they would listen to a *lecture spirituelle* and after supper they would recite the rosary. Bedtime came soon after.

During Lent, the faithful were expected to attend retreats at their parish church where, night after night for a week, they listened to extensive homilies, often delivered by visiting preachers of renown. At special retreats for women, the evils of birth control were dealt with at length, and wives were advised that they would roast in the flames of Hell "*si elles refusent leur mari*" (if they resisted their husbands' advances). In Catholic Montreal, a headache could never be an excuse. "*Empêchez-vous la famille?*" was a question the priest would ask a woman in the confessional when he sought to find out whether she was resorting to any "artificial" method of birth control. (The rhythm method was permitted, but it was notoriously ineffective.) One noted preacher at retreats, a Capucin friar, usually managed to horrify young wives with his story about a woman who had confessed that she was using a forbidden method of birth control. When he told her that this was a grievous sin, she said that her doctor had advised her that she would die if she had another child. "Then die, madam," the priest had told her. Another source of apprehension for women was knowing what might happen during a difficult childbirth in a Catholic hospital. If only one life could be saved, that of the mother or that of the baby, doctors were instructed to save the baby. Fortunately cases where this choice had to be made were extremely rare, but the procedure would be in keeping with a religion that always needed more souls to baptize. For French Canadian nationalists, the Church's advocacy of large families gave welcome support to the policy of *la revanche du berceau* – the revenge of the cradle – which would assure the numerical dominance of their people in Quebec.

In French Montreal, the Church seemed to have many more exhortations for women than for men. One priest, Father Tessier, gave frequent lectures on how iniquitous it was to allow one's house to become untidy. Even with a dozen children romping around, he said, a woman should keep her house spotlessly clean at all times; a surprise visitor dropping in at any time of day should always find the house in perfect order. Inspired by this vision, many women redoubled their efforts to become *ménagères parfaites*, perfect housewives. With a long tradition as a guide, each day had its specific tasks.

Monday was laundry day, an enormous chore in poor households that had many children but no washing machine. Working with reddened hands on the washboard, a woman might do not only her own family's clothes but also those of others, in order to earn a few extra dollars. Tuesday was ironing day, and the challenge to the perfect housewife was to make old, worn clothes look as though they had just been bought at Eaton's. Wednesday was for sewing and darning, not only replacing buttons but perhaps also creating a new dress for a daughter from yard goods and a Butterick pattern. And, of course, on this day as on all others, large meals had to be cooked for a large family. If all tasks had been achieved by Thursday, this was the one day of respite, a time to go shopping or to the hairdresser. Friday was a day for scrubbing floors and annihilating dust, and it might take until late afternoon to achieve perfection. Saturday was the day to go to market, to cook, to bake cakes, pies and biscuits. This was also the day that the children underwent inspection, a rigorous examination of shoes, clothes, hair, fingernails. All this, of course, was in preparation for church on Sunday, and the large festive meal afterwards. In this unending cycle of effort, the perfect housewife, frequently pregnant, was guided by the notion that *la paresse demeure un péché capital* – sloth remains a deadly sin.

An even more serious sin, on the part of a woman, was lack of modesty. The female body always had to be adequately covered, and the clergy was frequently dismayed by what it observed on the province's beaches. To put an end to this, the Archdiocesan Committee of Catholic Action announced, in 1946, that it had commissioned the design of a modest bathing suit suitable for respectable women and girls. This news was received with delight by Jacques Francoeur, that enterprising young journalist, who immediately queried a number of American newspapers, asking if they would like to buy his story about Montreal's "Catholic bathing suit," when it was unveiled. The American editors all said yes and asked for the story as soon as possible, but Francoeur never got to write and sell it; Church authorities, being advised that their project was engendering widespread hilarity, quietly abandoned it. Most Quebec women, however, didn't require a Church-sanctioned suit. They were innately modest, and they did not have to be told that undulating flesh was provocative. This modesty perhaps accounted for statistics released in 1949 by the Dominion Corset Company: in Quebec, 61 percent of women wore corsets, as opposed to only 14 per cent in bouncy British Columbia.

Yet Bruce Hutchison, the British Columbia author, had to come to Montreal to find perfection in womankind. In his 1943 book *The Unknown Country*, he told readers what they might see if they observed two women at lunch in a downtown restaurant. "You will gawk and stare at these two ladies of Montreal," he wrote, "sipping their wine and exchanging gossip (in French, of course) with such a tinkling music of language, with gestures so exquisite, with such a perfect wearing of clothes and sparkle of jewels, with such a touch of felicity as will be found nowhere else except in the movies, where it is rehearsed. And watching these incredible creatures, you long for a life more fortunate, more exciting, more splendid than you can ever hope to see."

~

The elegant women that Hutchison described were almost certainly members of the Outremont elite, chatelaines of the big rich houses, the French houses, on the northern flank of Mount Royal, across the mountain from Anglo Westmount. Outremont and Westmount seldom came into contact with each other, except perhaps at Holt Renfrew's as the social season approached, when the ladies came to select gowns and finery for balls and dinners. While Mrs. Mackenzie would be preparing for the St. Andrew's Ball, Madame Mercier would be getting ready to dazzle them at the Bal des Petits Souliers at the Ritz. This annual event, sponsored by La Ligue de la Jeunesse

6

6

6

Féminine, took its name from the charity for which it raised money – a fund to purchase shoes for poor children.

Bruce Hutchison was not the only visiting author to be impressed by Montreal's French elite. In his 1946 book *The French-Canadian Outlook*, the American historian Mason Wade wrote about male members of the upper crust, rather than the women. "The elite of priests, lawyers, doctors, scholars and other highly educated men includes some of the most cultivated and charming beings on this continent," he wrote. "Perfectly bilingual, at home with the cultural heritages of France, Britain and the United States, and adding Gallic gaiety and wit to the North American mixture of traits, the best of this elite is a leavening influence in Canada."

Monsieur Mercier and Mr. Mackenzie differed in many ways, not the least of which were their after-work pursuits. For the English gentleman, it was likely to be golf and horses, but his French counterpart was often more interested in art and literature, subjects which, in Westmount, were generally thought best left to the ladies. As Hugh MacLennan once observed, describing men of the Anglo elite, "Their incomes [are] large . . . their minds unclouded by any of the doubts or perplexities arising from undue absorption in philosophy or the arts." But in French Montreal, where artists and intellectuals were held in higher esteem, doctors, lawyers and businessmen were known to write amateur works of history, as well as novels and poetry. Jean Lallemand, who became president of the Montreal Symphony Orchestra in 1941, personified the businessman-aesthete of the time. Visiting artists were frequently his guests, writers like Saint-Exupéry, actors like Charles Boyer, musicians like Yehudi Menuhin. On one occasion, to mark the conclusion of the orchestra's Beethoven festival, he invited two hundred people to a candlelight dinner, with plenty of space to accommodate them in the art gallery of his big Sherbrooke Street house. The refinement of Jean Lallemand's taste was evident in everything he did. When his prized beige-and-black Rolls-Royce became difficult to start on cold winter mornings, he decided to dispose of it and replace it with a more practical Packard. But he insisted that the new car also had to be beige. Why? To go

with the uniform of Albert, his chauffeur, which, of course, was beige
– with black puttees.

Lallemand's wealth was inherited, as a great deal of the bread
baked in Montreal had for many years risen with yeast made in the
Lallemand yeast factory. It was old money, as was the wealth of
most of the French Canadian rich of the 1940s. But the prosperous 1950s saw new fortunes being amassed by self-made men like
J. Louis Lévesque, who rose from humble beginnings to become an
insurance magnate and financier. Like others among the *nouveaux
riches* Lévesque displayed Anglo-like tastes, being more interested
in breeding racehorses than in reading poetry. Other new tycoons
included the six Miron brothers, who made their millions in the
post-war construction boom and were among the first Montrealers
with large private airplanes – a DC-3 and a Canso flying boat.
When Adrien Miron couldn't find the kind of Chinese food he
liked in Miami, he would have it flown down from Ruby Foo's in
Montreal. Although they weren't nearly as numerous as their
Anglo counterparts, enterprising French Canadian businessmen
were slowly making headway.

The wealthy, educated elite comprised only a small fraction
of the city's French-speaking population. In his book, Mason Wade
contended that this elite could be likened to that one-ninth of an
iceberg that was above water. "The submerged eight-ninths of the
social iceberg," he wrote, "the great mass of the French-Canadians,
are underprivileged economically and intellectually. Their standard
of living is well below the North American norm." The severe
housing shortage that persisted through the '40s made life particularly miserable for the working poor, who were usually confined
to ancient, rotting slums. In 1946, a survey by the Ligue Ouvrière
Catholique found that 94 percent of homes in the east end were
woefully overcrowded, with people sleeping in kitchens and hallways. After the war, desperation to find space and housing often
resulted in the creation of new, instant slums, places like Ville
Jacques Cartier, across the river on the South Shore. This was a
shantytown of wretched little dwellings, little more than shacks,
covered in tarpaper designed to look like brick. They stood on unpaved

streets which, after a rainfall, were deep in mud. Without a proper water supply, residents collected rainwater in barrels or bought it from passing water carts. On hot summer days, in the absence of sewers, a stench would arise from the privies behind the houses. These conditions fuelled the rage of Pierre Vallières, who grew up in Ville Jacques Cartier. In later years, Vallières would become a committed Marxist and one of the founders of the Front de Libération du Québec (FLQ), whose nationalist bombs would resound through the streets of Montreal.

As the 1940s progressed, the earnings of workers rose, to the point where, in 1950, the average weekly wage in Montreal was $43.38, almost 65 percent more than it had been ten years earlier. Prices, of course, were also rising, after the lifting of wartime price controls, but still there was a new feeling of prosperity in the air, and by 1949 the city was in the midst of a housing boom, with more dwellings being built in Montreal than anywhere else in Canada. In Ville St. Laurent alone, a cluster of apartment buildings under construction would house 1,100 families, and new duplexes nearby would house another 750. While Anglos who wanted to better themselves were moving westward on the island, French Canadians were moving to new areas north and east. For members of the working class, the aim was to move up from *en bas de la côte*, away from the decrepit, slummy houses of the Hochelaga-Maisonneuve area, away from the river and the factories and up the slope toward Sherbrooke Street East and, preferably, beyond – the farther north the better. During the 1950s, the population of Montreal North more than tripled, while that of Ville St. Michel increased fivefold. At the beginning of the decade, there were 37,000 people living on Ile Jésus, across the Back River, but by 1960 enough farmland had been vacated to make room for almost 125,000.

Besides labourers, factory workers and truck drivers, the new suburbs were also attracting many *cols blancs*, men who wore white collars and neckties. These men, thanks to better education and some ability to speak English, worked in banks and offices. They were the ones whose mothers had urged them to seek *une position* rather than *un job*. At several levels of French Canadian society there were now, in the post-war period, new aspirations toward social mobility, especially through education of a different kind. Traditionally, the well-educated elite had considered its privileges hereditary, and had little concern for the schooling of the masses. The sons of Outremont took the eight-year course of the classical *collèges*, which prepared them to become doctors, lawyers, notaries and politicians, but this kind of schooling was too expensive for those outside the charmed circle.

Now, however, there were new paths, in more affordable technical schools where science, commerce and mathematics were featured, rather than Latin and philosophy. Graduates of these schools might head for university, and careers in engineering, architecture or chemistry, which in the past had few French Canadian practitioners. And these new professions, as well as finance and business, would before long enjoy as much social prestige as the old professions, like medicine and the law. Slowly but surely, in the 1950s, the long-submerged portions of Mason Wade's "social iceberg" were coming to the surface, and a hitherto small middle class was getting bigger. At Christmas and New Year's you could see its members, big families and friends, feasting in the dining room of the Queen's Hotel, where they knew they would be received in French. Traditionally, sumptuous holiday meals were eaten at home, but this new bourgeoisie wanted better things in every realm, including the legendary viands and sauces from Chef Bourdayron's kitchen.

Lucette Lagacé was ten years old when her widowed mother put her into a convent. She paid only twelve dollars a month for the girl's room, board and education, and so Lucette, like all the girls, was expected to undertake a great many housekeeping chores. Soon after her arrival, the nuns took her into the steamy laundry room and told her to feed wet bedsheets through the mangle. But Lucette had heard that hands and arms could be crushed by the big rollers of the mangle, and one look at the monstrous machine was enough to make her faint. When she came to she was given a less threatening chore – ironing uniforms. Life in the convent was austere. All meals were eaten in total silence and the girls washed their dishes in cold water. A day off, to visit the family and get a decent dinner, came only once a month. But what was most distressing for Lucette was the moral instruction she got from the nuns. She would never be happy in life, they told her, because she was *trop orgueilleuse* – she was too proud, and pride was the deadliest of sins. As seen by the nuns, this pernicious pride was probably similar to something that a future generation of educators would try to foster in children – self-esteem.

By 1957, Lucette Lagacé had been married for four years and had three children. Like other housewives, she attended retreats in her parish church and heard preachers promise eternal damnation for anyone who practised birth control. It was about this time that she began to wonder why priests were so obsessed by sin, and it occurred to her that the few people she knew who no longer practised their religion seemed more charitable, more humane. Others, like Pierre Vallières, were being assailed by much more profound doubts about the Church. By the mid-'50s, as he would later write, he had concluded that Catholicism was nothing more than a "vast enterprise for hoodwinking the masses." Vallières's anti-establishment passions would propel him toward the doctrines of revolution, but most of the young intellectuals who were questioning the Church had more moderate goals. It was reform that they sought, in moderation, a "democratization" of religion. In this they found inspiration in the new breed of worker-priests in France and Belgium, and in the works of progressive Catholic writers in Europe.

"Our education, based on monkish authoritarianism, favoured silence," Gérard Pelletier would write, years later. "The rule of silence applied not only to theology as such, but to all areas of life in which the clergy had a hand. Respect for what was sacred protected the doctrine of the Church; respect for authority made sacred anything that had to do with the clergy. But the clergy had to do with everything, so that it was impossible to touch on any subject without risking an interdict." But now that was starting to change, thanks in part to an organization called Jeunesse Etudiante Catholique – Catholic Student Youth. At meetings of the JEC, young people with little or no clerical supervision discussed topics like work, love, literature, the cinema. Members were encouraged to think for themselves, to arrive at decisions about their lives without constant consultation of the authorities. For some bishops, this was disturbing; the JEC was too intellectual, not religious enough. But in the 1950s the Church in Quebec was far from being monolithic in its attitudes toward society. Liberalizing influences were in evidence, especially among younger priests in the cities, and whereas the Jesuits might deplore any departures from the most rigid traditionalism in the realm of education, the Dominicans would be quietly encouraging the exploration of new paths.

Members of the intellectual elite formed l'Ecole des Parents, where parents could meet to discuss the upbringing of their children. Hitherto, guidance in this matter came almost exclusively from folk wisdom or from the Church, but now psychologists were being consulted and modern, secular approaches were being considered. And while these middle-class intellectuals were reading and debating the works of Mounier, Ricoeur and Maritain, young people of the working class and their parents were being subjected to another kind of liberalizing stimulus, something very new – television. From the time of TV's arrival, in 1952, French Montrealers were, in effect, glued to their sets. Their limited, parochial vision of the world was suddenly and explosively widened. The manners, morals and way of life in the rest of North America were now on display in Quebec, especially for those who watched the American programs. As for the programs in French, being produced in Radio-Canada's studios in the old Ford Hotel, here was a new art form, born in great haste and much less shackled by the constraints and self-censorship imposed on the older media. "We don't think like the Church," members of the JEC would say, and the same was certainly true of television, where discussion programs touched on subjects that hitherto had been out of bounds. For the French of Montreal, the 1950s brought ever-growing freedom of thought and action. It was still not exactly a liberal, freewheeling society, but as Bernard Côté, a former priest, summed it up: "In 1940 in Quebec everything that wasn't explicitly permitted was forbidden. In 1960, everything that wasn't explicitly forbidden was permitted."

Nowhere was the craving for freedom more acute than among young women of the middle class, always subject to more restrictions than anyone else. Mothers always watched more vigilantly over their daughters than over their sons, and in some families, as late as the 1940s, when a suitor came calling on a girl, to sit with her in the living room, they would be chaperoned by an aunt or an older sister sitting along with them, or, thanks to a strategically placed mirror, parents in the kitchen could keep an eye on what was going on in the parlour. But now, with a few young women even being admitted to university, they were kicking over the traces. They wanted above all to see the world, and for some the only way to do it was through a hitherto forbidden activity – *faire du pouce*, hitchhiking. In the summer of 1947, Marcelle Brisson, an eighteen-year-old student at Collège Basile-Moreau, set out for the Saguenay-Lac St. Jean area with her two friends, Jacqueline Leduc and Denise Thibault. They rode in trucks with farm animals and their parents would have been horrified to know that in Percé they were given shelter for the night in the town jail, in the morning joining the convicts in peeling potatoes. Seeing Europe was the ultimate dream, but an expensive one. By 1955, when Suzanne Côté was twenty-four, she had saved up seven hundred dollars, enough to keep her in France for six months, riding through the countryside on a motor scooter – a freedom unimaginable to her mother's generation.

There were new professions for women, too. In 1945 Marguerite Daigle came back from studies in the United States to become the first French-Canadian physiotherapist. She worked at the Hôtel-Dieu Hospital and also visited patients at home. To do this she bought a car, becoming one of the first women drivers to be seen in east-end Montreal. When she stopped at a traffic light the man in the car beside her would sometimes roll down his window and shout, "*Va donc laver ta vaisselle!*" – "Go home and wash your dishes!" After a few successful years in her career, in which she had been helpful to young men crippled in the war, Marguerite Daigle married a wealthy businessman and, as he insisted, she gave up her work. If his wife worked, he said, the world would think that they needed the money, that he had gone bankrupt.

During the war, many French Canadian women escaped the confines of the kitchen by finding well-paying work in factories that made arms and ammunition. After the war they were expected to go back to being housewives, and most of them did. But French Montreal was now more willing to accept the idea of working women, and a number of notable careers took root in the post-war period. Judith Jasmin travelled the world to report for radio and television, a field hitherto reserved exclusively for men. Marielle Fleury became a successful designer of women's clothes, insisting on promoting her own creations rather than the copies of Paris and New York fashions that clients asked for. The Farand sisters, Juliette and Madeleine, founded Les Chocolats Andrée, creating the city's most delicious bon-bons. Some of the most militant labour leaders were French Canadian women, like Yvette Charpentier of the garment workers and Madeleine Parent of the textile workers, who kept being arrested by the Duplessis police while on the picket lines. The 1952 strike at Dupuis Frères, the big east-end department store, was in effect a women's strike, with the city astonished by the courage of the picketing saleswomen as they resisted the onslaught of police and strikebreakers. After thirteen weeks of the walkout, the company gave in and the underpaid and overworked employees got a satisfactory collective agreement. Sympathizers of the strikers had managed to discourage at least some Dupuis Frères shoppers by bringing in little green frogs to jump around in the ladies' lingerie department.

∽

"Can you imagine anything more boring than to be English?"

"Even their language is boring. There's no beauty in it. It's good only for doing business."

"It's worse than boring, it's hard on the ears. The English don't speak their language, they spit it."

It was the kind of conversation one might hear (in French, of course) at a Sunday dinner table in Villeray or Ahuntsic. As the family dug into its succulent *gigot* or *rôti de porc*, an elderly aunt would express pity for the English, rather than contempt, because they ate so poorly; only on Thanksgiving did they get any kind of decent meal. They ate mutton, Maman would point out, which tasted of wool. The conversation then might take an etymological turn, when a child asked why the English were called *têtes carrées*. A learned uncle would explain that this expression referred to the uniquely square bone structure of the Anglo-Saxon skull, but Papa would disagree: it was because *les Anglais* refused to learn French that they were called blockheads. Older children might then contribute some angry anecdotes about how poorly the French were treated in factories with unilingual Anglo foremen. But the conversation would become more benign as Maman brought out the stunning dessert, lathered in whipped cream. Now it would be time to again pity the poor Anglos, so lacking in *l'art de vivre*.

"They are not allowed to do anything at all on Sunday," Uncle Fernand would say. "They can't enjoy life, like us. I saw them once, those Presbyterians, when I drove through NDG on a Sunday. They just sit on the balcony, like statues. They are not even allowed to smile."

The Presbyterians might contest this appraisal, but there were a few Anglos who would probably agree with Uncle Fernand. One of them was Maureen Forrester, who wrote, in her autobiography: "I often wonder if the reason I have such a lust for life is that I grew up in the boisterous jollity of Quebec. Back home on Rue Fabre I would find any excuse to drop in on the French-Canadian families around us. They welcomed me like one of their own. The kitchen was always the biggest room in the house and family life seemed to revolve around mealtimes. . . . Everybody would gather around the kitchen table and tell the stories of the day and guffaw. They seemed so lusty and good-natured — my idea of what a family should be. Their meals weren't like ours where somebody was always looking at somebody else the wrong way and stalk off from the table in a huff, slamming doors."

But there were few Anglos who grew up, like Maureen Forrester, on French streets in east-end Montreal. And most Anglo opinion was much less charitable than hers. French Canadians were widely regarded as being rowdy, uncouth, backward and – above all – priest-ridden. Even those who professed affection for them were often condescending, like William Henry Drummond. It was half a century since Drummond, a Montreal physician, had written his immensely popular books of verse about French Canadian life, but people still liked to quote lines like "For de boulanger's got heem une jolie fille / mos' bes' lookin' girl on paroisse dey say. . . ." All of Drummond's voluminous doggerel was in this vein, and down the years jokes and recitations that made fun of Johnny Bateese's accent were always good for a laugh at Anglo parties. The 1940s and '50s saw little diminution of this form of entertainment.

But French spoken with an English accent was less subject to ridicule among French Canadians, probably because they heard it so seldom. Anglos just didn't try very hard to learn the language. French was certainly taught in English schools, but it was taught very badly. These Protestant schools would not hire Catholic teachers and hence could not have French taught by French Canadians, who were actually able to speak it. Instead, Anglo teachers taught mainly written French, as though it was a dead language like Latin; a graduate might be able to understand the difference between the *plus-que-parfait* in the *indicatif* mood and in the *subjonctif*, but be unable to conduct even a rudimentary conversation with the janitor. But nobody worried too much about this. An ambitious young person would have no need to speak French; in the Montreal of the time, anything one wanted to accomplish in life could be accomplished in English. There were a few people who didn't agree with this outlook, like Leslie Buzzell, a prominent accountant, who addressed the Class of 1939, graduating from Montreal West High School. To find and keep a job in Montreal, Mr. Buzzell said, it was essential to have a good command of French. But few people took him seriously.

At the International YMCA on St. Catherine Street, opposite the offices of the newspaper *La Patrie*, it was English that new immigrants were being taught, not French. This was noted, approvingly, in 1941, in an article in *Canadian Business*. "Perhaps more than other cities," the article said, "Montreal has developed a natural formula for cooperation between races, and there lies its strength. In this one city, living side by side, are representatives of all the races which go to make up the Dominion of Canada. Montreal, in miniature, presents a picture of a new nation and offers leadership in solving a new nation's problems."

Just how unimportant it was to be able to speak French in the world of Montreal business and industry is illustrated by the fact that in 1961 the average annual earnings of a bilingual Anglo were only about 3 percent more than those of a unilingual Anglo. How important it was to *be* English as well as speak English is illustrated by the fact that a unilingual Anglo earned 37 percent more than a bilingual Francophone. Big business was almost entirely in the hands of the English. Although there was an increase in French enterprise during the 1950s, at the end of that decade only 13 percent of Montreal's manufacturing establishments were owned by French Canadians, and these were mostly small, marginal companies with relatively few employees and a modest volume of sales. In his 1947 booklet *Who Owns Canada?*, Watt Hugh McCollum listed only three French Canadian names among his "Fifty Big Shots."

When asked why this disparity should exist, an Anglo businessman might have said that the French were educated in a system that prepared them for life in the Kingdom of Heaven rather than in the Dominion of Canada. Children of the Outremont elite, who might have been expected to become business leaders, went to private schools, the classical *collèges*, where they dwelt on Latin, Greek and philosophy rather than on practical subjects. As for working-class children, the elite was generally indifferent to their educational needs and was unwilling to spend much money on them. Under Quebec's separate Catholic and Protestant school systems, each funded by taxes levied on its own community, the more prosperous English had more to spend on public education than did the French. Thus the better jobs generally went to English graduates. As for the universities, their creation of new faculties or courses to train French business executives was hampered by Premier Duplessis's refusal to accept funding from Ottawa for higher education, something he did in the sacred name of Quebec autonomy. Aware of this educational deficit, most French Canadians lacked confidence in their business abilities, and those who managed to accumulate some wealth were often more ready to invest it in Anglo enterprises than in those of their compatriots. In the east end, the Bank of Montreal generally chose English managers to run its branches, having found that French businessmen would rather deal with Anglos than with French managers.

English signs outside stores gave downtown Montreal an almost completely English face, to the point where foreign visitors were surprised when they were told that the language of most of the population was French. In the big department stores, French customers often found that they couldn't be served in their own language, but it was the simple inconvenience of the situation rather than its political implications that formed the basis of most complaints. For most French Canadians, English domination of the economy was a fact of life, and from this fact flowed disabilities that had to be endured, like the necessity of working in English if one wanted a good job. When protests were formal and vocal, they dealt not with issues like the language of work and business but with "face" issues like the language of signs and the labels on commercial products. Organizations like the Société Saint-Jean-Baptiste and the Comité Permanent de la Survivance Française merely wanted street and business signs to be bilingual, so that Montreal, in effect, would look at least half-French.

This goal, which would seem ridiculously modest to the next generation, was not easily attainable. The biggest battle waged by the linguistic nationalists in the 1950s was one that they ultimately lost. It concerned the huge new structure going up on Dorchester Boulevard, which its owner, the Canadian National Railways, said would be named the Queen Elizabeth Hotel. In a remarkable display of obtuseness, the CNR's president, Donald Gordon, said that this name had been chosen because it would "symbolize the unity between the two language groups in our country . . . the Crown [being] the symbol of that unity." But one of the two language groups didn't quite see it that way. "How would you like it," Mayor Jean Drapeau wrote to Gordon, "if in Toronto the CNR established a hotel and called it the Dollard-des-Ormeaux or the Louis-Joseph Papineau?" This hotel, owned by the federal government, should have a French name, and the Ligue d'Action Nationale collected 200,000 signatures on its petition demanding that it be named Le Château Maisonneuve, after Montreal's founder. When Donald Gordon continued to reject this suggestion, some five hundred shouting students paraded down McGill Street, assembled under his office and hung his effigy from a lamppost. Looking down on the near-riot, Gordon dismissed it as an amusing student prank – and the hotel was duly christened in honour of Her Britannic Majesty.

A more serious demonstration with racial overtones took place on March 17, 1955, when a mob surged down St. Catherine Street, smashing the windows of dozens of stores, looting and starting fires. The rioters were voicing their displeasure with a decision by Clarence Campbell, president of the National Hockey League. Maurice "Rocket" Richard, starring scorer of the Canadiens and Montreal's revered hockey idol, had been involved in a brawl on the ice and had struck a linesman who had been trying to break it up. For this, Campbell had suspended Richard for the rest of the season, including the Stanley Cup playoffs. For French fans, this was an unreasonable penalty imposed on one of their own by a much-detested, arrogant Anglo. He would never have imposed it on, say, a rambunctious player of the Toronto Maple Leafs. When, two days later, Campbell unwisely showed up at the Forum for a Canadiens-Detroit game, a listless affair without the great Rocket, the NHL president was booed and pelted with every handy missile. When someone threw a tear-gas bomb, the fire department ordered the Forum evacuated and the crowd surged out onto St. Catherine Street, hotheads ready to riot.

Besides the Forum and the Queen Elizabeth Hotel demonstrations, there were no outbursts in the 1950s that could be attributed to linguistic tensions. The French nationalist cause had not yet generated enough popular support for concerted political action. In his book *Montreal, Seaport and City*, Stephen Leacock examined the language question and drew a metaphor from the belief that in pre-historic times Mount Royal had been a volcano. "The soil under the feet of its people covers ashes never extinct," Leacock wrote. "Its real volcano still smolders." Leacock wrote his book in 1942, two years before his death. By the end of the 1950s, the volcano was still only smouldering. The full eruption was still a few years down the road.

8

A Third Solitude: The Jews

Who made the best smoked meat? Was it Etinson's or Rogatko's, Chenoy's Brooklyn Delicatessen or the Hebrew National? It was a question that was passionately debated on St. Lawrence Boulevard, the artery better known as the Main. On a warm summer evening in 1939, if you were to walk north on the Main from Prince Arthur, your nostrils would be assailed by the aroma of hot, spicy smoked meat wafting out of no fewer than seven delicatessens in less than a mile. Each had its own secret recipe, its own combination of pickling spices to encrust the noble brisket of beef. And as the clients of Putter's or Shagass's bit into their ten-cent sandwiches (rye bread, lots of mustard), they argued about quality and authenticity, just as they argued about everything else under the sun, such as Trotsky versus Stalin. And, of course, they argued about just who it was that first brought smoked meat to Montreal from Romania, around the turn of the century, whether it was Old Man Kravitz or Old Man Wiseman.

Seven delicatessens in 1939, but by 1959 only three were left (including the incomparable, indestructible Schwartz's). The others had succumbed not because they had lost the brisket wars but because so many Jews were moving away from the old neighbourhood, to more affluent areas. In earlier years, the shabby streets on either side of St. Lawrence Main, at this latitude, were almost entirely Jewish, but this was no longer the case. Now it was Greeks and Hungarians who were coming to live here, new immigrants who were moving into dwellings vacated by Jews, newcomers who craved their own kind of food.

For many decades, the Main had been the long funnel that bore the tide of immigrants northward into the city, from the riverfront steamship piers and from the downtown railway stations. Since the turn of the century, Jews fleeing oppression in Europe constituted the largest group of immigrants to arrive in Montreal, swelling the number of Jews in the city, by 1941, to sixty-four thousand. Of these, two-thirds lived within a short walk of those seven smoked-meat dispensaries, to say nothing of the hickory-fired bagel ovens.

These were mostly working-class Jews – toilers in the sweatshops of the garment industry, fabricators of fur coats and handbags, shoemakers, deliverymen, mechanics. In the 1940s and '50s, prosperity brought new opportunities for these people, and now a cutter and a sewing-machine operator could thumb their noses at the tyrannical boss of the clothing factory and bravely start a little factory of their own. With their new affluence came the determination to finally abandon the dingy old dwellings of Villeneuve and St. Viateur and take their families westward into the sunshine of the new suburbs.

It was a sign of the times, in 1952, when Horn's Cafeteria, a landmark on the Main, finally closed its doors. This was where Irving Layton, A.M. Klein and other poets would hold forth, on Sunday morning, over tea with lemon. During the week, at lunchtime, the big clothing moguls would devour their *latkes* at a table in the back, Joe Guttman of Progress Brand and William Shatner's father, the pants man, discussing the price of broadcloth. But the clothing factories were moving northward, away from the old area, to more commodious quarters, and the bosses and workers would be taking their lunch elsewhere. As the 1950s progressed, the exodus of the old businesses gathered momentum, although some die-hards seemed determined to stay put. At the end of the decade, the Globe Sponging Works and the Better Made Button Hole Company were still operating in the Balfour Building, and the Cute Hat Manufacturing Company was still doing business just up the street from Abie's Sanitary Barber Shop. But now the Main was acquiring a different ethnic complexion, with establishments like the New Greece

People poured out into the streets to celebrate victory in Europe on V-E Day, 1945. The crowd was especially thick in Phillips Square, across the street from Morgan's.

The war is over! Celebrations on St. Catherine Street hold up traffic, May 7, 1945. The sale of liquor was forbidden that day, so rejoicing would not get out of hand.

The Royal Montreal Regiment, among the first units to go to Europe in 1939, comes home in September, 1945. During the war, 104 men of this regiment lost their lives.

Bakery, the Dutch Pastry Shop, the Budapest Meat Market. Berman's Caterers might still be strictly kosher, but Sepp's sausage shop was strictly Teutonic.

Nine or ten streets parallel to St. Lawrence Main, and on either side of it, once constituted a long, narrow Jewish buffer zone between English Montreal to the west and the French city to the east. In 1939, there were virtually no gentiles living on St. Urbain Street, between Pine Avenue and St. Viateur, and the same could be said about neighbouring streets, like Clark and Esplanade. But twenty years later, most of the Jews were gone. A few stubborn old people lingered on, deaf to the entreaties of their upwardly mobile children, but now on St. Urbain it was the Evangelistas and the Kriarises, not the Cohens and the Rosens, who climbed the steep outdoor staircases to the second floor. And on Clark there was now very little Yiddish to be heard, certainly not from new residents like Pasquale Verruto or a man who rejoiced in the name of Steve Satan.

~

The poorest Jews, in the 1940s, lived on streets east of the Main. The Aronovitches were on the notorious De Bullion Street, but well north of the red-light district. When they opened the door and entered their flat they would clap their hands and make a lot of noise, to frighten the rats back into hiding, so they wouldn't scurry across their feet. Coming home at night, their neighbours, the Resniks, would send their daughter Doris in first, to turn on the light to make the cockroaches flee from the dining-room table. Doris Resnik and Goldie Aronovitch would shudder together over the tale of the neighbour's baby whose ear was partly chewed off by a rat while he was asleep.

These were cold-water flats, heated by a single coal stove in the kitchen. In winter the house was never warm enough and Doris would sleep with several hot water bottles in her bed. In the morning, her mother would warm up her clothes for her on the stove before she put them on. Heating water in the boiler cost money, so after Goldie and her sister had their bath together their brother

Irving would have his in the same water. There was no hot water in the summer and so the girls would go to the public baths for a shower. During a July heat wave, outside the Schubert Bath, the body odour from perspiring blue-collar workers lined up to get in was legendary, and people said they could smell it as far down as St. Cuthbert Street. It was an aroma familiar to all of the city's sixteen public baths, all in poor districts where hot water was at a premium.

Street life in the Jewish streets was lively and noisy. The milkman, the breadman and the iceman, with their horses and wagons, all made a hearty clatter as they plied their trade. In the back lanes, the ragmen, their wagons drawn by the scrawniest of horses, uttered incomprehensible cries to alert housewives that they were ready to buy old rags, bottles, bones and junk of any description. Meanwhile, on the street out front, the fruit man would be coming by, delighting the children whenever he could announce, at the top of his voice, that today he had "vadermelon" in his wagon. The iceman, in the days before refrigerators, was a key figure in the household economy. But his life was not an easy one. Louis Aronovitch – using his Yiddish name, they called him Laibel the Iceman – couldn't afford a horse, so after buying blocks of ice from a wholesaler he would load them onto a handcart, which he pulled through the streets to his customers' doors. The customers, he would say, drove him crazy. Gripping a great block of ice in his tongs, he would lug it up three flights of stairs, only to be told by the housewife that it was too small. He would stagger down the stairs to get a bigger piece, consoled perhaps by the knowledge that he might make four cents profit on this block rather than only three.

For the children, the streets were playgrounds and their sporting equipment was homemade. Old rags stuffed into an old sock made a football, and any long piece of wood could be a baseball bat. Strips of rubber cut from old automobile inner tubes became slingshots, and scooters were made out of orange crates and roller-skate wheels. A complex device involving a length of thread, a button and a thumbtack could cause mysterious clickings on the front window of a house, and the children, hiding, would wait to see the housewife come rushing out to see what was going on. On Napoleon Street, women on their way to the grocery store would be horrified when a big rat came slithering across the sidewalk, right in their path – actually a dead rat at the end of a long cord, manipulated by enterprising boys across the street.

More formal sport was to be had on the long expanse of Fletcher's Field, where there was room for much simultaneous baseball, soccer and lacrosse. And across Park Avenue, on the grass at the foot of the mountain, there were military band concerts on summer evenings, and Wednesday-night singalongs where Mister Murphy, from the Kiwanis Club, would lead three hundred young Jewish voices as they rendered "Deep in the Heart of Texas." On Friday night, dressed in their best, the young folk would promenade up and down Park Avenue, from Mount Royal to Bernard, to engage in heavy flirtation and perhaps line up a date for the Saturday-night dance at the YMHA.

For young mothers, the centres of their social life were those long outdoor staircases, so peculiar to Montreal. They would sit there, on hot summer days, feeding their babies, scolding the older children for getting dirty on the street, and – above all – gossiping with the neighbours. The limitations of icebox refrigeration made it necessary to make frequent trips to the corner grocery store, to buy a quarter of a pound of butter, and a woman's neighbour would watch her children while she was doing her errands. At the grocery store, credit was usually extended, and the grocer might keep his accounts on the back of a brown paper bag. Some grocers had reputations as psychiatrists, listening to customers' problems and offering advice. The grocer at the corner of Villeneuve and Jeanne Mance was said to know if a woman was pregnant before her husband learned of it.

While still at school, in 1939, John Liberman worked weekends at one of Steinberg's groceries, from 4:00 p.m. to 11:00 p.m. on Fridays and from 8:00 a.m. to midnight on Saturdays. For this he received a total of $2.50, which he turned over to his father, who was "tickled pink," because this was 10 percent of the monthly rent for the family's cold-water flat. The Depression was not yet over, and paying the rent was a problem for many families, some of them solving it by taking in a boarder. Even as the early 1940s finally brought a measure of prosperity, many Jews felt that it wouldn't last, that it might all somehow evaporate. One legacy of the Depression was the habit of thrift, and Harry Stillman, as a student, walked from his home to McGill and back every day – more than two miles each way – to save on carfare. Rather than spend seven cents on a street-car ticket, Mary Segall would walk a similar distance on her way to work at the family business on Ontario Street, where they sold bales of hay to caleche drivers at one cent a pound.

Optimism about the future grew as the 1940s progressed. At Baron Byng High School, where almost all the students were the children of working-class Jews, more students than ever before felt they had a chance to go on to university. Their older brothers and sisters usually had had to leave school to go to work and help support the family, but for this generation the possibilities seemed unlimited. They would become not only doctors, as their mothers fervently hoped, or lawyers, as their fathers hoped, but they would venture into fields much less traditional for Jews. Among graduates in the Class of 1944 there were several future scientists and university professors, a world-class mathematician, a foreign-service diplomat and even a ship's captain. Harry Stillman, a member of that class, wanted to become an architect – not, as he put it, just to make money, but to help build a better world. Idealism was rife among the 1944 graduates; it was up to them, once the war was won, to build a new world – the One World where the Four Freedoms, as enunciated by Franklin Roosevelt, would prevail, especially the freedom from want.

Much of the students' idealism was inherited from their parents. During the week, their fathers might work in butcher shops or drive taxis, but on Sundays they put on their carefully pressed blue serge suits and went to the Jewish Public Library to listen to lectures and poetry readings. They aspired to culture and they thrived on argument, always ready with a devastating question for the lecturer ("Excuse me, sir, but the way you describe this Mr. Lenin, I do not recognize him. Is it the *Russian* Lenin, or maybe some Irishman Lenin?"). The majority of the working-class Jews were certainly leftists, the only question being how far left one should be on a spectrum from faint pink to bright crimson. But if debates were hot, a certain European formality prevailed in the older generation, where people who had been friends for thirty years still referred to each other not as Max and Sophie but as *Mr.* Borenstein and *Mrs.* Glickman.

Most Jewish children went to elementary schools of the Protestant School Board, but a substantial number were sent to parochial schools, day schools where half the day was spent on the English curriculum and the other half on Jewish subjects. These day schools, half a dozen of them, reflected different political beliefs and different degrees of religious observance. The Talmud Torah school espoused Orthodox Judaism and traditional Zionism, while the Jewish People's School was more secular and somewhat to the left with its Labour Zionist credo. But the Morris Winchevsky School, for the children of communists, had no use for either Zionism or religion. A young communist's religious education was apt to be like that of Harry Gulkin who, at the age of eleven, was taken to a synagogue for the first time by his father. "This is where the rabbis make a lot of money," Peter Gulkin told his son. "Never set foot in here again." (Gulkin *père*, owner of a Main Street photo studio, went even further one year, on Yom Kippur, that holiest of days, by marching up and down in front of a synagogue eating a ham sandwich.)

The Jewish part of the parochial schools' instruction was almost always in Yiddish, which was, in effect, Montreal's third language. It had been brought to the city in the waves of immigration from Eastern Europe that began in the last decades of the nineteenth century, a Germanic vernacular spiced with an admixture of Hebrew and Slavic words. In the 1940s it was still the language most often heard up and down the Main, over the grocer's pickle barrel and in the sweatshops of the clothing factories. Charitable institutions and community groups of every kind functioned largely in Yiddish, and the Jewish Public Library housed an ever-growing collection of Yiddish books and periodicals. But as the 1950s progressed, less and less Yiddish was being spoken. Young Jews of the new generation, born in Canada, had become anglicized at school, and most of them had little use for the "old country" language of their parents. Some would even pretend that they couldn't speak it and, embarrassed by the distinctive cadence of Yiddish, were determined to banish any traces of it from the English that they spoke. English was the passport to professional or commercial success and it was widely predicted that Yiddish would soon fade away, completely.

Still, the *Kanader Adler*, Montreal's Yiddish daily newspaper, soldiered on defiantly. In 1957, the paper, which called itself the *Jewish Daily Eagle* in English, celebrated its fiftieth anniversary. "We who guide the Eagle in its flight choose to believe that we still have a valuable contribution to make," its publisher, Max Wolofsky, said in his introduction to the English section of the paper's thick Golden Jubilee Edition. He scorned the sages who were predicting the demise of Yiddish. "We recall that these prophets of doom and gloom were with us generations back," he wrote. "H. Wolofsky paid them little heed when they were wont to importune him to desist from tilting at windmills and to engage in a less taxing and more profitable venture." H. Wolofsky was Max's father, Hershel, an immigrant from Russia who founded the *Kanader Adler* in 1907.

The fledgling Eagle had had a difficult birth, rendered no easier by the pressmen at the *Herald*, where the paper was printed, who had difficulty comprehending that Yiddish, written in Hebrew characters, read from right to left and what they produced as a front page was actually the back page. The initial technical and financial difficulties were eventually overcome, and the *Adler* became the mainstay of Yiddish culture in Montreal and a guiding light for immigrants trying to make their way in a bewildering new world. Besides offering its readers international, national and local news, the *Adler* published poetry, fiction and essays which helped make Montreal, in the years before the Second World War, a centre of Yiddish literature that ranked with Warsaw and New York. Montreal's Yiddish writers – Sholem Shtern, Ida Maze, Israel Rabinovitch and many others – often differed from their more reserved English and French contemporaries by being vociferously active in community affairs, politics and labour disputes. Far from inhabiting ivory towers, many of these poets seemed to be involved in every squabble that enlivened their community. Their arguments echoed up and down the Main.

Preeminent among the Yiddish poets was J.I. Segal, who may have been the most prolific Canadian versifier that ever lived. By the time of his death, in 1954, Segal had published ten books of Yiddish poetry, not slender chapbooks but thick volumes of three hundred pages or more. And there were two more volumes to come, posthumously. To those who dared ask him why he felt he had to publish so much, Segal would reply that a poet was judged by his ability to produce. Much of this torrential output was suffused with melancholy, with the loneliness of the outsider, the immigrant who can never feel at home in a strange new country. There was much sentiment for the village in Poland where Segal grew up, the *shtetl*, and he found echoes of it in some of Montreal's old, narrow streets, where he saw signs of decay – "Rotting fences, bent boards / Sad – the window eyes / of the factories that stand closed. . . ."

Yiddish theatre in Montreal, vigorous in the 1920s, went into eclipse during the Depression days of the '30s but saw a revival in the '40s, especially toward the end of that decade, when a new wave of Yiddish-speaking immigrants, survivors of the Holocaust, started arriving in the city and would constitute a new audience. Once again, touring companies were coming from New York. In 1950, in the same January week, they brought Sholem Aleichem's *Yosele the Nightingale* to His Majesty's Theatre and a Yiddish version of *Anna Lucasta* to the Monument National. Great stars were frequent visitors, like Menasha Skulnik, "The King of Laughter," who came with his musical comedy *My Wedding Night*, which boasted "a chorus of beautiful girls." In *Yosele* the star was the renowned Maurice Schwartz, a thespian so vain that he refused to be photographed with locally hired bit-players.

The Monument National Theatre, owned by the nationalist St. Jean Baptiste Society, was the venue for most of the Yiddish plays. In the early '50s its stage saw tragedies like Louis Freiman's *Two Mothers* and comedies like Abraham Blum's *Three Daughters*. Jewish audiences loved to shed tears in the theatre, and Freiman obliged them with plays like *Children without a Home* and *A Child for Sale*, about a blind girl in an orphanage. Audiences also filled the Monument National to see Chayele Grober's one-woman show. She had trained with Stanislavski in Moscow, and now, settled in Montreal, she offered dramatic monologues, folk songs and mime.

But the greatest performer of all was Hertz Grosbard, who took Yiddish Montreal by storm when he arrived from Europe in the early 1950s. A.M. Klein, the poet, could barely contain himself when he reviewed Grosbard's one-man show for the *Kanader Adler*. "Elocutionist? Reader? Diseur? Actor? Grosbard is all of these," Klein wrote. "As one recalls his varied program – monologue, dialogue, mass mise-en-scène, fanciful fable and Chassidic tale, exercise in naiveté, nostalgic poem, parody, satire – one hears him again reciting, intoning, whispering, sneering between the hyphens, weeping, almost weeping, thundering, confiding, even neighing. (Did you ever hear a horse neigh in Yiddish? A talking horse? A horse talking Yiddish with inflexions truly equine?)" Klein was particularly taken by Grosbard's reading of a poem about the contents of a cooking pot, where onions, beans and noodles spoke up with distinctive accents. "Many can mimic human speech," Klein wrote. "Grosbard ventriloquizes vegetables."

～

If the poorest Jews lived in the streets just east of St. Lawrence Main, their somewhat more affluent cousins lived in streets to the west, like St. Urbain and Waverley. There were not only working-class people here, but also small merchants and the owners of corner candy stores. Going farther west, one came to Park Avenue, an economic dividing line, for beyond that, again to the west, was Outremont, abode of Jews with healthy bank accounts, proprietors of clothing factories. It was to Outremont that ghetto boys from St. Dominique Street went in spring to steal lilacs from the gardens of prosperous Jews. This posh precinct was a different world where, the boys had heard, there was a synagogue whose rabbi didn't have a beard and who spoke with a British accent.

The youth of Outremont went to Strathcona Academy, not Baron Byng High School, and there was little contact between the two groups, although they did meet occasionally over hot chocolate at

Archie's soda fountain, at Hutchison and Bernard, on the border between the two domains. Strathcona girls told each other that it was beneath them to go out with Baron Byng boys, but surreptitiously some of them did. If they married them they would be "marrying down," but Baron Byng students were consistently getting some of the highest exam marks in the province, and that held out the promise of careers with swift upward mobility. Marriage was an imperative for Strathcona girls, and if Arlene or Shirley went on to McGill she was expected to be wearing an engagement ring by the time she graduated. Then her mother could tell her bridge-club friends, "She got her B.A. and she got her diamond, too." (The diamond was called the "M.R.S. degree.") Another measure of a Strathcona girl's standing was how many cashmere sweaters daddy could buy for her. For poor girls, competing with cashmere could be intimidating. One of the poorer ones, a girl who was at the top of her class when she graduated from Baron Byng, won a scholarship to Sir George Williams College, but she didn't take it up, worried that she wouldn't be able to keep up with the Outremont girls at Sir George when it came to clothes. So instead she took a commercial course at a secretarial school.

Outremont might be "comfortable," but Westmount was rich, very rich. But exactly where *was* Westmount and how did you get there? Jules Foxman and his teenage friends, boys from the cold-water flats, had to find out after being invited to a B'nai B'rith social at the home of Norma Betty Grover, daughter of the mighty Hyman Grover, president of Grover Mills and Knit-to-Fit. It took the boys two hours to make the trip, on unfamiliar streetcars like the exotic No. 14. Finally they had to trudge up a steep hill in a heavy snowstorm. When a man opened the door for them, they thought it was Mr. Grover himself, but no, it was the butler and he handed them Kleenex to wipe their runny noses. The house was as opulent as anything they had seen in the movies. When they went to the bathroom they noted the limitless amount of toilet paper; at home they seldom had toilet paper, getting by with squares of newspaper on a spike or wrappers from oranges retrieved from the grocery store. A maid in a white cap served some snacks and the party was just warming up when, at ten o'clock, Mr. Grover, president of synagogues and governor of hospitals, came into the room, sat down at the piano and played "God Save the King," indicating that the party was over. Trudging back home through the snowstorm, after only an hour of near-fun, Jules Foxman and his friends could only conclude that rich Jews lived on a different planet.

Nevertheless, it was a planet to which the ambitious could aspire, and a mother was apt to say to her son, "If you study hard, Morris, you could become a Bronfman." She would be referring, of course, to Sam Bronfman, the Seagram's whiskey magnate. Richer than Croesus, lavishly philanthropic and president of the Canadian Jewish Congress, Bronfman was, in Montreal, the acknowledged King of the Jews. In his house on Belvedere Road he kept seven servants, and there was a woman who came in frequently to wash, starch and iron their uniforms. There was a Rembrandt, a Monet and a Degas in the drawing room, and in the basement the recreation room was fitted out like a nightclub, with a coat-check room that seemed bigger than that at Ruby Foo's.

The Bronfman fortune was relatively new money, but there was also old Jewish money on the slopes of Westmount. Some of it dated back almost two hundred years, when the first Jews arrived in Montreal after the British conquest of New France. Aaron Hart came as a lieutenant in General Amherst's army, and he went on to Trois-Rivières to become a prosperous businessman. When he went north with some Indians to trade for furs, he took kosher food with him in his canoe. Other Jews, from England and the United States, also prospered and achieved stature, and in 1837 Moses Judah Hays and Benjamin Hart became city magistrates. People like these, relatively few in number, were well accepted by the city's Anglo-Scottish elite and were the anglicized forerunners of what came to be known as the "uptown Jews." The downtown Jews – Yiddish-speaking, poor and with less-polished manners – were the immigrants who came later, in large numbers, from Eastern Europe.

In the 1940s, uptown Jews could be found, smoking their Havanas, in their Montefiore Club on Guy Street. They took great pride in this luxurious, leather-armchaired replica of a London gentlemen's club, and in the fact that no fewer than twelve of its members appeared in the first King's Honours List issued after the war, having been awarded the Order of the British Empire for wartime services or being made MBEs. But some of the older members were uneasy about new trends in the community. They could recall a time, early in the century when the club was young, when its members conformed closely to the conservative manners and dress code of their Anglo-Scottish neighbours in the Square Mile. Now, uptown Jews seemed to feel perfectly free to wear disconcertingly brighter plumage. In his book *The State of Quebec*, Peter Desbarats quoted a fashion authority's description of the stunning – "but somehow slightly vulgar" – gowns that she had observed at the Angels' Ball, the Jewish high-society event. "It was fantastic," she said. "You've never seen more opulence." By comparison the ladies at the St. Andrew's Ball looked tatty. As the fashion expert explained it, when an Anglocrat woman bought a Balenciaga gown at Holt Renfrew's, she would have everything removed that would make it stand out, but a Jewish woman would add beads to it.

Some downtown Jews liked the idea of having their own aristocracy up there on the hill, with King Bronfman snug in his palace, attended by his courtier lawyers, each with his own little castle. But there could be sharp conflict between the two groups. Downtown Jews who were passionate Yiddishists could not easily forgive the Montefiore clubmen for their machinations in the separate-schools issue of the early 1930s. Most Jewish children, those who did not attend parochial schools, had always gone to schools of the Protestant School Board. In the 1920s, downtown Jews agitated for the creation of a tax-supported separate Jewish school system, with the same status as the Protestant and Catholic systems. The idea was anathema to most uptowners, one of whose rabbis denounced its proponents as "the worst enemies of their country." What they wanted, he said, was "the revival of a ghetto and the return of the dark ages of ignorance and superstition . . . the perpetuation of their horrid jargon known as Yiddish." The battle went on for years, and by 1930 the Quebec government was prepared to give Jews their separate school system. But the uptown Jews, working behind the scenes with their considerable political influence, finally managed to have the idea scuttled once and for all. Jewish children would continue to go to Protestant schools, even if it meant being exposed to Christian teachings. Thus, when Arlene Cooperberg's very orthodox grand-mother asked her to sing a song for her, little Arlene, aged six, obliged by singing "Jesus Loves Me, This I Know." "That took a few years off her life," Arlene said, recalling the incident half a century later.

Labour conflicts in the clothing industry, where uptowners were the employers and downtowners the workers, were even more bitter and more prolonged than the dispute over separate schools. By the 1940s tensions had diminished considerably, but memories of almost half a century of industrial strife were still vivid and contributed to the uneasiness of relations between these two classes of Jews. Many an old cutter or presser remembered the strikes of yesteryear, the miserable wages, the fifty-five-hour work weeks, the filthy and dan-gerous working conditions in the sweatshop factories of an indus-try that was largely Jewish. Pitted against the Westmount factory owners were immigrant Jews from Poland and Russia who had brought with them radical socialist ideas. One factory owner, early in the century, was so incensed by his workers' demands that he sug-gested that "foreign agitators" be deported, meaning, of course, fellow Jews.

Jews were vigorous organizers of labour unions, and none was more effective than Lea Roback, a firebrand ideologue involved in the formation of the Montreal branch of the International Ladies Garment Workers' Union. In its 1937 strike, when four thousand workers were out for three weeks, the new union made important gains that helped humanize the industry. Jewish and French Canadian workers were now drawing together in their battles against the bosses, and in this atmosphere Lea Roback was an ideal organizer, being fluent in French as well as English and Yiddish. When she heard a French worker cursing his employer as a *maudit Juif*, she corrected him by explaining that this boss was evil not because he was a Jew but because he was their enemy in the class struggle, just as bosses called Trottier and Tremblay were their enemies. When she heard that an employer had refused to hire a qualified seamstress because she happened to be black, Roback stormed into his office and cursed him in Yiddish, pointing out that his morals were identical to Hitler's. The employer relented, hired the black woman and later admitted that she had become one of his most valuable workers.

Uptown-downtown friction was also present in politics, especially in the epochal federal by-election of 1943 in Cartier, a riding that was almost 60 percent Jewish. Fred Rose was running for the Labour-Progressive Party, a new name of the Communist Party, while Lazarus Phillips, a duke in the court of the Bronfmans, was carrying the Liberal banner. A number of artists and writers were on the communist side and they concocted, for door-to-door distribution, a replica of *Life* magazine entitled *Life in Cartier*, featuring a picture of a slum house on De Montigny Street beside a picture of Lazarus Phillips's mansion on Murray Hill in Westmount. There was a third Jewish candidate in the election, David Lewis, who would one day be head of the NDP and was now running for the CCF. A fourth candidate, Paul Massé, represented the new nationalist party, the Bloc Populaire, and his pamphlets, in five languages, denounced his rivals as Jews and conscriptionists.

Election day promised to be as spirited as ever, and Lazarus Phillips was prudent enough to have a doctor in his committee room, standing by all day to attend to any injuries his workers might sustain in the inevitable fighting. Phillips had more money than the others with which to buy votes, but still he finished a poor third in the race. It was Fred Rose, the downtowner-communist, who won, but with the Jewish vote split he got only 261 votes more than the anti-Semite Massé. David Lewis, an innocent from outside, was shocked at the crookedness of a Cartier election. His workers had discovered, on the voters' list, the name of a seven-month-old baby listed as a bookkeeper, eleven voters listed as residing in a barber shop and any number of dead people. "They inscribed everyone from the cradle to the grave, inclusive," Lewis complained. But for more seasoned campaigners, this only proved that Jews were becoming just as adept at Quebec-style politics as their Christian counterparts in ridings like St. Ann's or St. Jacques. As one happy warrior from St. Urbain Street put it: "Buy, slug and steal – and it's kosher if you're elected."

~

"We never heard a bird on De Bullion Street," Goldie would say. "There was no grass. We lived right off the pavement." But now there was grass, and the chirp of birds, and fresh air without the stink from the stables behind the houses. Goldie was married now, she was Goldie Libman, and she had finally left the old neighbourhood to settle in a new suburb. She and her growing family were part of the great Jewish migration northwards and westwards in the city. Growing up amid the decay of De Bullion Street, she had always dreamed of escape. "We didn't want big things," she recalled, decades later. "We just wanted to have that picket fence and wear a pretty little apron and have the kids come home from school and have milk and cookies." Now she was having it all, in Ville St. Laurent.

It was post-war prosperity that made the Jewish migration possible and, finally, the availability of new housing. The desperate housing shortage of the war years, and the years immediately after, was now coming to an end, in the late '40s, with houses and apartment buildings sprouting all over the island in a building boom like nothing that had ever been seen before. Government-subsidized apartment buildings in Côte des Neiges attracted many working-class Jews from the old area. Goldie's friend Doris Resnik was among them, moving with her parents to an apartment on Legare Street, where there were still large open fields nearby. There was still no central heat in Doris's new dwelling, and the oil stove in the hallway wasn't enough to keep them from shivering on cold winter days. But there was a refrigerator here, not a leaky old icebox, and the bathroom had a shower – and there were no cockroaches.

In five years, 1951 to 1956, fourteen new synagogues had been built or were under construction to accommodate migrants moving west to Snowdon, Hampstead, Notre Dame de Grâce, Côte St. Luc. In 1951 there were thirty-four Jews living in Côte St. Luc; ten years

later there were 8,307. This was to become the most Jewish part of
Montreal, with many towering apartment blocks, but in the early
'50s it was the far-western frontier, and women who became pregnant
out there worried whether they would be able to get into town, to
the hospital, in time.

Three-quarters of the city's Jews had once lived within a one-mile
radius of Jeanne Mance and Villeneuve streets, but now they were
dispersed over a vastly wider area. Paradoxically, in its dispersion the
community seemed to be achieving a greater cohesion. The old area
had been a welter of small synagogues, mutual-aid and cultural societies, and political clubs, many of them competing with each other
with no small degree of acrimony. Opposing viewpoints still existed,
but now the mood was more temperate. As poor Jews became more
affluent and as labour problems were more or less resolved, uptowners became less offensive in the eyes of downtowners. And downtowners of the new generation – better educated, no longer speaking
Yiddish and with manners more North American than European –
were more acceptable to the snobbish uptowners. Even more important in drawing the city's Jews together was the shock of the
Holocaust, the post-war revelation of the monstrousness of the Nazi
crime. This led to increased fervour for the creation of a State of
Israel, and this, too, was a unifying force.

In Doris Resnik's modest home on De Bullion Street, much of the
furniture had been bought from the junk man. Now, as they were
moving westward, her parents left much of it behind – "for the D.P.s."
The D.P.s were Displaced Persons, Jewish refugees from Europe,
many of them survivors of the concentration camps. With thousands
of them arriving in Montreal between 1947 and 1952, many of them
moved into premises near the Main vacated by Jews moving to Côte
des Neiges and Snowdon, but soon the newcomers, quickly adapt-
ing to local ways, also started making the trek westward.

In the late 1950s, a new wave of immigrants started to arrive,
Moroccan Jews fleeing the rising anti-Semitism of North Africa.
Jean-Claude Lasry, aged twenty, was one of the first to come, and he
soon found that integration into the Jewish community was far from
easy. At Saturday-night dances at the YMHA, girls that he asked to

dance would refuse him, and he concluded that they didn't think he was Jewish, especially as his language was French rather than English. But at the Union Française dances, the French Canadian girls were happy to dance with him, and other French Canadians were more than hospitable, inviting him home, helping him to look for an apartment and finding him a job. Years later a survey would show that most Moroccan Jews – and they would become a fifth of the city's Jewish population – would prefer to have French Canadian employers than bosses who were Canadian Jews or Anglos.

Had Jean-Claude Lasry come to Montreal twenty years earlier, he might not have had as warm a welcome from French Canadians. At that time, in the late '30s, anti-Semitism in Quebec was at its height, emanating not only from Adrien Arcand's homegrown Nazis but also from publications like *L'Action Nationale*, an intellectual magazine that spoke frequently of the Jewish plot to take control of the whole world. In *Le Devoir*, the elite daily, readers learned how cunning Jews could be both communists and capitalists at the same time and how they were pushing the world toward war, as part of their plot. Over the years, in hundreds of articles, *Le Devoir* asserted, among other things, that Jews had a distinctive and repugnant body odour and that their crooked noses denoted criminality. One article said that Jews were planning to take over St. Joseph's Oratory and turn it into a synagogue. In *La réponse de la race*, a 1936 book, it was revealed that Jewish scientists, working in a secret laboratory, were preparing to inject the germs of venereal disease into sanitary napkins sold to French Canadian women. The book was dedicated to Abbé Lionel Groulx, the racist priest so beloved of Québécois nationalists. Father Groulx was second to none in the volume and intensity of his anti-Semitic utterances, which found sympathetic ears during the Depression when the unemployed and the impoverished wanted scapegoats to blame for their misery.

In 1939 the St. Jean Baptiste Society sent Parliament a petition, signed with 128,000 names, demanding that Jewish refugees be kept out of Canada. Of the 800,000 Jews who managed to escape from Germany from 1933 to 1939, Canada accepted only 4,000, far fewer than any other country that was willing to admit them. In his cold rejection of pleas to accept desperate refugees, Prime Minister Mackenzie King was largely influenced by fear of offending Quebec.

During the war, the tenor of prejudice became less strident, but in March 1942, a mob of youths who had been attending an anti-conscription rally surged down St. Lawrence Main, breaking store windows and shouting, "A bas les Juifs!" In the Quebec legislature, Laurent Barré, the minister of agriculture, complained that his son, on joining the army, had had to suffer the indignity of being examined by a Jewish doctor. The experience had rendered him physically ill. Yet other French Canadians sought out Jewish doctors, thinking them more proficient than their own.

"The French-Canadians, who were our enemies, were not entirely unloved," Mordecai Richler wrote, in 1960. "Like us they were poor and rough and spoke English badly. . . . But bring round the most insignificant little Anglo-Saxon fire-insurance inspector or cop and even the most powerful merchant on the street [the Main, of course] began to scrape and bow and say, 'Sir.' " If French Canadian anti-Semitism was vociferous, its English equivalent was silent, subtle and, in practice, more destructive. The Frenchman might shout it aloud, but the Englishman would quietly close the door in a Jew's face when he came round to ask for a job. "Frankly, we don't take Hebrew boys in this bank," the manager told Saul Rubin when, in 1953, he applied for a job as junior clerk in a branch of the Bank of Toronto, located in a very Jewish district. When Rubin asked why that was, the manager said, "Most Hebrew boys wouldn't stay here long. They go into business with their in-laws."

When the Canadian Jewish Congress wrote to the British Rubber Company, in 1952, to ask why their employment application form asked the applicant's religion, its president, one A. Stuart McLean, replied that it was to indicate, in the event of a death in an employee's family, "whether flowers or masses would be appropriate." When the Congress wrote to the Government of Quebec's superintendent of insurance to ask why applicants for insurance were asked, on forms to fill in, their "racial extraction," the superintendent replied, succinctly: "This question is asked in order to enable the underwriter to appreciate the nature of the risk involved." Jews, it seems, had a reputation for insurance fraud, although statistics did not bear this out. Robert Hampson and Son, Limited, underwriters, was surprised that the Congress deplored prospective clients being asked their racial extraction and suggested that people should take pride in their origins. Jewish high-school graduates had to have higher marks than gentiles to be admitted to McGill, and when there was grumbling about this the McGill registrar came to Baron Byng to explain that it was simply to motivate Jewish students to excel. Anglo anti-Semitism lacked both the frankness and the inventiveness of the French Canadian brand.

Eventually there were breakthroughs. In 1954, Lazarus Phillips became a director of the Royal Bank, and that same year Jews mingled with the Anglostocracy at the Museum of Fine Arts Ball. There were young Jews in the city now who were destined for undreamed-of accomplishments. Two would some day become ministers in Quebec governments, two would become principals of Montreal universities and one would become publisher of the *Gazette*. Ben Greenberg, the Jewish policeman, would rise to the rank of Detective Inspector, and Alan Gold, born on St. Dominique Street, would become Chief Justice of the Superior Court of Quebec. In the discriminatory 1940s and '50s, anyone predicting achievements like these for Jews in Quebec would have been considered seriously deranged.

9

Novelists, Poets:
New Views of the City

In the 1940s and '50s, the best novels that had ever been written in Canada were being written by Montreal authors. The best short stories were also coming from a Montreal writer and the best poetry from Montreal poets. It was in those pivotal decades that Hugh MacLennan produced his major works, while Mavis Gallant, Brian Moore and Mordecai Richler were at the beginning of their careers, precursors of the burgeoning of Canadian literature that would take place in the decades to come. The early work of these Montreal authors attracted international attention, in sharp contrast to the forgettable historical romances that had constituted most of CanLit up till then.

"We need to see the festering sores in our social body, as well as its areas of healthy tissue," the critic Desmond Pacey wrote, in 1945. "Our novelists of the past, with a few honorable exceptions, have been cautious souls, afraid to incur the wrath of the public, and producing either sugar-coated tracts or novels of escape." But there was no sugar-coating on the realities that were being depicted by MacLennan, Gallant, Moore and Richler. And Gabrielle Roy's books, translated from the French, were giving English readers their first views of how sombre the life of the working class could be in French Montreal.

But the first Montreal novel of this new era came from a lesser author, Gwethalyn Graham, whose *Earth and High Heaven* was the literary sensation of 1944. "The first reader at Lippincott's [its publisher] greeted the manuscript with vocal delight," according to the blurb on the book's jacket. The editor who bought serial rights for *Collier's* magazine went even further: "Collier's fiction department is dancing in the streets!" he wrote. "If this book doesn't sell, I'd better have my heart examined." His instinct was sound: within six months *Earth and High Heaven* sold 600,000 copies in Canada and the United States and, after being translated into nine languages, sold 1,250,000 copies worldwide – a phenomenal achievement for a Canadian writer. The book won the Governor General's award, as had Graham's previous novel, *Swiss Sonata*. But, seemingly overwhelmed by her success, she never wrote another novel.

The theme of *Earth and High Heaven* was the anti-Semitism that was so prevalent in Canada in the 1940s. Gwethalyn Graham, daughter of a prominent Toronto family, had herself been injured by it. When she fell in love with a Jewish lawyer, her father, known as a man of culture and liberal ideas, angrily refused to meet him, and the love affair came to an end. Moving to Montreal in 1934, Graham set her novel in this city, which she found fascinating. Her heroine, Erica Drake, member of an upper-class Westmount family, also falls in love with a Jew, Marc Reiser. Erica's father, like Graham's, does everything he can to sabotage the romance. Erica and Marc desperately want to marry, but readers in the 1940s could accept the proposition that parental disapproval could keep the lovers apart for 288 pages, this despite the fact that Erica is a twenty-eight-year-old career woman, a journalist, and Marc a thirty-three-year-old lawyer. A Jewish husband would simply not "fit in," Erica is told, over and over, by her family. And, as for Jews in general, "once they get a foot in your door, there's no way of getting rid of them." In the end, Erica and Marc do manage to overcome the opposition and give the novel a happy ending.

In its praise for the book, *Quill and Quire*, the publishers' trade paper, said that Graham was "the master of dialogue that is smooth and convincing, without once straining to be too witty." The absence of wit, and the endless and repetitive dissection of the main problem, apparently did not deter readers hungry for anything that would break new ground in the somnolent world of Canadian fiction. Despite its literary shortcomings, *Earth and High Heaven* could be seen as a courageous venture by a woman who was prepared to expose the unsavoury prejudices of her own people, upper-class Anglo-Saxons, and cast some light on a dark corner of Montreal life that had hitherto been unexplored.

Tensions between English and French, always a dominant feature of life in Montreal, had also been unexplored by writers of fiction. But in 1945, the year after Gwethalyn Graham's success, Hugh MacLennan published *Two Solitudes*, his penetrating examination of relations between inhabitants of Quebec's two worlds. Here again was a literary sensation. "[It] may well be considered the best and most important Canadian novel ever published," said the critic of the Toronto *Globe and Mail*. Ecstatic reviews like this led to the book's entire printing being sold out on the day of publication. Again, in *Two Solitudes*, the prospect of an interracial marriage is a source of conflict. Again the young woman is an upper-class Anglo Protestant, but this time her lover is a Catholic, not a Jew, half French and half Irish. But the romance between Heather Methuen and Paul Tallard, important as it was to the book's jacket and publicity, comes toward the end of the story, and is much less interesting than earlier conflicts in the book, between members of the generation preceding that of the young lovers. Here the struggle is between French Canadian traditionalists, like Father Beaubien, who want life in their village of Saint Marc to continue unchanged, as it had for centuries, and English Canadian entrepreneurs who want to build a textile mill and turn the placid village into a modern industrial town.

MacLennan was at his best in his depiction of life in the French Canadian village, and in evoking the sounds, smells and colours of the streets of Montreal. Readers who were familiar with the city were struck by the accuracy of his accounts of everyday life, of his descriptions of a hockey rink, a hotel dining room, the McGill campus, the heat of a summer day – "hotter here than in Singapore." People in London, Paris and New York were accustomed to recognizing their cities in novels, but in Montreal this was something new. Another novelty was MacLennan's picture of the tedium of life among the super-rich Anglo-Scottish inhabitants of the Square

Mile. There was both humour and insight in his account of the rites of this reclusive tribe:

> Each great city had some special way of demonstrating its communal spirit and showing its face to the world. London used the Lord Mayor's Show, New York the procession of a hero up Broadway, the French section of Montreal the parade on the day of Saint-Jean-Baptiste. But in McQueen's opinion, his own Montreal reserved itself for an occasion more personal and significant. Only on the death of one of their own number, did the real controllers of the nation, the businessmen who were as unobtrusive as a hierarchy, gather in force before the public eye.

These are the ruminations of Huntly McQueen, one of MacLennan's characters, who was to be a pallbearer at the momentous funeral of Sir Rupert Irons, the richest of the rich, a character probably modelled on Sir Herbert Holt. Men like McQueen and Irons, MacLennan wrote, were regarded by French Canadians with a mixture of envy and suspicion: "Dollars grew on them like barnacles, and their instinct for money was a trait no French-Canadian seemed able to acquire." But for one French Canadian in the book, economics did not matter. "A pure race," Marius Tallard muses, "a pure language, larger families, no more connection with the English, a greater clerical control over everything – with these conditions Quebec could reach the millennium." Marius, the bitter, impoverished, "nerve-shot" nationalist, is one of the novel's most memorable characters, but, in general, characterization was the weakest part of *Two Solitudes*. There was little real drama in the book, and most of its characters lacked dimension. As one American critic put it, the novel was "more workmanlike than gifted." One of MacLennan's characters, an aspiring novelist, observes that "a novel should concern people, not ideas," but what MacLennan himself had written was essentially a thesis novel, a novel of ideas.

In dealing with a peculiarly Canadian problem, MacLennan had held out little hope for the book's success in the United States, yet a number of American reviewers were extravagant in their praise for it. "If a better novel than Mr. MacLennan's – or one as good – has been published this year by an American writer, I have not read it," J. Donald Adams wrote in the *New York Times*. Mason Wade, the American historian, wrote that the book was "required reading for every Canadian who is concerned with the fundamental problem of his national life." In Montreal, *La Presse* called it "*le grand livre de l'heure*," and most French reviewers, including Abbé Arthur Maheux, were outspoken in their praise for it, many noting MacLennan's respect and sympathy for the French Canadian way of life. But not *Le Devoir*. In its eternal mission to foster ethnic friction and national disunity, *Le Devoir* took exception to the book's thesis that reconciliation was possible between the two solitudes. MacLennan had taken the memorable title of his novel from Rainer Maria Rilke's poem which said: "Love consists in this, / that two solitudes protect, / and touch, and greet each other." But for ultra-nationalists like the editors of *Le Devoir*, nothing could be more upsetting, or more inimical to their ambitions, than the thought that the English and the French might some day be able to get along together.

Ironically, the thesis embodied in Hugh MacLennan's novel was destined to be overlooked and forgotten. The phrase "two solitudes" would enter the Canadian vocabulary, but rather than hold out hope for love and reconciliation, it would come to signify something quite contrary – an unbridgeable chasm, an insoluble problem.

∾

He pictured the end of April, when there would be a great exodus into the street. From all the houses, from damp cellars and mean garrets, from the tenements on Workman Street and the stone apartment houses on Sir Georges-Etienne Cartier Place, from dismal alleys near the canal, and tumbledown shacks on the railroad tracks, from quiet squares, here, there and everywhere, the crowd would emerge. . . .

It was the coming of spring, the long-awaited liberation after a harsh winter in St. Henri, the working-class district, that was the scene of Gabrielle Roy's novel *The Tin Flute*. Here was another literary landmark of the 1940s, a revelation, for English readers, of the despair of the French Canadian poor, struggling to emerge from the grip of the Depression. In its accurate depiction of urban poverty, it was unlike anything that had ever appeared before in Canadian fiction.

Written in French, as *Bonheur d'occasion*, the book was received with immediate acclaim when it came out in 1945. The English translation was published two years later and, in the United States, it became a selection of the Literary Guild, which meant an initial printing of 500,000 copies. As the *New York Times* observed, selection by the Guild would assure its having the widest readership in the United States of any French Canadian work since *Maria Chapdelaine*. The *Times* critic admired Gabrielle Roy's "vivid characterization, unflinching honesty and dry-eyed compassion," but predicted that readers would be disappointed by "its total lack of humor." Another leading American critic, Edmund Wilson, generally approved of the book but took exception to its lengthy descriptions of the Montreal scene. "A young man walking from his lodging to a rendezvous at a cinema," Wilson wrote, "is described at a length of ten pages, which involves exact specifications as to all the streets through which he passes, and careful accounts of the river boats, the railroad, the grain elevators and the telegraph wires – with all of which this young man must have been so familiar that at such a time he would have scarcely have noticed them."

Yet for many readers, Gabrielle Roy's descriptions of St. Henri were the most memorable parts of her book. As a struggling freelance journalist, she lived in lower Westmount, but before writing her book she went down the hill to St. Henri and spent weeks walking its streets, absorbing its sights and sounds, visiting stores and factories, listening to conversations. The result was down-to-earth, evocative description, a gritty realism unprecedented in serious French Canadian literature, most of whose authors preferred vagueness, lofty symbolism and high-flown abstraction. Roy wrote vividly about mundane events like the first of May, Montreal's traditional moving day:

> Too often they had moved. Too often their faded mattresses and rusted bedsprings, their dilapidated chairs, scratched tables, and discolored mirrors – the visible signs of their poverty – had joined the parade . . . a part of the motley caravan that filled the streets on May first, rags flying in the wind, grease spots exhibited for all to see.

The book was about the Lacasse family, and it is they who are moving – once again. The father of the family, Azarius, is unemployed, and his wife, Rose-Anna, is pregnant for the twelfth time; three of her babies died in infancy, and eight children survive. As they move on to cheaper lodgings, she reflects bitterly on the fact that the larger the family grows, the smaller and darker their home. Now they will live in a miserable little house hard by the railroad tracks where "sometimes the freight trains would come to a halt outside the door, and then move backward and forward as individual cars were switched to another track, and while this went on the house was beset by the sound of bells ringing, couplings banging, hissing steam and clouds of soot." When express trains roared by, "the window panes vibrated, the pictures swayed on the walls, even the contents of the drawers were tossed about." In this neighbourhood, "thin, sad-looking women appeared at evil-smelling doorways, blinking at the sunlight that lay among the garbage cans. Others with listless faces sat at the windows, giving suck to their babies. Everywhere there were windowpanes stuffed with rags or sealed with oiled paper."

But this harrowing poverty is about to diminish. War has broken out and this – toward the end of the book – will be the salvation of the Lacasse family, with both father Azarius and Eugène, the eldest son, joining the army, where the pay is good. But it is Florentine, the nineteen-year-old daughter, a waitress, who is at the centre of the book with her desperate search for love. For her, too, war comes as a blessing. Pregnant by a man who has abandoned her, she solves her problem by reluctantly marrying Emmanuel, a soldier who will give her not only unquestioning love but also financial security.

Writing about *The Tin Flute*, Mavis Gallant said that it was probably the most authentic picture of the working class ever to come out of Canada. And, she pointed out, French critics who praised it seemed hurt to discover that poverty was not necessarily an ennobling circumstance. Gallant, then a reporter for the *Standard*, a Montreal weekly, read the book, in French, shortly after it first came out, and was so impressed by it that she persuaded her editor to let her do a picture story about it. Enlisting actors from the Montreal Repertory Theatre, she took them to St. Henri, where they reenacted scenes from the book, to be photographed by a *Standard* photographer. For most English Montrealers, it would be their first glimpse of life in a part of the city that was completely foreign to them, and of a story that was destined to become a classic of Canadian literature.

Mavis Gallant's own literary works, in the years to come, would achieve much wider recognition than those of Gabrielle Roy. But now, in her early twenties, Gallant was making a name for herself as a journalist, as one of Montreal's most innovative and versatile feature writers. No topic was outside her scope, as can be seen by the titles of some of the dozens of articles she wrote for the magazine section of the *Standard*: "What Is This Thing Called Jazz?" "Our Shameful Old Peoples' Homes," "Shyness Isn't Normal," "Dilemma in the Shipyards," "Is Romance Killing Your Marriage?" "The Making of a Hoodlum." Gallant wrote articles exposing many varieties of social injustice, especially the mistreatment of children and of new immigrants to Canada. She caused a sensation (and a libel suit) with her exposé of a sinister "baby farm" in Nova Scotia, a maternity home for unwed mothers whose babies were sold to couples who had been turned down by legal adoption agencies. Another article, in 1946, that aroused widespread comment was entitled "Why Are Canadians So Dull?" Canadian audiences at plays and concerts, she said, were "the coldest in the world." Canadian clothing designers turned out fashions that were "derivative, dull, ugly and depressing." And, she said, "Caution and neutrality, our most distinctive traits, have kept us from producing anything new and original in every field except radio, and the heavy hand of conservatism will probably fall here any minute. If it does, there will probably be a faint protest but not much action, for Canadians are quick to recognize injustice but slow to act."

Gallant worked for the *Standard* for six years, from 1944 to 1950. Besides her prodigious output of magazine articles, news reports and criticism of theatre, films and radio, she was also writing fiction. Her first published short stories appeared in *Preview* and *Northern Review*, Montreal literary magazines, and in 1950 she sold a story to the *New Yorker*, the first in a long stream of stories that she would contribute, in the decades to come, to that most prestigious vehicle for short fiction. Even before her coup with the *New Yorker*, she had decided to leave the security of the *Standard*, go to Europe and, for a two-year period, see whether she could earn her living writing fiction. After the two years, and more sales of stories, her course was clear, and Paris became her home.

Most of Mavis Gallant's stories and novels would be set in Europe, but in some of her best work she would harken back to Montreal. As a child, she had attended both English and French schools, and she was equally at home in both languages. When it came to insight into French Canadian family life, no writer in English (and very few in French) would be her equal. In her book *Across the Bridge*, the stories about the Carette family show how well she understood class differences in the French Montreal of her youth, and the nuances of life on Rue Saint-Hubert:

> Mme. Carette looked out upon long façades of whitish stone, windowpanes with bevelled edges that threw rainbows. In her childhood this was how notaries and pharmacists had lived, before they began to copy the English taste for freestanding houses, blank lawns, ornamental willows, leashed dogs. She recalled a moneyed aunt and uncle, a family of well-dressed, soft-spoken children, heard the echo of a French more accurately expressed than her own. She had tried to imitate the peculiarity of every syllable, sounded like a plucked string, had tried to make

her little girls speak that way. But they had rebelled, refused, said it made them laughed at.

Writing about an English Canadian Quebec family in her novella *Its Image on the Mirror*, Gallant is equally trenchant. Here the narrator is one of the daughters, Jean Duncan, and she says:

Our sameness was stamped on our faces and spoke in our breath: Eastern Canadian. Protestant, Anglo-Scot. The seed of our characters came from another continent. Like the imported daisies and dandelions, it was larger than the parent plant. Flowering in us was the dark bloom of the Old Country – the mistrust of pity, the contempt for weakness, the fear of the open heart. . . . Our father believed that Scottish blood was the best in the country, responsible for our national character traits of prudence, levelheadedness, and self-denial. If anyone doubted it, our father said, the doubter only had to look at the rest of Canada: the French-Canadians (political corruption, pusillanimity, hysteria); the Italians (hair oil, used to bootleg in the 'twenties, used to pass through Allenton); Russians and Ukrainians (regicide, Communism, pyromania, the distressing cult of nakedness on the West Coast); Jews (get in everywhere, the women don't wear corsets); Swedes, Finns (awful people for a bottle, never save a cent); Poles, hunkies, the whole Danubian fringe (they start all the wars). . . .

The only immigrants Mr. Duncan approved of were the Dutch, who kept quietly to themselves on celery farms in Western Ontario and who were so unobtrusive that one hardly knew they existed. But incisive as such generalizations were, the true excellence of Mavis Gallant's writing, besides her graceful style and her exploration of character, lay in her mastery of the telling detail, the minutiae that can reveal a world. Here is the Duncan family at the dinner table:

My mother, presiding over covered vegetable dishes, received the passed-along plate on which my father had placed a dry slice of salmon loaf. The vegetable dish covers were removed to reveal creamed carrots, and mashed potatoes piled like a volcano, with a pat of salty butter melting inside the crater. The ritual of mealtime mattered to us more than the food. None of the women in our family could cook, and we felt that women who worried about what they were to eat or serve were wanting in character.

Images like the salty butter melting in the potato crater could make a page sparkle, a family unforgettable.

~

REFRESHING GUST OF RAGE
FROM YOUNG MONTREALER

The headline appeared in the Toronto *Telegram* in 1954, over a review of a book called *The Acrobats*, a review that began by saying, "Arrogant, opinionated, rebellious, scornful, resentful and refreshingly angry, 23-year-old Mordecai Richler announces in his first novel that his writings will never be infected by what he belligerently terms 'mediocrity draped in the Maple Leaf.'" And the *Telegram's* review concluded by saying, "Richler has written a good book. His next book will be better and the one after that – perhaps great."

In Montreal, three years earlier, after spending a year at Sir George Williams College, Richler had decided that if he was going to be a writer a university had nothing to teach him, and so he pulled up stakes and headed for Paris. Here, living was cheap and in the sidewalk cafés one could compare notes with other expatriate writers like Mavis Gallant, James Baldwin, Herbert Gold, Alexander Trocchi. "I was only a callow kid of nineteen when I arrived in Paris in 1951," he would write, years later, "and so it was, in the truest sense, my university. Saint-Germain des Prés was my campus, Montparnasse my frat house." But Richler never had much money in his pocket, and from Paris he went to Spain, where living was even cheaper and wine could be delivered to one's door daily, like milk, at eighteen cents a gallon. It was during his sojourn on the island of Ibiza that he began writing his novel.

The Acrobats was first published in England, where the *Spectator* said that "Mr. Richler has a fire and a frenzy all his own which, when they truly take hold of his characters, produce a powerful effect." But the reviewer found echoes of Dos Passos and Hemingway in the book, which was set in Spain, and concluded by saying, "I would like Mr. Richler to go back to Canada and write about the things he really remembers, knows, feels about." A few months later, Richler wrote to a friend that "I'm halfway through a book about Montreal . . . trying to trace the development of the ghetto. . . . I'm not interested in passing judgements or shouting – I'm simply observing. The only people who could consider this book anti-Semitic – there are, of course, good and bad people in it – are those Jews who are very frightened."

Montreal Jews, it seemed, could easily be frightened by a novel like *Son of a Smaller Hero*, which came out in 1955, and if not frightened, enraged. The book was about Noah Adler, a young Jew trying to escape from the limitations of his background. In the course of the story we meet a number of unsavoury Jewish characters and observe scenes like the beach at Prévost, a summer resort in the Laurentians frequented by Montreal Jews, where "plump, middle-aged women, their flesh burned pink, spread out blankets and squatted in their bras and bloomers, playing poker, smoking and drinking cokes." Richler, predictably, was denounced as an anti-Semite and a "self-hating Jew." *Congress Bulletin*, the organ of the Canadian Jewish Congress, said the book was a caricature worthy of *Der Stürmer*, one of Hitler's newspapers. In the *Montreal Star*, a Jewish reviewer said the book was without any literary merit and should be "sold under the counter at the corner news-stand." But in London, the critics saw it differently. The *Times Literary Supplement* said "there can be no doubt of his prodigal talent," and the *Daily Telegraph* spoke of "some really superb studies of Jewish family life."

For those Montreal readers who were not offended by it, *Son of a Smaller Hero* was a valuable addition to the new portrait of their city that was being created by the novelists of the 1940s and '50s, as in one passage where Richler deftly describes a new staging area in the Jewish migration westward through the city:

> On Saturday afternoons the well-to-do Jews walked up and down Decarie Boulevard, which was their street. A street of sumptuous supermarkets and banks built of granite, an aquarium in the lobby of the Snowdon Theatre, a synagogue with a soundproof auditorium and a rabbi as modern and quick as the Miss Snowdon restaurant, neon drugstores for all your needs and delicatessens rich in chromium plating. Buick convertibles and Cadillacs parked on both sides: a street without a past. Almost all these Jews, who had prospered, craved for many lights. Wishing away their past and the dark.

Four years after *Son of a Smaller Hero*, Richler published *The Apprenticeship of Duddy Kravitz*, again to critical acclaim and Jewish displeasure. It was the story of a poor young Jew's ruthless struggle to achieve success, to "be somebody," and it was told with great comic flair. From this book, the streets of Richler's youth came to be firmly engraved on the literary map of Montreal – and of Canada:

> To a middle-class stranger, it's true, one street would have seemed as squalid as the next. On each corner a cigar store, a grocery, and a fruit man. Outside staircases everywhere. Winding ones, wooden ones, rusty and risky ones. Here a prized plot of grass splendidly barbered, there a spitefully weedy patch. An endless repetition of precious peeling balconies and waste lots making the occasional gap here and there. But, as the boys knew, each street between St. Dominique and Park Avenue represented subtle differences of income. No two cold-water flats were alike. . . . No two stores were the same, either. Best Fruit gypped on the scales, but Smiley's didn't give credit.

Again, Montreal's Jewish establishment was outraged. Best Fruit's cheating on the scales, and even darker doings by Duddy Kravitz himself, were the sort of thing one could discuss within the tribe, but not out loud, so the *goyim* could hear. Some of the pundits who denounced the book seemed never to have read a novel before, and didn't realize that good novels often contained social criticism. Others could not imagine that there could be Jewish fiction that wasn't warm and sentimental, with fiddlers on the roofs. Even though *Duddy Kravitz* solidified Richler's reputation, at the age of twenty-eight, as one of Canada's most important authors, it would still be a good few years before the Jews of Montreal would feel secure enough to start taking pride in him, as one of their own.

~

As Coffey pushed open its doors he was met by a beer stench and a blast of shouted talk. Two waiters in long white aprons, each balancing a tray containing a dozen full glasses of draught beer, whirled in and out among the scarred wooden tables, answering thirsty signals. . . . The customers put him in mind of old Wild West films: they wore fur caps, peaked caps, toques. They wore logging boots, cattle boots, flying boots. They talked in roars but they numbered also their solitaries. These sat alone at smaller tables, staring at the full and empty bottles in front of them as though studying the moves in some intricate game.

It was a typical tavern – men only, beer only – in Brian Moore's novel *The Luck of Ginger Coffey*, a formidable contribution to the literary cityscape of Montreal. It was Moore's third novel, but the first to be set in the city where he was living, his two previous books having been set in his native Belfast. Moore had been living and working in Europe when, in 1948, he decided to emigrate to Canada. In Montreal, he found work at the *Gazette*, first as a proofreader and then as a reporter. He soon distinguished himself as the paper's most versatile reporter, covering everything from politics and economics to the shipping beat and the dreary speeches at the Kiwanis Club that were so cherished by his editors. "As a reporter, he was enterprising, accurate and – above all – fast," a colleague recalled, years later, after Moore had established himself as one of Canada's leading authors. "He would come into the office at high speed and seemed to start typing while still in the process of sitting down at his desk. He'd have his story finished while the rest of us were still staring blankly at that old Underwood, and adding more sugar to our coffee. Because he was fast he was prolific and the *Gazette* appreciated this. For the puny salary they were paying him, they were getting a lot of words to fill the space between the ads."

But Moore's ambition was to write fiction, not journalism, and in 1952 he left the paper to become a free-lance writer. Three years later he published *The Lonely Passion of Judith Hearne*, and the book was greeted with an intensity of applause seldom accorded a first novel. "Awe-inspiring," the Toronto *Globe and Mail* said in its review of this story about a sad, middle-aged Belfast spinster, the first of many of Moore's books in which, as a male writer, he showed an unparalleled ability to depict female characters. "Only astonishment can greet the fact that *Judith Hearne* is Brian Moore's first novel," the *New York Times* critic said, while in London the *Sunday Times* said the book was a triumph, by a born novelist. Moore's second novel, *The Feast of Lupercal*, equally praised, was also set in Belfast. But now he was ready to attempt a book set in Montreal, where he had been living for almost ten years. "It took me a long time to have the courage to do Ginger Coffey," he later told an interviewer, "and it was the most difficult book to write in many ways, simply because I had to do an awful lot of sociological explanation to tell people what Montreal *was*." The book would see the city anew, from a view-point very different from those of MacLennan, Roy and Richler, from the viewpoint of an immigrant. For James Francis (Ginger) Coffey was, like Brian Moore, a newcomer from Ireland. It was a strange, unexpected city that he found, where the policemen, in winter, wore tall black fur hats that made them look "like Russkis":

It amused him now to think that before he came out here, he had expected Montreal would be a sort of Frenchy place. French my foot: it was a cross between America and Russia. The cars, the supermarkets, the hoardings; they were just as you saw them in the Hollywood films. But the people and the snows and the cold – that woman passing, her head tied up in a babushka, feet in big bloothers of boots, and her dragging the child along behind her on a little sled – wasn't that the real Siberian stuff?

These are the observations of Ginger Coffey, who comes to Canada with his wife and child in search of a better life. A man of limited abilities, he is an optimist with grandiose ambitions, and he goes from failure to failure in a series of comic misadventures, in an environment he can't quite understand. Coffey, Moore once told an interviewer, "represents what I was terrified would happen to me. I've always felt myself to be a misfit." In an article he wrote for *Holiday* magazine, in 1958, Moore told how, as a new immigrant ten years earlier, he had decided to go back to Europe. Then – suddenly – he fell in love with Montreal. He had come to the city with a fellow immigrant called Arthur, after a disappointing first winter working in a bush camp in Northern Ontario. But Montreal, with its slushy springtime streets, was unappealing, and they decided to look for a boat that would take them back to England. Trudging along St. Catherine Street, they came to the Gayety Theatre, where Lili St. Cyr was presenting her renowned interpretation of Leda and the Swan. They went in:

A baby spot felt its way around the curtains and, to the gut-bucket chuckle of *Sugar Blues*, the first stripper strutted onstage with a gait as mannered as a Lippizaner riding horse. "*Baptême!*" yelled the man beside me in hearty, un-Anglo-Saxon approval. "*Tabernacle!*" roared a man down front. There was an explosion of laughter and I pulled at Arthur's sleeve. "Do you realize," I whispered, "they still swear liturgically here?"

When we came out of the theatre, the snowbanks were still filthy, the gruel on the streets more watery than ever. The neon lights of the Boulevard Saint Laurent stretched before us, a midway in midafternoon. In a restaurant named *Le Roi des Frites*,

we sat down to French fries and an excellent meat pie called *tour-
tière*. Above us a sign read: *Chiens Chauds – Hot Dogs*. I was falling
in love. . . .

Hugh MacLennan was another novelist who was fascinated by
Montreal's bilingualism. He, too, wrote an article about the city for
Holiday, entitling it "City of Two Souls," asserting that

I am more or less free to live wherever I choose, but I stay in
Montreal because no other place I know is quite like it. It is wonderful and utterly deplorable. It is magnificent and ridiculous. It
is a rowdy man in a boiled shirt and a mature diplomat who has
solved impossible problems with a cynical urbanity no European
city can equal. . . . Two proud races, different in religion and
history, once bitter enemies – they *are* Montreal. And for nearly
two centuries this bilingual city has continued to grow without
bloodshed, each race bringing out the best in the other.

Morley Callaghan, the Toronto novelist, was also intrigued by the
bilingual face of Montreal in the 1950s, that era of relative linguistic peace. In 1958, he wrote an article entitled "Holiday Weekend
in Montreal" for *Maclean's*, and in it he sought to reassure prospective tourists about the language situation: "A lack of French," he
wrote, "is no handicap to the visitor. French-Canadians all seem to
speak serviceable English. Even the street signs are bilingual; French
on one corner, English on the other. . . . Even in the east-end beer
halls below the Main, where the patrons are all French, the waiters,
if you speak to them in English, will answer in that language."

Callaghan was a frequent visitor to Montreal, and the city was the
scene of his 1951 novel *The Loved and the Lost*, the story of a young
woman who gets into trouble with the Anglo community because
of her friendship with the black jazz musicians of St. Antoine Street.
Now, in his magazine article about "the continent's most flavorful
city," the novelist gave a detailed account of a weekend he and his
wife spent there, paying particular attention to what things cost. At

first they thought of staying at one of the cheaper downtown hotels, like the La Salle or the Berkeley, but finally they decided to splurge on the opulent old Ritz, even if it would cost them a whopping $51.60 for three nights' lodging. In his meticulous list of expenditures, Callaghan noted that a taxi from the hotel to Old Montreal and back cost $2.00 and dinner for two at the Ritz $7.00. One of his biggest expenditures – $11.00 – was for Saturday-night drinks at Dunn's Birdland, a St. Catherine Street nightclub above Dunn's steak house, where the entertainment was unusual – a poet reading from his work while a band played jazz in the background. "In the main he read love poems," Callaghan wrote, describing the performance of Leonard Cohen, "and he read well, just like a pro." After his performance, Cohen sat down to have a drink with the Callaghans and told them that business had been good at Dunn's during his gig and that even the waiters stopped to listen to him.

Now twenty-three years old, Cohen had been writing poetry seriously since he was sixteen. At McGill he took a course in modern poetry given by Louis Dudek, himself an established poet, and when young Leonard showed the professor some of his efforts, Dudek immediately recognized talent. As the two walked down a corridor in the Arts Building, Dudek suddenly commanded Cohen to kneel down in front of him. Tapping the puzzled student on the shoulder with his rolled-up manuscript, Dudek knighted him and dubbed him "poet." The new young star's ascent into the literary firmament was swift, and in 1956 he published his first collection of poems, *Let Us Compare Mythologies*. That year he also recorded some of his work for a Folkways album entitled *Six Montreal Poets*. The other poets who recorded for the album – all long-established practitioners – were A.M. Klein, Frank Scott, Louis Dudek, A.J.M. Smith and Irving Layton. These men, and some of their colleagues, made the 1940s and '50s a golden age for poetry that was without precedent in Montreal – or, for that matter, anywhere in Canada.

Besides Louis Dudek, Leonard Cohen had another mentor – the rambunctious Irving Layton. It would be hard to imagine two Jews with more dissimilar backgrounds. Layton, twenty-two years older than Cohen, had grown up in the poorest part of the ghetto, in a house too poor to have electricity, while Cohen, as a rich boy in Upper Westmount, had been attended by maids, chauffeurs and nannies. But Cohen was hankering for the bohemian life and Layton had much to teach him. Already an established poet, Layton often took Cohen with him on reading tours and to conferences, and Cohen quickly learned that these literary events offered excellent opportunities to meet girls. By now, in the mid-'50s, Layton's renown was growing; he had already published half a dozen slim volumes, and his scatological bellowings and his proclamations of priapic prowess were being heard well beyond the bohemia of Stanley Street. He had been breaking new ground in the prissy world of Canadian poetry ever since he published his first collection, *Here and Now* (1944), where his likening a Montreal church and a corner mission to "hemorrhoids on the city's anus" could not fail to attract attention.

Layton and Dudek were among the contributors to *First Statement*, a little magazine founded by John Sutherland in 1942 because, it was rumoured, one of his poems had been turned down by *Preview*, the already-established little mag of Montreal poets. The two "magazines," actually mimeographed sheets, stayed locked in battle until they merged, in 1946, to create *Northern Review*, and the tensions between them made for the liveliest era ever in the annals of the politics of poetry. The new boys of *First Statement* wanted poetry that was visceral, masculine, based on personal experience, and they snapped at the heels of their elders, *Preview* practitioners like Scott, Smith, P.K. Page, Patrick Anderson, Neufville Shaw and Bruce Ruddick, whom they considered overly intellectual and too admiring of British poets like Eliot, Auden and Dylan Thomas. The *First Statement* group, as Layton phrased it, wanted "celebration not cerebration," and their idols were Americans like Walt Whitman, Carl Sandburg and Hart Crane.

Both groups, however, had one aim in common – to create *modern* poetry in a Canada where literature, in the early 1940s, had not yet emerged from the Victorian Age. As one critic said, "The bulk of poems written in Canada may be briefly classified under four heads. They are, Victorian, Neo-Victorian, Quasi-Victorian and Pseudo-Victorian." This summation aptly described the contents of *Montreal in Verse*, a book published by the Canadian Authors' Association in 1942, a book that, for the modernist poets, was beneath contempt. As they saw it, the book's poems extolling the virtues of the city, by thirty-two authors, were nothing more than the timid effusions of romantic poetesses and gentleman versifiers, Establishment bores who could write things like "Over Saint Catherine Street soft clouds go by / Clouds, ermine and grey, like a gentle sigh." As an antidote to this kind of pap, the modernists welcomed – at least the *First Statement* group welcomed – bold sallies like Irving Layton's celebration of crotch and rectum.

~

Meanwhile, there was other poetry being written about Montreal, besides that of the rhymesters of the Canadian Authors' Association. On occasion the moderns would also take the city as their subject, but no one wrote about it more felicitously than A.M. Klein. Another graduate of the Jewish ghetto, Klein was one of the editors of *Preview* and a contributor to its pages, but he was considerably less bohemian than his fellow poets, usually dressing in a dark blue suit, as befitted a man who was not only a poet but also a lawyer and a speechwriter for Samuel Bronfman, the whiskey king. His poetry, spanning three decades beginning in 1926, came into full flower in the 1940s, when E.K. Brown, widely regarded as Canada's leading literary critic, called Klein the best Canadian poet of his generation. And other critics concurred.

Besides his highly original interpretations of standard Montreal subjects, like the view from Mount Royal and the spring breakup of ice on the river, Klein found inspiration in unexpected places, like a store of the Quebec Liquor Commission and a grain elevator on the waterfront ("Up from the low-roofed dockyard warehouses / it rises blind and babylonian / like something out of legend . . ."). He was an admirer of Mayor Houde, and in a poem entitled "Political Meeting" he explains how the charismatic Houde would captivate his audience: "jokes also on himself, speaks of himself / in the third person, slings slang, and winks with folklore; / and knows now that he has them, kith and kin." Among the English poets, Klein was unique in the depth of his understanding of French Canadians, his sympathy for their problems and his love of their language. In "Doctor Drummond," he excoriates William Henry Drummond, the popular writer of comic verses about habitants, wondering whether Drummond, in making them into "a second class of aborigines, / docile, domesticate, very good employees," understood anything at all about the French. In "The Sisters of the Hôtel Dieu" Klein gives thanks to the nuns of the hospital who looked after him during childhood illnesses ("me little, afraid, ill, not of your race"). In "The Cripples" he speaks of "the lame, the unsymmetrical, the dead-limbed" who come to be cured at St. Joseph's Oratory – and he laments his own inability to share their faith.

Above all, A.M. Klein revelled in language, was intoxicated by words – English, French, Latin, Yiddish, Hebrew. He rejoiced in the bilingual nature of his city, and in one of his most memorable poems, simply entitled "Montreal," he tells how he cherishes the "music" of the city, its voice:

> . . . double-melodied vocabulaire
> Where English vocable and roll Ecossic
> Mollified by the parle of French
> Bilinguefact your air!

10

On Stage, On the Air:
Theatre, Radio and the Birth of Television

As every Canadian artist knows, there is no greater validation for one's work than to have it mentioned in the House of Commons. For Rupert Caplan and Mac Shoub, the accolade came when Henry Hosking, MP, rose to his feet in the House and said, "This is the filthiest program I have ever heard on any radio." Hosking was referring to *Anvil into Sorrow*, a three-hour anthology of the work of the great American playwright Eugene O'Neill. In Montreal, Shoub had adapted the material for radio and Caplan had produced it for the CBC. "In twenty-two places they took the Lord's name in vain," Hosking told Parliament.

The year was 1954, toward the end of a decade in which Canadian radio drama developed into an art of phenomenal originality and vitality. It was an art whose appeal petered out only when radio was pushed aside by a new and irresistible medium – television. In Montreal, Rupert Caplan and Mac Shoub were among the boldest contributors to that golden age of radio. Although Toronto was the main production centre, Montreal, Winnipeg and Vancouver also produced plays for the CBC's networks. These programs, in the words of the playwright Len Peterson, "shattered the awful silence that characterizes Canada." It was an era so puritanical, in some parts of the country, that radio listeners might complain if they heard the word "pregnant" on the air, but dramatists writing for the CBC were encouraged to tackle controversial themes. Lister Sinclair's play *Apple Pie, Home and Mother* even satirized those holiest of subjects. On American radio, which was widely listened to in Canada, guidelines issued to writers by the networks specified that there could be no controversial treatment of religion, race, politics, sex and several other topics. Canadian writers were not shackled by restrictions of this sort, but in Toronto, Andrew Allan, the national drama supervisor, still had to wage what he called guerrilla warfare with the CBC's front office, which was frequently upset when his programs trod dangerous political paths, particularly those that seemed to advocate socialistic solutions to Canadian problems.

In the 1940s, before television, it was radio that supplied the family's evening entertainment. There was comedy from Amos 'n' Andy, Jack Benny, Edgar Bergen and Charlie McCarthy, the Aldrich Family. There was mystery from Nero Wolfe, horror from *The Inner Sanctum* and interplanetary adventure with Flash Gordon. Competing with these hugely popular American shows was a host of Canadian musical, variety and comedy shows, and even home-grown soap operas like *Laura Limited*, produced in Montreal. But above all there was drama – the CBC's *Wednesday Night* series and, on Sunday night, the *Stage* series – *Stage 46*, *Stage 47*, and so on. In contrast to American shows like *Boston Blackie* and *Bulldog Drummond*, the CBC's dramas included adaptations of works by Shakespeare, Sophocles, Dickens, Wilde, Ibsen, Voltaire, Cervantes. For some listeners all this was hopelessly highbrow, but there were times when listenership for the *Stage* series was second only to the CBC's most popular program – Saturday-night hockey.

Original plays, written for radio, were heard more frequently than adaptations of the classics, and many of these new Canadian works were highly innovative. Len Peterson's *Burlap Bags* was an angry drama about people dehumanized by their work, people so demoralized by the slavery of modern life that whenever the light of emancipation started to glow they would pull burlap bags over their heads so as not to see it. It was theatre of the absurd, except that Peterson wrote it in 1946, some years before that phrase was coined and before the production of plays by Ionesco and Beckett. Other CBC plays also explored worlds of fantasy and dreams, like the much-acclaimed *Mr. Arcularis*, which took its protagonist on a voyage through the stars toward his rendezvous with death. But the most famous of the *Stage* productions was *The Investigator*, by a Montreal writer, Reuben Ship. It was a savage satire on the methods of Joseph McCarthy, the American senator whose witch-hunt investigation of suspected communists was mesmerizing America. In Ship's play, the infamous senator, his voice mimicked with deadly accuracy by John Drainie, interrogates Socrates, Milton, Luther, Spinoza and other illustrious figures, finds them all guilty and consigns them to the fires of hell. With plays like this – and by 1952 the CBC was producing more than three hundred plays a year – radio had, in effect, created Canada's first national theatre. Young actors who would later go on to careers on Broadway and in Hollywood were frequently heard in these plays, among them Christopher Plummer, John Colicos, Arthur Hill, Lorne Greene and William Shatner.

Montreal's contribution to this theatre was prodigious, largely through plays produced by Rupert Caplan. The versatile Caplan, in his long career with station CBM, directed soap operas, dramatizations of the Bible and difficult plays like O'Neill's *Long Day's Journey into Night*. His production of *The Trial* was the first time Kafka's work had ever been offered on the radio. A Montreal writer, Mac Shoub, provided Caplan with many of his best plays, works that often attempted ambitious themes involving suffering, death and redemption. In Shoub's *Death and Transfiguration*, a dead soldier comes back to life and is shocked to find that the world is at war again. *Born to Be Hanged* was about a man awaiting execution. *Death – Handle with Care* and *Fall Down, Friend – You're Dead* were other evidences of Shoub's preoccupation with mortality and bereavement, themes that could make Sunday-night radio listening a sombre affair. But in the 1940s, radio drama went much farther than most Canadian novelists did in dealing with real social problems and deviations from accepted codes of behaviour.

It was a time before the kitchen-sink school of playwriting, and many of the CBC's plays were more allegorical than realistic, being set in places that could be called Anywhere and with heroes who could be called Everyman. Almost all of Mac Shoub's plays could be set anywhere in North America, betraying little evidence of his native Montreal. In sharp contrast, plays in French being broadcast by Radio-Canada were earthy, realistic and set in a Quebec with which listeners could easily identify. While English radio listeners may have heard some unsettling notions being expounded in *Burlap Bags*, by characters named Authority and Cautious, French listeners to *Faubourg à m'lasse* followed the doings of realistic characters like François Rivard, in the poverty-stricken streets of Montreal's east end. This series, written by Pierre Dagenais, pioneered in having characters who spoke the colourful, slangy speech of working-class French Canadians. (This was twenty years before Michel Tremblay was acclaimed for introducing *joual* to the stage.)

Other aspects of Montreal life were vividly depicted in *La Pension Velder* and *Métropole*, two series by Robert Choquette who, besides being a prolific writer (six thousand scripts!) for radio, was one of Quebec's most highly regarded poets. In both these *radioromans*, Choquette drew telling portraits of the French Canadian middle class and of the *haute bourgeoisie* of Outremont. Like nothing else on radio, Choquette's dramas took their listeners into Montreal's restaurants and bars, into Notre Dame Church and the Ritz-Carlton, into business offices, exclusive clubs and police stations. As a series, *Métropole* was popular enough to keep it on the air from Monday to Friday for thirteen years, and when a character died, listeners would phone the station to inquire where the funeral was being held. Other series had even longer runs. *Ceux qu'on aime* ran for twenty years, *Rue Principale* for twenty-two and *Jeunesse dorée* for twenty-six. Claude-Henri Grignon's series *Un Homme et son péché* was the most popular of all. Throughout Quebec everything was said to stop at seven o'clock every weeknight for the fifteen minutes that the show was on the air, and country priests would not commence any services until after it was over. Its main character, Séraphin, a villainous miser, was so detested by listeners that the actor who played him, Hector Charland, was often threatened on the street, while Estelle Maufette, who played Donalda, his long-suffering wife, received a steady stream of gifts from a sympathetic public.

These *radioromans* were, in effect, soap operas, and as such were held in contempt by intellectuals. But although they lacked the high seriousness of the English *Stage* series, and its French counterparts like *Nouveautés dramatiques*, they had their defenders, among them Rupert Caplan, who said that the so-called soaps could contain "a lot of deep wisdom, human warmth and good writing." Caplan had excellent credentials as a man of the theatre, working not only for radio but also for the stage, directing plays by authors like Anouilh and Tennessee Williams for the Théâtre du Nouveau Monde. In his busy career he also directed a number of Montreal soap operas. "I sometimes wonder," he told an interviewer, "whether people who call such serialized dramas 'corny' or 'sloppy sentimentalism' are not a little limited in their capacity for emotional expression." People who sneered at the soaps, he said, were taking refuge from their emotional impoverishment behind an artificial screen of derision.

∾

When television first came to Montreal, in 1952, there were fewer than three thousand TV sets in the whole city, bought in anticipation of the launching of this astonishing new medium. It was a magical medium, everybody knew, but its capacities were poorly understood by the public. On the night of September 6 of that year, when the city's first station – CBFT – was to be formally inaugurated, some people put on their Sunday-best clothes before sitting down in their living rooms to watch the opening ceremonies. They knew that Prime Minister Louis St. Laurent would be speaking, and if they, the audience, could see Mr. St. Laurent, surely Mr. St. Laurent would be able to see *them*, and so casual attire would certainly not be in order.

The city had been waiting impatiently for this event, which had taken an inordinately long time in coming. Soon after the war, in the United States, people were happily gawking at the buffoonery of Milton Berle and Red Skelton, in living black-and-white, and by 1951 there were 108 TV stations in the U.S. – but not a single one in Canada. Since 1945, the CBC had been eager to get started with the new medium, but the large amount of money this would require was not forthcoming from Ottawa, which seemed to regard television as a luxury that could be dispensed with. Private broadcasters were ready and anxious to enter the field, but the CBC, which had authority in such matters, refused to grant them the licences they needed. Privately owned television, the CBC suspected, would simply fill the airwaves with programs imported from south of the border, and the CBC wanted Canadian television to be largely Canadian. Finally, at the end of 1949, the federal government, sensitive to public clamour, gave the CBC the green light – and four and half million dollars with which to get started, with two stations, one in Toronto and one in Montreal.

It was not until the spring of 1952 that CBFT was ready to begin test broadcasts from its studios in the old Ford Hotel on Dorchester Street. But there was hardly anything to broadcast *to*, as there were so few TV sets in the city. Montrealers had to be encouraged to buy them, and in March they were invited to the Palais du Commerce, on Berri Street, to see this new household boon in action. Large crowds came and gaped at the display of TV sets being offered by various manufacturers – the squat boxes by Crosby and Phillips and a tall, handsome piece of furniture by Emerson, something that looked like a grandfather clock, with the little screen high up on top and bookshelves underneath. And these things worked! As the eloquent Raymond Laplante delivered his spiel to the camera, you could see him doing it on screens across the room. But TV was going to be expensive, with a set costing more than four hundred dollars at a time when the average worker was making less than fifty dollars a week.

At 3:42 p.m. on June 2, the test pattern went on the air from Dorchester Street. Television, of a sort, had come to Montreal. The test pattern, with its lines and circles surrounding the drawing of an Indian's head, would be useful in adjusting the picture on your new TV set. Later that week, a few test broadcasts were cautiously begun. Henri Bergeron, he of the mellifluous voice, would read the news in both French and English. The Toronto Symphony Orchestra, always popular on radio, could now be seen via film. A magician performed tricks on a program entitled *Watch This One*. And *Le Seigneur de Brinquevilliers*, a historical comedy written and produced by Pierre Pétel, may well have been the first Canadian play written specifically for television. It was performed by actors destined to become some of Quebec's most luminous stars – Guy Hoffman, Jean Duceppe, Charlotte Boisjoly. But the biggest hit of all came on July 25 when CBFT broadcast the Montreal Royals–Springfield Cubs baseball game from Delormier Stadium, with Larry O'Brien voicing the play-by-play in both languages. Crowds of spectators watched this telecast, the first of its kind in Canada, on sets in department-store windows on St. Catherine Street, and many sports fans were thrilled enough to go inside and buy a set – for forty dollars down and three dollars a week.

Television had been born, but it remained to be baptized. That solemn event took place on September 6, when viewers could see a great assemblage of dignitaries in the downtown studio, including Mayor Houde and Archbishop Léger. Davidson Dunton, chairman of the CBC, addressed the audience, as did J.J. McCann, the minister of national revenue, who was doling out the money to finance this dubious enterprise. Finally the prime minister, the avuncular Louis St. Laurent, said a few words in which he recognized the potential power of the new medium. "This force," he said, with his usual incisiveness, "could be harmful to the nation, or it could be of great benefit." As though to prove that the CBC was determined to bring culture to Canadians, the evening's program concluded with a locally produced version of Jean Cocteau's play *Oedipus Rex*. Like all television drama in those days, it was done live, and the play was further enlivened when one of the cameras conked out.

Regular programming, which began the following day, would start at 5:30 in the afternoon with a half-hour show for children. At six o'clock the station would go off the air and the test pattern would fill the screen until eight o'clock, when adult programs would begin and run until sign-off time at ten. This would be the regular pattern for the months to come, except for special days like Sundays, when there would be football in the afternoon, and Tuesdays, when the immensely popular wrestling show would begin at 10:00 p.m. The first hockey game, in October, was in French only, but the variety show *Holiday in Paris* was bilingual. English children as well as French eagerly watched the puppet show *Pepinot et Capucine*. Adult fare in the evening might include an English newsreel, a French newsreel, *The Big Revue* from Toronto, a drama entitled *La Fenêtre ouverte* and *The March of Time* from New York. Audiences during the first months were uncritical, so fascinated by the little screen that they would stare at anything, including, for long periods of time, the test pattern.

The new medium's greatest moment came on June 2, 1953, when viewers were able to watch the most lavish spectacle in living memory, the coronation of Queen Elizabeth in London. As the lengthy ceremonies proceeded, three jets of the Royal Air Force carrying film of the event took off at intervals for Montreal, allowing CBFT to get it on the air that very afternoon. In Verdun, Doug and Betty Whyte stood outside a furniture store, with dozens of other people, to watch the splendour of the coronation on TV sets in the window, and it was exciting enough for them to decide to finally buy a television set of their own. For Frank Conlon, it was Eaton's Santa Claus Parade on TV that made him decide to make the investment. Other people bought sets mainly to get their children back into the house; otherwise they would disappear for hours on end into the houses of neighbours with television. Once people installed their TV sets, they often found friends and neighbours dropping in uninvited and, with a minimum of greeting, sitting down to watch the show.

After the first few months of television, when its novelty had led viewers to forgive all its defects, the bilingual programming began to irritate both communities. The French said there was too much English and the English said there was too much French. Finally, in January of 1954, the problem was solved with the inauguration of CBMT Channel 6, an all-English channel for Montreal. CBFT would now become all-French, while English viewers could have their fill of what they wanted most – American shows. On Friday night they would watch the Dave Garroway show, on Saturday night the Jackie Gleason show and on Sunday night the biggest treat of them all, *The Toast of the Town*, starring Ed Sullivan. In Toronto, CBC programmers bravely tried to counter the American invasion with variety shows featuring homegrown talent like Gisèle MacKenzie, Bob Goulet, Don Messer, Cliff McKay and Shirley Harmer.

There was an endless menu of song-and-dance shows, but Canadian television was more original and successful with public-affairs programs and programs with some intellectual content, like Nathan Cohen's *Fighting Words*. Documentaries from the National Film Board showed aspects of life the public had never seen before, like cardiac surgery in a Montreal hospital. *Tabloid*, an evening magazine show that served up information in an entertaining way, was most successful of all. It was *Tabloid* that produced Canada's first TV star, Percy Saltzman, the weatherman who used chalk and blackboard to make his forecasts. Other Canadian stars of the 1950s were Johnny Wayne and Frank Shuster, the comedy team that brought "Shakespeare" to the masses with their own version of *Julius Caesar* and their immortal baseball sketch ("O what a rogue and bush-league slob am I who has ten days hitless gone").

It soon became apparent that television was radically changing daily life. Children were neglecting their homework and refusing to go to bed. Movie theatres were largely empty, bowling alleys were quieter and lawns were not being mowed. Kitchens and dining rooms were being abandoned for folding "TV tables" in the living room, so one could eat and watch at the same time. Mothers reported that their babies ate better while viewing Howdy Doody. Dinty Moore's Restaurant announced a new home-delivery service for its famous barbecued spareribs (complete with pineapple rings) and called it "Telefeasting."

When Toronto's station CBLT went on the air, in 1952, Torontonians were already familiar with television, many with antennas on their roofs that could pick up American programs from a station across the lake, in Buffalo, New York. But in Montreal, with the nearest American station too far away to be accessible, the new medium was much more of a novelty. Aurèle Seguin was one of the many thousands of Montrealers who had never laid eyes on TV before the first experimental transmissions, and Seguin was director of television for Radio-Canada. Most of the people Seguin hired as producers had also never seen TV, never having gone to New York, like some Toronto producers, to learn how it was done. Instead, it was their policy to develop their own techniques and create something entirely original. And within five years their efforts would make Montreal the world's third largest television centre, in terms of volume of production. Only New York and Hollywood produced more original material, with Toronto in a distant fourth place.

Aurèle Seguin and his producers wanted to create French Canadian television that was original, and not an imitation of what was American. And in many ways they succeeded. What could be more original – and popular – than their rollicking show *La Rigolade* (Fun Time)? In one episode, before a live audience, four nervous wives were given cameras with which to photograph their nervous husbands as each man, in his turn, embraced a very sexy blonde actress. The most passionate embracer would win a twenty-four-inch TV set. The studio audience was convulsed with laughter as they listened to the wives urging their husbands to be more – or less – vigorous as they took the blonde into their arms. Meanwhile Denis Drouin, the master of ceremonies, gave a running commentary replete with double entendres that would have had a Toronto broadcaster banished for life.

By the standards of the time, French television was frequently daring, even capable of taking a gentle jibe at the unassailable fortress of the Catholic Church. In the long-running serial *Le Survenant* the hero was in frequent conflict with the village priest, portrayed almost as a villain. Many other dramatic serials were immensely popular, especially the Monday-night doings of the detestable miser Séraphin Poudrier, too stingy to provide a doctor for his ailing wife. Séraphin, famous from his *radioroman*, was now in a *téléroman*. On Wednesday nights, ratings for the family saga of *Les Plouffes* were so high that one could conclude that there was nobody in French Quebec who wasn't watching. But there was serious drama, too, on *Téléthéâtre*, with original works by local playwrights as well as adaptations of works by authors like Shaw and Graham Greene.

CBFT's outstanding public-affairs show was its weekly *Point de mire* (On Target), which offered reportage and analysis of international events by René Lévesque. The future Quebec premier had made a name for himself in radio by reporting from the front lines in the Korean War, and now he adapted easily to television with commentaries on crises from Suez to the Hungarian revolution. His style was that of a university lecturer, making ample use of maps and a blackboard, but his audience was enthralled by what one critic described as "a harsh voice, a piercing look that seems to read your mind, a sharp gesture that expresses a whole mess of ideas, the dishevelled hair, a cigarette, twenty cigarettes." Critics were unanimous in their praise for *Point de mire*, one of them stating: "There has never been anything like René Lévesque before, and there will probably never again be anyone like him on television anywhere."

~

The death of Jean-Baptiste Laframboise, wrote a columnist for *La Presse* in 1945, heralded the end of the nineteenth century in Quebec. Years later, another critic wrote that the event marked the birth of French Canadian literature. But the fictional Jean-Baptiste Laframboise was not a character in an epochal novel or in a major dramatic work. Instead, he was the hero of one of the sketches in a musical-comedy revue brought to the stage of the Monument National Theatre by Gratien Gélinas. Each year, from 1938 to 1946, French Montreal was convulsed with laughter at the annual revue – the *Fridolinons* – that Gélinas wrote, produced, directed and acted in. His comic sketches were sometimes slapstick, often satirical, but in *La Vie édifiante de* [the Edifying Life of] *Jean-Baptiste Laframboise* he brought tears to the eyes of his audience. Dedicating the work to "all those young French Canadians who don't want to waste their lives," he touched on a deep vein of frustration and pessimism in the Quebec psyche.

The sketch was actually a short play in twenty-five brief tableaus, tracing the life of Jean-Baptiste from the day he is born in a quiet Quebec village. As a boy, he would rather read a book than milk the cows, which makes him a big disappointment to his parents. Satire helps make the play's serious points, as when the boy's devoutly Catholic mother frets about his obvious intelligence. "It's not good," she says, "for children to be too bright: they start to sin earlier." But perhaps the boy's studiousness could make a priest out of him, and so he is sent off to a college in the city. But here he is caught reading Baudelaire's *Les fleurs du mal*, a book forbidden by the Church, and he is sent home, obviously a youth without a vocation. By now, however, Jean-Baptiste, sure of his talent, has decided to become a poet rather than a priest. This notion shocks his parents, who assure him that becoming a poet would turn him into a beggar, the ultimate disgrace. The parish priest points out that if the youth had been meant to be a writer, "God would undoubtedly have enlightened your parents."

Defeated, Jean-Baptiste gives up his dreams and becomes the village notary, resigned to a boring life and a loveless marriage. He earns the respect of the villagers, and eventually, after a long life and many honours, he dies. In heaven, he appears before God to account for his life, and it was here that the play's audiences were deeply moved, with sadness now supplanting satire. "My Lord," Jean-Baptiste says, "you have before you a notary who should have become a poet. And I have the impression that this does not please you. . . . Looking back at the scorecard of my life, I see, among the column of sins of omission, the works that you gave me a mission to write, and that I did not write. . . ." As he continues his speech, the penitent dead man explains that his father never had confidence in him, the village never had confidence in him, no one had confidence in him. And so he gave up. Through the pathos of his hero's final confession, Gratien Gélinas was telling French Canadians to cast aside prejudice and ignorance, and overcome their inferiority complex, so they could aspire to more fulfilling lives.

Before 1945, Gelinas's revues were entirely and raucously humorous – he was often compared to Chaplin – but there was almost always some social comment with which his audience could identify. The fact that French Canadian women were expected to have many babies was a frequent theme. In one of his 1940 sketches, Madame Pitre tells her neighbour that her husband is away, having joined the army. She misses him, she says, in the morning, when he could be unblocking her kitchen sink, but she does not miss him at all at night, happy that he is not in bed with her. "*Huit-z'enfants,*" she says. "*C'est une sacreé bonne affaire que le père couche à la caserne. . . .*" ("Eight children. . . . It's a damn good thing their father has to sleep in the barracks.") Yes, Madame Pitre's neighbour agrees, for some people war is a blessing.

What audiences liked best in the *Fridolinon* revues was Gélinas himself in the starring role of Fridolin, an impoverished, impudent teenage ragamuffin living in an east-end slum. Dressed in short pants and a ragged hockey sweater, wielding his slingshot, Fridolin was the leader of a band of urchins always seeking adventure amid the garbage cans of the back alleys. He was a dreamer and innovator of grandiose projects to raise his gang out of their abject poverty, but his schemes always failed. His optimism, however, never flagged, and he was always ready to rise up from defeat, anxious to try again. If there was pathos in Fridolin's lot it could always be made bearable by laughter, and here again the audience found much it could identify with.

Although he was only fourteen or fifteen years old, Fridolin had opinions about everything that was going on in the world, and he made frequent comments about politics. When Quebec nationalists formed a new party, the Bloc Populaire, Fridolin formed the Flop Populaire. In 1945, when family allowances were first introduced, he noted that many English Canadians had qualms about the new law, and he set out to allay their doubts by addressing them (*les Blokes*) in their own language ("*la langue de Tchékespire*"). "Us French pea soups," he said, "we have big families of twenty-five children minimum. So we receive from the gouvernement big *poches* of money, big, big. And you, with many dogs but small families of two children, one children or not at all, *p'en toute*, you have a small *poche*, flat, flat." But Fridolin had a solution for the unprolific Anglos, a form of equalization payments: if they helped elect his Flop Populaire Party they needn't have babies to get money from Ottawa as there would be a family allowance cheque every month for each and every Anglo dog.

After the 1946 edition of the *Fridolinons*, Gélinas decided to abandon the revue form and try his hand at something more ambitious – a full-length play. During the 1940s, a number of French theatre companies had arisen in Montreal, but almost all the fare they offered consisted of the classics or imported works; the few locally written plays they attempted enjoyed little success. Quebec was waiting for its first major playwright, and Gélinas would attempt to fill that role. In his last revue he had included a sketch about the difficulties encountered by a conscript returning from the war and trying to adjust to civilian life. It was this theme that would form the basis of the new play – *Tit-Coq*.

It opened at the Monument National in May 1948, to the acclaim of critics and public alike. It was, by general agreement, the first great French Canadian play, and it ran for two hundred performances, with Gélinas himself in the title role. As in his revues, comedy and pathos were mixed, and the all-powerful Catholic Church was instrumental in bringing the play's central conflict to a melancholy resolution. The hero of the play, Tit-Coq (Little Rooster), is a lonely figure, born illegitimate and raised in orphanages, never having known his parents. His belligerence and cockiness are a mask for his feelings of inferiority in a society where a bastard is held in universal contempt. As a conscript in the army he befriends Jean-Paul, who takes him home at Christmas, when they are on leave. Here Tit-Coq encounters, for the first time in his life, the warmth of a large, happy family, something he craves more than anything else. And here he meets his buddy's sister, the lovely Marie-Ange. The two fall passionately in love and vow to marry as soon as Tit-Coq comes back from the wars. When he does come back, after long service overseas, he finds that Marie-Ange has been coerced into marriage with a man she does not love. She and Tit-Coq now love each other more than ever, and, with divorce impossible in Quebec, they decide to run off and risk living in sin. But a priest dissuades them, pointing out that Marie-Ange's family would disown her, and Tit-Coq would never have the warm family life he craved so much. Also, their children would be illegitimate, bearing the stigma that had so blighted Tit-Coq's own life. Convinced by these hard truths, the young lovers sadly part, leaving the Little Rooster, as always, alone.

An English version of the play opened in Montreal in November

1950, and two months later it opened at the Royal Alexandra Theatre in Toronto, where the title *Tit-Coq* lost its second T, becoming *Ti-Coq*, so that people who didn't know how the French should be pronounced would be spared embarrassment. The play was a big hit, with audiences fascinated by this unfamiliar view of life in Quebec, and by French actors speaking heavily accented English. In his review in the *Globe and Mail*, Herbert Whittaker had unstinting praise for Gélinas. "As an actor of unusual personality and talent," he wrote, "as a producer of taste and imagination, as the author of as strong and earthy a play as *Ti-Coq*, Gratien Gélinas stands at the top of the Canadian theatre today."

≈

While Gélinas kept French Montreal chuckling for most of the 1940s, English theatregoers had to wait until 1957 for a sustained burst of laughter. It finally came in February of that year, with the opening of the annual musical revue staged by students at McGill. Revues of this sort generally ran for six nights, with friends and relatives of the cast being the most appreciative members of the audience. But *My Fur Lady* was very different from any of its predecessors and, in heaping praise on it, Sydney Johnson, critic of the *Montreal Star*, said it was so good that it could easily tour from coast to coast. And that, to the delighted surprise of its creators, was what came to pass. After their great success in Montreal, they turned their amateur production into a professional one, and during the next eighteen months it was seen by 400,000 people, from Charlottetown to Victoria. With 402 performances in 82 venues, including the Stratford Festival, it was the longest run ever achieved by an original Canadian production.

My Fur Lady, its title a parody on the Lerner and Loewe Broadway hit, was cooked up by four McGill law students. The book was by Donald MacSween, Timothy Porteous and Eric Wang, with music by James Domville. Choreography and direction were by Brian Macdonald, who one day would be director of Les Grands Ballets Canadiens. For a student musical revue, its theme was ambitious: the

efforts being made by nationalists of the time to define what constituted the Canadian identity and Canadian culture. The exploration
of these weighty topics, through song, dance and satire, would
be precipitated by the heroine of the piece, Princess Aurora of
Mukluko, an independent principality somewhere up in the Arctic.

As there are no eligible men in Mukluko, Princess Aurora is sent
south, to Canada, to find a husband, and during her search the
country is revealed to her. "Teach me how to think Canadian,"
Aurora sings, plaintively, as she arrives in Ottawa. She is immediately
taken in hand by the Culturality Squad – "two effeminate men and
a masculine woman" – whose job it is to explain Canada, which
they do in song, with British accents. The Squad takes Aurora to
Parliament, where the members are debating the need for a distinctive Canadian flag. Emotions run high as Ontario refuses to consider
any flag without the Union Jack on it, while Newfoundland "Will
fly no flag that does not boast / That noble fish the cod." At the
Department of National Defence, Aurora learns that the Canadian
navy is always on high alert, high not only on rum but also on Aqua
Velva, methyl alcohol and duplicating-machine fluid.

Exploring Quebec culture, Aurora meets the cinema censor, who
wields his scissors as he sings, "Let's not admire womankind, snip!
snip! / Not Russell's front or Monroe's behind, snip! snip!" At McGill
she listens to a reading by Dylan Laydeck, the farmer poet, who is
inspired by the milking of cows ("Oh thou grubby teat / sucked by
man and bit by flea"). At the Governor General's Ball, debutantes
sing the praises of their fathers' abilities to make money on St. James
Street ("For what a father does not earn / His daughter cannot
spend"). Charmed by all this Canadiana, Princess Aurora falls in
love with the country – and with the governor general, whom she
marries. Her Arctic principality, Mukluko, now becomes part of
Canada, and the princess and the entire cast join in the show's
rousing finale, singing "To be specific, it's the most terrific / Country
in the world today."

∼

"Un acteur de grande classe . . . Une interprétation magistrale," Jean Béraud wrote in *La Presse*, describing Christopher Plummer's performance as Oedipus in *The Infernal Machine*, by Jean Cocteau. This young actor, Béraud prophesied, could have a great future in the theatre. The play he was reviewing was part of the Montreal Repertory Theatre's 1950–51 season. Plummer, then twenty-one years old, was already a leading light in the Montreal theatre. He had made his debut with the MRT at the age of seventeen, in Mauriac's *Asmodée*, and the following year had appeared in *A Midsummer Night's Dream*, staged by the Open Air Theatre on Mount Royal. Before long, Plummer would be on his way to the new Stratford Shakespearean Festival, as would other Montreal actors like Hume Cronyn, William Shatner, Leo Ciceri, Richard Easton, Robert Goodier, John Colicos, Eric Donkin, Amelia Hall, Pat Galloway and Joy Lafleur. Over the years, more than twenty actors who served some of their apprenticeship with the Montreal Repertory Theatre, in the 1940s and '50s, would make their way onto the Festival stage at Stratford.

In the decade that followed the war, theatre in Montreal flourished as never before. There was still no professional theatre, but the productions of amateur companies attracted appreciative audiences. In 1946, the Shakespeare Society came into being with a sold-out production of *Much Ado About Nothing* at McGill's Moyse Hall. That same year the Trinity Players, established for almost half a century, presented *The Hasty Heart*, while the YMHA Little Theatre offered Thornton Wilder's *The Skin of Our Teeth*. But, as always, the most noteworthy productions were those of the largest of the amateur companies, the Montreal Repertory Theatre, whose 1946 program included William Saroyan's *The Beautiful People* and Goldsmith's *She Stoops to Conquer*.

The MRT had been founded in 1929 by Martha Allan, daughter of Sir Montagu Allan, head of one of the city's wealthiest families. Martha, who had studied theatre in the United States and France, held rehearsals for the MRT's first productions in the stables of the family mansion on the flank of Mount Royal. The company began as something of a hobby for members of the Square Mile elite, but by the 1940s it was attracting talent from other parts of the city and its productions were achieving near-professional polish. Its choice of plays was always ambitious, and over the years it offered its audiences works by Giraudoux, O'Neill, Shaw, O'Casey, Ibsen, Molière, Wilde, Lillian Hellman, Tennessee Williams, Arthur Miller. There was also lighter fare from authors like Kaufman and Hart, Mary Chase, Lindsay and Crouse. In 1949, a banner year for the MRT, it offered four major and two studio productions. In addition, it ran a theatre club in its Guy Street Playhouse, housed a theatre library, published a magazine of the theatre, and gave courses in playwriting, stagecraft, fencing, make-up, costuming, voice and diction.

Besides this local non-professional theatre, Montrealers enjoyed a steady stream of performances by touring companies from London and New York, playing at His Majesty's Theatre. In 1940 they saw Katharine Cornell in *No Time for Comedy*. In 1944 they saw Paul Robeson and Jose Ferrer in the greatest *Othello* that anyone could remember, and in 1947 there was *The Importance of Being Earnest*, with John Gielgud and Margaret Rutherford. Reviewing the Oscar Wilde play, the *Gazette*'s critic, Herbert Whittaker, said that "perfection is a word that everyone should use sparingly, and critics most sparingly of all," but Whittaker allowed himself to use the word in describing Gielgud's performance and direction. (Gielgud reciprocated by telling people that Whittaker was the best critic in all North America.)

In the 1940s, Whittaker was Montreal's quintessential man of the theatre. Besides reviewing and writing about the stage, he was also busy designing sets and directing plays. For the MRT he designed *The Glass Menagerie, Ah Wilderness!* and *I Remember Mama*; for the Shakespeare Society he designed major productions at McGill's Moyse Hall; and for the Negro Theatre Guild he designed *Green Pastures*. He directed and designed Priestley's *The Linden Tree* for the Trinity Players and, the same year, for the Young Men's Hebrew Association, *The Dybbuk*. The YMHA players had wanted to tackle Noel Coward, to help perfect their diction and smooth over any vestiges of Jewish accents, but Whittaker persuaded them to do this Jewish classic instead, and it became one of the triumphs of the

Montreal season. Thus Whittaker was at home in many enclaves of a multi-ethnic city, including the one most inaccessible to an Anglo – French Montreal. In 1946, L'Equipe, a rising young company, invited him to direct Shaw's *Le Héros et le Soldat* (*Arms and the Man*), with a cast that included some of the city's best French actors, like Denise Pelletier, Yvette Brind'amour, Guy Maufette, Nini Durand and L'Equipe's brilliant young director, Pierre Dagenais. "I directed *en Anglais*," Whittaker recalled, many years later, "and they acted *en Français* – and very well."

Besides reviewing, designing and directing, Whittaker interviewed visiting stars of stage and screen for the *Gazette*, among them Greer Garson, Mary Pickford, Tallulah Bankhead, Conrad Veidt, Ramon Novarro, Kay Francis and Katharine Hepburn who, he found, didn't live up to her sophisticated screen image but was "young, opinionated and sandy with freckles." Some of these stars became friends, like the great German actress Elisabeth Bergner, who volunteered her New York phone number. Irina Baronova, one of the three celebrated Baby Ballerinas on the Ballet Russe de Monte Carlo, was pleased to accept his invitation to an evening at the Samovar, the Russian nightclub. They had a wonderful time, although Baronova caused a fuss by smashing wine glasses in her exuberance. (The Russian response to a birthday toast demanded that the recipient down her drink and smash her glass.) And, Whittaker discovered, ballerinas were not easy to partner on the dance floor.

Years later, in a memoir, Whittaker spoke of those heady days. "I recall," he wrote, "walking past the formidable fortress of the Canadian Pacific's Windsor Station one night, in a state of exaltation, on my way home from my work at *The Gazette*, past the Anglican buttresses of St. George's Church, past the Archbishop's Palace behind St. James's Basilica, past the Sun Life's wedding-cake building on Dominion Square, past the proud old seedy Windsor Hotel. 'This town,' I boasted, 'belongs to me.'"

But in 1949, when an offer came from Toronto to become the drama critic of the *Globe and Mail*, Whittaker knew that the time had come to move on from Montreal. French theatre was on the rise, with more and more important productions, and he felt that the feeble French he had learned in high school, at Strathcona Academy, had not prepared him to do justice to these productions as a reviewer. Also, the important touring companies from London and New York were now making fewer visits to Montreal and more to Toronto. Herbert Whittaker's departure was, in a way, prophetic of the decline of English theatre in Montreal. The 1950s were less lively than the '40s, and by the end of that decade the lights were starting to dim. More people were staying home, watching television; more of Montreal's best actors were moving to Toronto, where there was more work available on the stage and in TV; and less money was forthcoming to finance even modest productions. After its 1959-60 season, the Montreal Repertory Theatre went out of existence. The following year, the Trinity Players also gave up the ghost, after a distinguished history that spanned fifty-two years. In 1964 Her Majesty's Theatre closed its doors. This historic playhouse, on Guy Street, had opened in 1898, in the reign of Queen Victoria. It became *His* Majesty's during the reigns of four kings and now, with a new queen on the throne, it was again *Her* Majesty's. But finally the old lady had to go, to be torn down to make way for something that would be more profitable in downtown Montreal – a parking lot.

~

While Montreal's English theatre faltered in the 1950s, French theatre went from strength to strength. New companies proliferated, talented actors became more polished and audiences grew in size. The building of this audience was well under way in the 1940s, thanks largely to the initiative of Father Emile Legault, a Catholic priest whose parish was, in a sense, the theatre. In 1937, at a time when the Church in Quebec was highly suspicious of any kind of playgoing and the immorality it might encourage, Father Legault founded Les Compagnons de Saint-Laurent, a troupe of young actors that would present "Christian theatre." At first they performed the religious dramas of authors like Claudel and Ghéon, but eventually they ventured gingerly into secular works by writers like Molière, Musset and Shakespeare. Actors received rigorous training under

Father Legault, who had studied theatre in Paris, and alumni of his Compagnons de Saint-Laurent went on to create their own companies, and decades of outstanding theatre for Montreal.

One of Father Legault's most talented players was Pierre Dagenais who, in 1942, formed a company called L'Equipe. Dagenais, an actor-director-playwright, was only nineteen, but he was determined to create a professional theatre where there had only been amateurism before. L'Equipe was a success from the start, frequently filling the Monument National with its productions of the classics and contemporary plays, some of these avant-garde enough to make the Church uneasy. In 1946, Dagenais produced Jean-Paul Sartre's *Huis clos*, and after its run was over, when Sartre himself arrived in Montreal on a lecture tour, L'Equipe staged the play one more time, in the ballroom of the Windsor Hotel, especially for the author. Sartre applauded the performance and observed, cryptically, that if their religion deprived French Canadians of "the tragic sense," this deficiency was certainly not present in the talented actors who had performed for him.

After L'Equipe, the most notable of the new companies was the Théâtre du Rideau Vert, founded in 1947 by Yvette Brind'Amour and Mercedes Palomino, the first two women to assume positions of authority in a new Québécois theatre that was completely dominated, offstage and on, by men. Brind'Amour was not only a brilliant actress but also a brilliant administrator, adept at handling bankers and bureaucrats. Her company would achieve renown with its production of Parisian boulevard comedies as well as works by Garcia Lorca, Cocteau and Montherlant.

But the greatest acclaim was reserved for the next new company, the Théâtre du Nouveau Monde, founded in 1951 by other graduates of Father Legault's troupe, Jean Gascon, Jean-Louis Roux, Eloi de Grandmont and Georges Groulx. Their first production, in October of that year, was Molière's *L'Avare*, starring, among others, Guy Hoffman, perhaps Montreal's greatest comic actor, and Denise Pelletier, certainly its greatest actress. Four years later the company was bold enough to perform Molière in Paris, to loud applause. "In

Paris, our actors from [French] Canada are treated like adults," according to S. Morgan-Powell, the venerable critic of the *Montreal Star*. They showed much more maturity than their English Canadian counterparts, he said. Barbara Moon, writing about the Théâtre du Nouveau Monde actors for *Maclean's*, marvelled at how worldly and debonair they were. "An English-speaking actor in Canada," she wrote, "is apt to wear clothes that range from sober to scruffy. But Jean Gascon . . . artistic director of the TNM, is renowned throughout Quebec for his rich, Italian-style suits, cut narrow in the lapel and leg. Thus clad, with his battered nutcracker face, he *looks* like a star." Quebec didn't share English Canada's reluctance to treat its artists like stars, and in French Montreal the public, even people who didn't go to the theatre, doted on gossip in the press about the foibles, flamboyance and amours of Gascon, Roux and company.

In 1958 the TNM made a triumphal tour that took it not only across Canada but also to New York, France and Belgium. In New York, its performance of *Le Malade imaginaire*, in French, was called "delightful" by one newspaper and "an import of great import" by another. But the most trenchant appraisal of the Montreal actors (an appraisal that was typically Canadian) came from a Toronto matron who saw them perform at Stratford and was quoted by Barbara Moon. Asked what she thought of them, the woman pondered for a while and finally said, "They're so . . . so French. . . ."

The one element that was lacking in the lively French theatre of that era was plays by Quebec playwrights. Except for *Tit-Coq*, the few that were attempted from time to time made little impression, until the emergence of Marcel Dubé. His harsh, melodramatic play *Zone*, performed by a new young company called La Jeune Scène, was good enough to win first prize at the Dominion Drama Festival, in Victoria, in 1953. Set in a bleak urban world of poverty and degradation, the play dealt with a gang of young cigarette smugglers. Dubé's later plays of the 1950s, like *Un simple Soldat* and *Le Temps des lilas*, also told harsh stories of deprivation and alienation, and they won for him recognition as Quebec's major playwright. In the restrictive atmosphere of the Quebec of Maurice Duplessis, Marcel

Dubé presented a picture of an unhappy society, peopled by insecure men and women. Audiences found truth and relevance in his plays, and they filled the theatre to see them.

There were no government subsidies for the theatre in the 1940s and early '50s, and there were times when it appeared as though the authorities were trying to hinder the theatre rather than help it. One night, just before the beginning of a performance by L'Equipe, city inspectors arrived at the theatre to demand that amusement tax on receipts from ticket sales be handed over immediately. The company's young director, Pierre Dagenais, refused, saying he could not afford to pay the exorbitant tax. In that case, the taxmen said, the curtain could not go up. "All right," Dagenais said, "but you'll have to come out onto the stage with me and tell the people why they're not going to see the show." By now, while the argument was going on in the office, the taxmen could hear the impatient audience clapping and whistling as it waited for the curtain to go up. Meekly, the taxmen crept away, and the show began. But later the police came for Dagenais and he made the first of his three short sojourns in Bordeaux Jail, all for his refusal to pay the hated amusement tax.

By the late '50s, governments were becoming more enlightened and subsidies for the theatre were finally forthcoming from the city, the province and from Ottawa, through the new Canada Council. It was with the help of the provincial government, in 1958, that Gratien Gélinas was able to create a new theatre, the Comédie-Canadienne. It was here that Gélinas produced his second full-length drama, *Bousille et les justes*, an intense, bitter play whose pathetic underdog hero, Bousille, was the victim of society's hypocrisy.

In looking for a home for his new theatre, Gélinas had chosen the former Gayety, on St. Catherine Street just west of St. Lawrence Main. With the decline of vaudeville, the frisky old Gayety had closed its doors a few years earlier. Then, briefly and unsuccessfully, it had become first the Mayfair and then the Radio-Cité. Now, much refurbished, it was the Comédie-Canadienne, Montreal's confident answer, perhaps, to the venerable Comédie Française in Paris. But as they watched gripping new dramas on this stage, some members of the audience might have been distracted by memories of the boisterous burlesque that had once cavorted on these same boards. Where Gélinas's poor Bousille was now being drawn toward his doom, Lili St. Cyr – the divine Lili! – had once stripped with such sinuous insouciance. The frivolity of the '40s had yielded to the seriousness of the '50s. As some might say, with regret, Montreal was growing up.

I I

Ideologies:
Far Left, Far Right

Paulette Buchanan never got used to it. She was always afraid. The
knock on the door might come at any time, probably after midnight,
and the RCMP would be there. They would push their way past her,
stride down the hall and find what they were looking for – communists. Paulette's houseguests were always members of the Party, and
at any hour of day or night there might be three or four of them
sitting in her living room, endlessly palavering, studying the latest
edicts from Moscow, composing pamphlets to acquaint Canadians
with the wisdom of Joseph Stalin.

It was the fall of 1940. The Communist Party of Canada had
been illegal since June, and its leaders – men like Joe Salsberg, Tim
Buck, Leslie Morris – were frequently on the run from Toronto.
Paulette revered these men and their ideals, and when they came
to hide out in Montreal she was always ready to put them up in
her spare room, where they might stay for days, weeks, and even
months. But their presence frightened her. If and when that knock
on the door came, she herself would be going straight to jail, along
with Joe, Tim and Leslie. In Quebec, the provincial police had
always been a menace for the Reds, but now the Mounties had
joined in the hunt, and they were far more efficient than the illiterate thugs on the provincial force. Across Canada, more than a
hundred members of the party were arrested in 1940 and, under the
Defence of Canada Regulations, jailed without trial or locked away
in internment camps.

In Montreal, the ranks of the communists had swelled dramatically during the 1930s, during the miseries of the Depression. Marxism, they fervently believed, was the only alternative to an economic system that had brought on horrendous unemployment and, for those who did have jobs, brutal exploitation by the capitalist bosses. The extent of this exploitation in one of the city's largest industries, the textile industry, came to light in 1937, in the report of the Royal Commission on Price Spreads. One witness, Ovide Lemay, a weaver for the Montreal Cottons Company, told the commissioners that after thirty years with the company he was now earning only fifty-two dollars a month. With this sum, of which thirteen went for rent, Lemay had to support his wife, his mother-in-law and fourteen children. During those same thirty years, the commission observed, shareholders in the company made consistently huge annual returns on their investments. Labour and wage conditions in this industry "should not be tolerated in any state that calls itself civilized," the Royal Commission said in its report. "Substandard wages mean sub-standard health," Stanley Ryerson, a communist activist, wrote in his book *French Canada*, published in 1943. "The poverty of the great mass of French-Canadians is mirrored in the widespread range of sickness in their midst." Malnutrition fostered tuberculosis, he said, and the death rate from this disease in Quebec was more than three times greater than in Ontario. The infant mortality rate in Trois-Rivières was higher than that of Madras or Bombay.

With unemployment approaching 30 percent in Montreal, there were frequent mass meetings at which communist orators told angry crowds that there was no unemployment in the Soviet Union. Organizations like the Friends of the Soviet Union heard this message from Louis Kon, a handsome, well-dressed speaker who looked more like a capitalist than a communist. And the dapper, diminutive Fred Rose, in his three-piece suit, looked more like a businessman than a worker when he addressed the Workers' Unity League, but his passionate oratory left no doubt about his hatred of injustice and his sympathy for the downtrodden. Other communist-front organizations, like the League Against War and Fascism, attracted large crowds that turned out to support the Loyalist cause in the Spanish Civil War. The defeat of the Loyalists at the hands of the Fascists at the beginning of 1939 was a crushing blow to those who saw the relentless march of fascism and Nazism as the supreme peril confronting the world. For communists, these ideologies where nothing more than extensions of capitalism, and so Montreal members of the Party rejoiced when, in September of 1939, Britain and France declared war on Nazi Germany.

On September 18, Tim Buck, leader of the Communist Party of Canada, urged its members to support an all-out war to defeat Hitler and the Nazis. But the previous month Germany and the Soviet Union, mortal enemies, had shocked the world by concluding a non-aggression pact, and two days after Tim Buck's call to arms Joseph Stalin denounced the war as imperialist and unjust. "In no country can the Communist Parties or the working class support the war," he said. In Canada, Tim Buck and his party immediately and obediently reversed themselves, and their slogan became "Withdraw Canada from the War!" In their oratory, communist speakers now said that the war was not against fascism but simply to preserve imperialist markets, to make profits for the rich. A manifesto issued by the party declared that the sons of the working class would rot and die in the trenches of Europe while Canadian capitalists would revel in luxury at home – "a degenerate, besotten, parasitical class . . . carrying on a traffic in death." Incensed by this rhetoric, Ottawa, on June 6, 1940, invoked the War Measures Act and declared the Communist Party illegal. And the RCMP set about arresting members.

As leaders of the Party went underground, Paulette Buchanan's small apartment on Bishop Street became a "safe house" where fugitives could be sheltered. Paulette, a schoolteacher, and her husband Jim, an advertising man, were true believers, and when the Party asked them to find a more appropriate residence they didn't hesitate to move. They found a larger place on Girouard below Sherbrooke with an excellent backdoor setup, where Tim Buck could effect a hasty exit if the cops came in at the front. But here the walls were too thin; Paulette could sometimes hear the neighbours in the next apartment, so it was likely that the neighbours would be able to hear Tim and Fred and Leslie in their loud debates about dialectical materialism. And so the Buchanans moved again, this time to an apartment on Sherbrooke near Royal, and this place was perfect, with good thick walls and three bedrooms. The RCMP never found this sanctuary, and there was brisk traffic in and out, and the meetings, loud and long, were fascinating for a low-echelon Party member like Paulette. The only doubts she ever had about her role were when Charlie Sims, a Party luminary, and his wife Irene moved in. Charlie was colourful in his speech as only a former Welsh coal miner could be, but unfortunately he never stopped talking; when Paulette wanted to go out to do some shopping Charlie would catch her by the sleeve and detain her at the door for at least an hour to hear more of his eloquent socialist anecdotes. Charlie and Irene were in hiding at Sherbrooke and Royal for several months.

On June 22, 1941, German armies suddenly attacked the Soviet Union, and for communists this brought on another abrupt reversal of policy: the unjust war was suddenly a just war, a "people's war"; the enemy was no longer capitalist imperialism but good old fascism. Tim Buck urged young communists to join the armed forces, and workers to redouble their efforts in factories making arms and ammunition. The Party became legal again, and on the platform at patriotic rallies communist leaders sat in smiling amity beside formerly "degenerate, besotten and parasitical" capitalist tycoons. During the "unjust war" period, Montreal communists had allied themselves with French Canadian nationalists who were militating against the possibility of conscription; now these same nationalists were suddenly fascists. Aid to Russia became a watchword in Montreal, and Eleanor Roosevelt came to the city to call for contributions toward "Russian relief," as did Cardinal Villeneuve, leader of the Church's unrelenting battle against atheistic communism. On St. Catherine Street, bastions of capitalism like Eaton's big store occasionally flew Joe Stalin's once-despised hammer-and-sickle flag.

In the fall of 1942, Montrealers listened apprehensively to their radios for news from the Russian front, where the greatest battle of the war was shaping up. Hitler had thrown a German army of more than 500,000 men against the city of Stalingrad and seemed poised to take it, after months of house-to-house fighting. But then General Zhukov mounted his counteroffensive and, after staggering losses of Russian lives, he succeeded in routing the Germans. It was Hitler's first major defeat and a turning point in the war; for the first time now, an Allied victory seemed possible. In Canada, Russia's prestige was never higher, and objections to the doctrines and ambitions of communism were muted. It was in this atmosphere that Fred Rose won the by-election in the federal riding of Montreal-Cartier in August 1943, becoming the first communist ever to sit in Parliament. He had run under the banner of the Labour-Progressive Party (LPP), the new, sanitized name that the Communist Party of Canada had given itself. In Ottawa, Rose, this former fugitive and firebrand, was agreeably docile, generally supporting the policies of Mackenzie King. "The Liberal government's speech from the Throne," he explained in a communist magazine, "met or came close to the demands and immediate aims of labour." In his avowed aim to foster national unity, Rose even denounced a motion by the socialist CCF Party to curtail the powers of the chartered banks, claiming that the time was not ripe for gestures of this sort. The class struggle had, in effect, been suspended for the duration of the war. But this new-found friend of the bankers was not above suspicion, and on March 30, 1946, Fred Rose, MP, was arrested – as a Russian spy.

In Ottawa, Igor Gouzenko, a cipher clerk in the Soviet Embassy, had defected, taking with him, from the embassy safe, documents that detailed Soviet espionage activities in Canada. Asking for asylum in Canada, Gouzenko gave the documents to the RCMP, which learned from them that Canadian scientists, military officers and others had for years been passing secret information to the Soviets. In the months that followed, twenty men and women were arrested, the most prominent being Rose, who was charged with persuading communists who had access to information of military importance to reveal it to the Soviet Embassy. In Montreal, the trial of Fred Rose, charged under the Official Secrets Act, lasted for three weeks and attracted international attention, with some fifty reporters in the courtroom. In his summation to the jury, the crown prosecutor denounced Rose as a recruiter of spies who was responsible for "many good men and women falling by the wayside," while Rose's defence lawyer denounced Igor Gouzenko as a man trying to serve up Rose's head on a platter in exchange for Canadian citizenship. The jury took only half an hour to reach its verdict of guilty, and the member of Parliament for Montreal-Cartier was sentenced to six years in prison.

Most of the good men "falling by the wayside" were members of the Communist Party's Section 13, a closed organization of middle-class intellectuals and professionals who did not take part in public demonstrations, being deemed more useful to the Party if their membership could be kept secret. It was from Section 13 that Fred Rose recruited Raymond Boyer, member of a prominent Montreal family and heir to a large fortune. Boyer was a brilliant chemist whose research at McGill had helped develop a new and better method for making the explosive RDX. For passing information about this to the Soviets, Boyer was sent to prison for two years. He was one of the ten communists found guilty; nine were imprisoned and one was fined. Charges against another accused were dropped, and nine others who had been charged were acquitted.

During the war, all those who had passed on secrets to the Soviet spymasters had shared a passionate desire to help the Soviet Union in its struggle against the German onslaught, and were dismayed by what seemed to be official Canadian reluctance to extend all-out aid to this ally. Despite protestations of friendship, and generous shipments of arms to Russia, much scientific information was being withheld, and some military men, among themselves, were saying that they must prepare for war with Russia, after Germany was defeated. But Fred Rose and his confreres could see nothing wrong with helping a beleaguered ally.

The prosecutions that followed the Gouzenko revelations involved an unprecedented suspension of civil liberties, with the accused being incarcerated, questioned and denied access to counsel for long periods of time before finally being charged. Men were even denied the right to communicate with their wives, and a royal commission made public its findings, condemning some of the accused in advance, before their trials. Yet the secrets passed on by Fred Rose and his agents were, experts were later to agree, of a trivial nature, many of them already public knowledge. Among the persons named in the Gouzenko documents, only Allan Nunn May, a physicist, gave the Soviets secrets of any consequence. He was privy to information about the making of the atom bomb, and it is believed that what he was able to tell the Soviets helped them perfect their own bomb a year or two earlier than they would have been able to do otherwise. But Nunn May was an Englishman who had done some of his work in Canada, and he was arrested and tried in Britain. But despite the fact that none of the Canadians accused had passed on any nuclear secrets, they came to be known in some newspapers as "atom spies," a potent epithet in the new, nervous post-war atmosphere. Three weeks before Fred Rose's arrest, Winston Churchill had made his famous speech in which he declared that an Iron Curtain had descended across the width of Europe. Churchill's use of this new phrase was, in a sense, the inauguration of another new concept, the Cold War, and Fred Rose's trial in the courthouse on Notre Dame Street in Montreal was one of the opening shots in that long-running war.

When Fred Rose and the other accused were arrested, they were immediately abandoned by the Labour-Progressive Party, which let it be known it would do nothing to aid their defence. To do otherwise, the Party reasoned, would bring further discredit on it. And so there were no demonstrations, no legal-aid committees, no defence fund. Rose and his fellow activists were on their own. When Rose emerged from prison, he was a broken man. Unable to adjust to life in Montreal, where he was under constant police surveillance, he returned to his native Poland in 1953, still protesting his love for Canada, still asserting that he had done nothing wrong. He would die in Warsaw thirty years later, and the Canadian government, still vengeful, would deny his widow's request that she be allowed to bring his ashes back, to be buried in Montreal.

~

After the spy trials, the federal and Quebec governments unleashed a relentless anti-communist crusade that would continue for ten years. In Montreal there were no more than about two thousand card-carrying Party members, one quarter of them French, but to Premier Duplessis they were the Devil incarnate, a deadly menace to Christian society. In harassing them, and blaming them for many of Quebec's ills, Duplessis was not only protecting western civilization but also helping factory owners maximize their profits, as communists were among the most militant union organizers, constantly clamouring for higher wages and better working conditions. Purging the unions of communist leadership was a government priority, and in this it was supported by both the Trades and Labour Congress and the Canadian Congress of Labour, which within five years managed to expel all big member unions that were dominated by communists.

It was the era of the Senator McCarthy witch hunt in the United States, and in Quebec Premier Duplessis warned of "reds under the bed" everywhere. He even blamed communist sabotage for the collapse of a large new bridge at Trois-Rivières, a bridge that had been shoddily built, probably thanks to the usual graft involved in the awarding of government contracts. The hunt for "subversive literature" never let up, and in January 1951, the provincial police proudly announced that in one day they had seized sixteen thousand communist books, leaflets and circulars in raids on the Victory Book Shop on Park Avenue, as well as the headquarters of the Labour-Progressive Party and the United Jewish People's Order.

Members of organizations like these found that they were barred from entering the United States, as the RCMP routinely supplied the American immigration authorities with lists of Canadians suspected of being communists. The poet Irving Layton was turned back at the border and was unable to enter the U.S. for fifteen years. As a young man, Denis Lazure, destined to one day be a minister in a Parti Québécois government, was also turned back at the border. The American authorities had been informed that as a student leader at the University of Montreal, Lazure had attended international congresses of students in Czechoslovakia and Poland at a time when very few Canadians travelled behind the Iron Curtain. As a result of these travels, the Jesuit magazine *Relations* branded Lazure, a medical student, as a communist, and he was abruptly dismissed from his internship at the St. Jean de Dieu Hospital. Writers and artists were favourite targets for the "red squads," and one night a joint raiding party of provincial and city police spent four hours in the apartment of Dan Daniels, a writer, going through his books and papers. Among the many items they took away with them was the manuscript of a work of fiction he had been working on for more than a year. When Daniels later phoned the police and asked if he could have his manuscript back, they told him they had burned it.

In June 1956, the communists of Montreal, like communists the world over, were struck by a thunderbolt from Moscow. A few months earlier, for the first time ever, the crimes of Joseph Stalin had been revealed: Nikita Khrushchev, first secretary of the Communist Party of the Soviet Union, had told delegates to a Party congress how Stalin, now dead for three years, had ordered assassinations, political executions, mass arrests, deportation of whole nations; he had been responsible for the murder of perhaps sixteen million Soviet citizens. Khrushchev's revelations had been made at a secret session of the Party congress, in February, but in June they became public knowledge when the *New York Times* obtained a copy of the speech and published it. In Montreal there was shock, horror and consternation in the ranks of the LPP. It had been an article of faith for Party members to believe that the Soviet Union was the workers' paradise, the perfect state which the rest of the world must struggle to emulate. Now it was shown to have been permeated with injustice and evil of staggering dimensions. The remedy for the world's ills had proven to be fatally poisonous.

All summer the Party in Montreal was in constant turmoil, with meeting after meeting to discuss "the revelations." The climax came in October, at a mass meeting in the Mount Royal Arena, when Tim Buck, national leader of the Party, told members that despite Stalin's crimes they had no right to question the fundamental tenets of communism. The meeting broke up in disarray, with members booing and shouting at their revered leader. The six paid officials of the Quebec party resigned, and hundreds of members tore up their Party cards. Communism in Montreal was a spent force; in the future, police and factory owners would have much less to worry about.

For most members, quitting the Party was a wrenching, traumatic experience. Communism had been the focus of their lives, their religion, and working on its behalf had occupied a large part of their waking hours. Now, bereft of its guidance, they felt disoriented, lost. One of these lost souls was Harry Gulkin, who had grown up in the faith, devout and devoted. He was the child of communist parents, a "red-diaper baby," and as a boy, at the International Workers Children's Camp in the Laurentians, he had acted in plays about unemployed people resisting bailiffs who were trying to evict them from their homes. In the 1940s he went to sea with the merchant navy and became an organizer for the Canadian Seamen's Union, a communist union. It was a great honour for him to be selected for training at the Communist Party's leadership school in Northern Ontario, an experience, he recalled decades later, that was like entering the priesthood. Leaving the Party, in 1956, was as difficult for him as for any priest renouncing his vows. "The hardest part," he would later say, "was what was I going to say to my mother? She always wanted me to be a revolutionary."

Like Harry Gulkin, many of the LPP stalwarts who saw the light in the 1950s had little difficulty in eventually making their way in the capitalist world, several of them becoming plutocrats in the realms of business and real estate. And the city's more relaxed attitude toward the red peril was reflected in its welcome for Fidel Castro in 1959, when he arrived to be guest of honour at a dinner given by the Chambre de Commerce des Jeunes, an organization of young French Canadian businessmen. "Our policy is humanism, not communism," he told reporters who asked about his politics. The thirty-two-year-old rebel leader, now prime minister of Cuba, was cheered everywhere he went in Montreal, from the lobby of the Queen Elizabeth Hotel to Ste. Justine Hospital where, puffing a large cigar, he visited the nursery. Castro praised the "Latin atmosphere" of Montreal and voiced admiration for members of the RCMP who were guarding him. Probably unaware that the RCMP was Canada's most implacable foe of communism, Castro said that it would serve as a model for the new Cuban police force. "The Mounties, they're wonderful," he said. "I never saw them before except in pictures. Their uniforms are the colour of our July 26th movement."

~

If there were a few thousand communists in Montreal in the 1940s and '50s, there were far more true believers at the other end of the political spectrum, people who sympathized with the aims of fascism. These were often persons of influence and power, and Count Jacques Dugé de Bernonville, a recent immigrant, found many kindred souls among them. On a Sunday afternoon, De Bernonville's new friends might come round to his Côte des Neiges apartment in a large black Cadillac and take him and his wife for a leisurely drive up to the Laurentians, pleasant countryside that might remind the count of his native France, of Saône-et-Loire, where, as a collaborator with the Nazis during the war, he presided so efficiently over the torture and murder of his fellow Frenchmen.

When told that De Bernonville had been sentenced to death in absentia in France for his crimes, and when confronted with affidavits signed by Resistance fighters he had tortured, his Montreal friends shrugged their shoulders and said that these charges were nothing more than another plot of *"les judéo-maçons et les communistes"* – the Jews, the Freemasons and the communists. The count, they insisted, was an authentic French hero: he had been a devoted servant of the wartime Vichy government in France, a regime much admired in Quebec; he was a devout Catholic and, above all, he was a relentless fighter against communism. But the Canadian government knew that he had also been a member of the Nazi Waffen-SS. Ottawa wanted him deported to France, as a war criminal, but his defenders, members of Montreal's French Canadian political and cultural elite, were ready to put up an energetic battle to prevent that from happening.

After the war, De Bernonville escaped from Europe through Spain and arrived in New York in the fall of 1946. He crossed the border into Canada carrying a false passport and calling himself Jacques Benoit. He was disguised as a priest and claimed to be a tourist. He had introductions to important people in Quebec who gave him shelter and found him a succession of jobs, and soon he was able to be joined by his wife and three of his daughters. But a year after his arrival, "Benoit" was recognized by a Frenchman who had known him in Paris before the war and knew who he was. Alarmed, De Bernonville presented himself to Canadian immigration authorities, confessing his deception and asking to become a Canadian citizen. After some months, the immigration department turned down his application and told him that he would have to leave the country within sixty days. When he failed to do so, he and his family were arrested on September 2, 1948, and confined to the St. Antoine Street immigration lockup. They were to be deported within a few days.

De Bernonville's supporters responded immediately and vociferously, in the press and on the radio. Their leader was Mayor Camillien Houde, who said that the count had simply been a soldier following orders, and now he was to be sacrificed "for political reasons." Houde said that there were twenty other heroes like De Bernonville living in Montreal, men who had been falsely condemned by France as collaborators, and he threw his support behind the newly formed Committee for the Defence of French Political Refugees. Lawyers were brought to bear, the deportation order was challenged in court and the count and his family were released on bail. This was the beginning of a legal and public-relations struggle between De Bernonville's friends and his foes that would rage for the next three years.

At the time, in Montreal, there were several French immigrants of another stripe, veterans of the Maquis, the French underground resistance that had fought so heroically against the Nazis. These men spearheaded the battle against De Bernonville, sending to France for documentary evidence of his crimes as a commander of the Milice, Vichy's paramilitary police. There were sworn statements from men like Maurice Nedey, a garage mechanic who had been arrested by the Milice and brought before De Bernonville at his headquarters in Chalon-sur-Saône. As De Bernonville sat behind his desk, his men tried to get information from Nedey about his fellow Resistance fighters. "They spat on me," Nedey said in his affidavit. "They hit me with their fists, kicked me in the stomach. . . . One of them lashed me with a whip across the stomach and I thought I would vomit out my guts." When none of this elicited the required information from Nedey, De Bernonville ordered his men to start applying electricity.

There were also accounts of De Bernonville leading troops of the Milice in raids on the Resistance, killing many of its members. Before these raids, the count was reported to have said to his men, "Aim well, but shoot without hatred, for these are your brothers." But none of this evidence impressed De Bernonville's supporters; it was all simply a forgery by the communists or the Jews. When the Montreal Jewish Youth Council protested Ottawa's lenient treatment of several collaborators other than De Bernonville, the Ordre de Canadiens de Naissance was quoted in the newspapers as saying that "young Hebrews should be deported as agents of Moscow." And René Chaloult, a member of the Quebec legislature, said that if Bernonville had been called Bernondsky he would have no trouble staying in Canada.

During the late 1940s and early '50s, the De Bernonville affair was the most prominent manifestation of conflict between the two soli-tudes, with Montreal's English newspapers calling for the count's expulsion and the French papers, with the exception of the Liberal Party's *Le Canada*, giving him strong support. Across Canada, war veterans' organizations and other patriotic groups passed resolutions calling for his deportation, but in Ottawa an informal poll of forty French-speaking members of Parliament showed that thirty-eight of them thought he should be allowed to remain in Canada. In Montreal, one petition in support of De Bernonville was signed by 143 members of the French Canadian elite, including many doctors, lawyers and members of the faculty of the University of Montreal, whose student society also approved of the count. Among those whose names appeared on the petition was that of a young Camille Laurin who, twenty-five years later, as a minister in a separatist government, would be in a position to punish the Anglos by drafting Quebec's new language laws.

Despite all the petitions, support for the count was waning. There was now concrete evidence that in the latter days of the war he had joined the Waffen-ss and had been in the pay of the Nazis. While there was much appreciation of other forms of fascism in Quebec, there was little support for out-and-out Hitlerism. By the summer of 1951 De Bernonville knew that he could not survive a renewed order for his expulsion, and in August of that year he abruptly left for Brazil, where he is said to have made contact with Klaus Barbie, the Butcher of Lyon, and other Nazi fugitives. The count, whose title was probably bogus, lived in Brazil for twenty-one years, until he was murdered by his cleaning lady's son.

~

In May 1942, when Montreal was celebrating the three hundredth anniversary of its founding, General de Gaulle sent the city "a message of hope and confidence" on behalf of the Free French forces he commanded from London. France, he said, had not forgotten those of her sons who had made her traditions known and beloved in lands across the seas. But the traditions De Gaulle had in mind – Liberty, Equality, Fraternity – were not necessarily those admired by most of Montreal's French Canadians, whose taste at that time ran more to the "Work, Family, Fatherland" of Marshal Pétain's regime in Vichy. De Gaulle was overlooking the fact that ever since the French Revolution of 1789, the Catholic clergy of Quebec had been instilling in the populace a profound disapproval of France, with its anti-clericalism and its free-thinking ways. But now, with the defeat of France at the hands of the Nazis and the establishment of a fascist government in Vichy, most Québécois could rejoice at the revival of the old authoritarianism in their mother country. After the fall of France in 1940, Montreal's *La Patrie* asked, "Why weep over the Third Republic which confounded liberty with licence?"

As the American historian Mason Wade observed, English Canadians were astonished that Quebec was so little moved by the fall of France. Marshal Pétain, hero of the First World War, was now entrusted by the Germans to govern the unoccupied portion of France, and in Quebec he was once again a hero. "Pétain wants to make his country French again," said a headline in *Le Devoir*, which admired Vichy's anti-Semitic legislation. Quebec could learn from Pétain's ethnic-purification measures, *Le Devoir* felt, and noting that refugees from Europe were seeking entry to Canada, it said: "Let's close the door and keep it firmly closed. We already have enough parasites, from whatever country, whatever their language, whatever their true ethnic origin." Henri Bourassa, the grand old man of Quebec nationalism, added his voice to the chorus of praise for Pétain. "In the face of the calumny of a great number of people interested in ensuring that France does not rise again," Bourassa said, "Marshal Pétain is accomplishing a gigantic work." The chorus reached its crescendo in an article by Doris Lussier in the review *La Droite*. "Following the examples of Salazar's Portugal," Lussier wrote, "of Franco's Spain and of France, of the dear sweet France of Pétain, all humanity will be born again in the radiant sun of justice and charity, under the saintly crown of peace, glory and immortality."

For English-speaking Montrealers, hope for the rebirth of France lay not in the fascism of Marshal Pétain but in the determination of Charles de Gaulle, whose Free French forces had joined the Allies in their effort to defeat Germany in the war. In August 1940, De Gaulle sent his secretary, Elisabeth de Miribel, to Montreal to open an office for the Free French and to enlist the support of French Canadians for his cause. But she was soon dismayed at the extent of Quebec's admiration for Pétain. "They consider any news that France is being enslaved by the Nazis to be the work of English propaganda," she wrote. "The men in power . . . are more anti-British than anti-German." The populace seemed to share the sentiments of their leaders. In July 1942, a public opinion poll showed that 75 percent of the people of Quebec approved of Vichy's policies. That year supporters of the Free French were denied permission to march in the big St. Jean Baptiste parade.

Some members of the elite had courage enough to swim against the current and lend vocal support to De Gaulle, among them journalists like Louis Francoeur, Jean-Charles Harvey and Edmond Turcotte, publisher of *Le Canada*. While many priests were unstinting in their approval of Pétain, and dubious about the aims of the Allies, Cardinal Villeneuve was a strong supporter of the Allied war effort. Toward the end of 1942, after the Germans had occupied the whole of France, support for the Free French started to grow in Montreal, and when General de Gaulle visited Quebec in 1944 enthusiastic crowds welcomed him. But admiration for Marshal Pétain hardly diminished, even after his arrest and conviction for treason. The Allied victory of 1945, and the revelations of Axis war crimes, did not dampen *Le Devoir*'s love affair with fascism. The paper deplored the way Italian partisans executed Mussolini and expressed admiration for his achievements. As for Hitler, while admitting that he had been "one of the great scourges of mankind," *Le Devoir* praised him for "galvanizing a humiliated people."

~

On June 22, 1944, Télésphore-Damien Bouchard rose in the Senate of Canada to make his maiden speech, startling his fellow senators with his radical message and unleashing an unprecedented storm of protest in Quebec. He was denouncing the Order of Jacques Cartier, a secret society which he said was coming to dominate public policy in Quebec with its insidious nationalist and separatist ideology. It was anti-English and anti-Jewish; it wanted a state run on the authoritarian lines of Spain or Portugal, perhaps a dictatorship. The order had the blessing of the clergy, Bouchard said, despite the fact that secret societies were forbidden by the Church.

This was the same organization that Jean-Charles Harvey's liberal newspaper *Le Jour* had called the Ku Klux Klan of French Canada. New members were initiated in a rite in which they were led, blindfolded, through a series of minor ordeals, like being made to drink an unpleasant concoction and being given a mild electric shock. Finally the blindfold was removed and, as a Quebec folk tune played in the background, they would be knighted with a sword and sworn to absolute secrecy. Even a wife must never know of her husband's membership in the Order of Jacques Cartier. By now, T.D. Bouchard told the Senate, the order had some eighteen thousand members, among them some of the most prominent and powerful people in Quebec. They included officers of the St. Jean Baptiste Society, of Catholic trade unions, of school commissions, of municipal councils, boards of trade and public administrations of every kind. Without the support of the order, Bouchard said, Maurice Duplessis's Union Nationale would not have come into power in 1936, "to give us the poorest and most abusive government in the history of the province." The ultimate aim of this secret society, the senator said, "is not only to disunite the people on lingual and religious matters, but also to disrupt Confederation, to abandon the more human North American concept of a large nation composed of people of different religious beliefs and racial origins, and to revert to the old European concept of smaller nations of the same religious and racial descent." The independent French and Catholic state that the order wanted, he said, would "bring us back to the social and economic status of the Middle Ages."

Bouchard was speaking in support of a motion calling for the adoption of a common textbook of Canadian history that would be used in the schools of all provinces. He denounced what he called the "false history" that was taught in Quebec schools and blamed it for the Order of Jacques Cartier's being able to attract so many recruits for its insidious program. "[False] history," he said, "should not serve as a tool of subversive propaganda in the hands of those who are aiming to disrupt Confederation and overthrow our form of democratic government." Bouchard then cited passages from Quebec history textbooks in which all the ills of French Canadians were blamed on the English and only the wrongs of British rule were mentioned and none of the advantages. As a student, Bouchard said, these things had been thoroughly instilled in him, and it was only after he went out into the world that he learned that "Canadians of

English descent were not all cloven-footed and did not wear horns, but on the contrary entertained the very same good sentiments as did we of French descent." And, he pointed out, "the founder of Christianity never preached that one man should rise against the other because of differences of race and language." As for politics, Bouchard said, most French Canadians did not subscribe to the separatist ideas of the intellectual elite, as embodied in the doctrines of the Order of Jacques Cartier. "A large majority of my compatriots," he said, "love Canada as it is, constitutionally and otherwise, and do not want any change in their allegiance."

In Quebec, Bouchard's speech provoked an immediate storm of protest from politicians, academics and journalists. Premier Godbout said that the senator's remarks were "absolutely unjustified," and Maurice Duplessis, now leader of the opposition, called them "despicable and reprehensible." Cardinal Villeneuve added the condemnation of the Church, and one of Bouchard's French-speaking fellow senators called him a madman, while another said that "a decent bird doesn't foul its own nest." Not surprisingly, the many organizations that he had named as being dominated by the secret society joined in the outcry, and before long Premier Godbout, with an election in the offing, yielded to their demands and dismissed Bouchard from his post as president of Hydro-Quebec. Predictably, most of the French newspapers applauded this punishment, while the English papers denounced it as a shocking abrogation of the freedom of speech.

No one could be more offended by Bouchard's assertions than Abbé Lionel Groulx, the priest who had been teaching history at the University of Montreal since 1915. His interpretation of Quebec's past would dominate the thinking not only of the senator's generation but also of generations of French Canadians yet unborn. A disciple of Charles Maurras and other European fascists, Groulx was a believer in the supreme importance of racial purity, and he issued constant warnings against the dangers of intermarriage, through which the unsullied French Canadian race would become mongrelized. French Canadians were endlessly victimized by the English, in Groulx's version of history, and the Jews were a particular menace.

"Jewish internationalism," he wrote, not long after Hitler came to power, "[is] one of the most dangerous forces of moral and social decay on the planet."

Writing about fascism in 1937, Lionel Groulx announced that "certain nations are currently very content, experiencing the most glorious kind of rebirth under this political system." Quebec could learn valuable lessons from Mussolini, he said, and he wondered whether French Canada would ever get the strong man it deserved. "A man! A leader! Will he ever come our way?" Groulx wrote. "Unlike other more fortunate nations, our present crisis has not resulted in a real man stepping forth from the crowds, a man capable of pulling us out of the mire in which we are foundering. . . . One is almost tempted to say, 'Lucky are the nations that have managed to find a dictator.'" And much later, in 1954, when the horrors of the Holocaust were common knowledge, Groulx was still writing about the perfidy of the Jews and what he called "their innate passion for money – an often monstrous passion that makes them totally unscrupulous."

During his lifetime, and after his death, Groulx's writings about Quebec's history, with their disregard for documented facts, were taken as gospel by most members of French Montreal's intellectual elite and served to fuel their nationalist fervour. "He was the spiritual father of modern Quebec," Claude Ryan wrote when the old priest died in 1967. "Everything noteworthy, everything novel on the Quebec scene carried the imprint of Groulx's thought," said Ryan, the Le Devoir editor who would later become leader of the Quebec Liberal Party. When Montreal finally got its subway, the Métro, one of its most important stations was named "Lionel Groulx." For Montrealers, seeing his name on the station would serve as a durable, everyday reminder of the historic affinities between nationalism and its cousins – racism, xenophobia and contempt for democracy.

12

End of an Era:
Drapeau Enters, Duplessis Exits

Frank Petrula, one of Montreal's most notorious mobsters, had just come back from Italy, where he had conferred with Lucky Luciano, the Mafia kingpin. Luciano, it was rumoured, had supplied him with a goodly stash of heroin for sale in Canada. And so the RCMP hastened out to Petrula's luxurious home, in Beaconsfield, to look for narcotics. After hours of patient searching they still hadn't found anything, but they did come across a hidden wall safe. Inside there was eighteen thousand dollars in cash and a few pages of notes, but no heroin. Hastily, Petrula told the Mounties that they could keep the money for themselves if only they would let him destroy the notes. But the policemen declined the offer; those bits of paper were too interesting to destroy, listing as they did the names of Montreal's leading underworld bosses and the amounts each had contributed, more than $100,000 in all, to a worthy but futile cause – the defeat of Jean Drapeau, the crime-busting lawyer who had just been elected mayor in the municipal elections. Also listed were the thugs who had been hired to intimidate Drapeau's supporters with their base-ball bats and the telegraphers who had been hired to stuff ballot boxes with fraudulent votes. For it was Drapeau, along with Pacifique Plante, who had led the attack on the underworld at the Caron commission inquiry, which resulted in the condemnation of senior police officers for condoning decades of widespread gambling and prostitution. In the wake of the famous "vice probe," the city's gangsters had been anxious to keep Drapeau from becoming mayor and further tightening the noose around their necks.

On election day, October 28, 1954, the police switchboard was swamped with calls – at least five every minute – complaining about violence and skulduggery at the polls. At one point, a dozen goons smashed the plate glass window of Drapeau's headquarters, in a store-front committee room, and came rushing in to overturn desks, smash typewriters and destroy files and electoral lists. They came when the solitary policeman who had been assigned to Drapeau's committee was out having a coffee down the street. But despite all the efforts of the underworld, and the apparent complicity of the police by denying him protection, Drapeau won in a landslide, with more than three times as many votes as his closest opponent. For Montrealers, who had followed the drama of the Caron inquiry for four years, Jean Drapeau was the hero of the hour, a mayor who would be corruption's nemesis, who would restore dignity to the city.

"The victory is not mine, it is the people's," Drapeau told cheering supporters at City Hall on the night he was elected. "A new page," he said, "has been written in our history." Much to the satisfaction of the religious organizations that had backed him, the new mayor appointed his sidekick, Pax Plante, as assistant chief of police. Plante immediately got busy raiding the gambling dens and whorehouses that had survived their exposure during the Caron inquiry. Two months after Drapeau's election, Al Palmer advised readers of the *Herald* that Montreal's gambling empire was crumbling. Ever the insider, Palmer noted that two leading gambling bosses had retired from the rackets to enter legitimate business. "Montreal isn't as pure as the driven snow that blanketed it last week," he wrote, "but it's as pure as it is likely to be for some time."

Putting an end to corruption at City Hall was more difficult. Of the ninety-nine members of city council, Drapeau could count on support from not many more than the twenty-eight who were members of his party, the Civic Action League. Although Pierre DesMarais, an ally of Drapeau's, was chairman of the all-powerful city executive committee, other committeemen were adversaries who could block projects or delay them. And some of them were eager to line their pockets. Historically, graft had been one of the cherished prerogatives of the executive committee, and years later

Pacifique Plante would explain how it worked in his book *Lutte à finir avec la pègre* (Fight to the Finish with the Underworld). "As soon as a new executive committee would meet," he wrote, "they would divide up *le gâteau des influences*." The most lucrative slice of the cake, that involving city finances and the negotiation of loans, would go to the chairman of the committee. Other members of the committee would be assigned territories like public works, changes in zoning laws, permits, expropriations, and so on. Plante claimed that these details had been divulged to him by a former committee-man who told him that as the most recently elected member he had been given *les rackets* as the trough from which he could drink. "Do you think I liked that?" he asked Plante. "No, but I thought that if I kept my mouth shut I might some day rise through the ranks and become chairman."

Without full control over the executive committee, Drapeau and DesMarais could not prevent some of its members from playing the old traditional games. These were prosperous years, with the city expanding rapidly, and there was good graft to be collected from land speculators who, having assembled large parcels of residential land, wanted to greatly increase their value by having them re-zoned for commercial or industrial use. Members of the executive committee were generally happy to arrange this – for a consideration. But there were no kickbacks to be garnered from projects proposed by the mayor, and the committee and the city council seemed to enjoy putting obstacles in their way. Still Drapeau did manage to effect a number of improvements in the way the city was run, especially in the matter of traffic control. Massive congestion downtown was relieved by the institution of one-way streets and coordinated traffic lights; new parking lots and underpasses were being planned, as well as an elevated Metropolitan Boulevard, which would traverse the north of the island.

While projects like these won wide approval for Drapeau, other measures proved to be highly unpopular. He was denounced for heartlessness when he decided to turn over garbage collection to private operators and fired two hundred city garbagemen just before Christmas. There was a similar reaction when he cut off $634,000 in grants to welfare agencies, arguing that expenditures of this sort were the responsibility of the provincial government, not the city, which could not afford them. In the eyes of the public it was a monstrous act, and it was denounced by charitable organizations and labour unions. The press, generally sympathetic to Drapeau before his election, was now starting to turn on him, delighted with every flaw it could discover. There were guffaws at his expense when, after he campaigned to have children immunized with the new polio vaccine, it was discovered that his wife refused to have their own children vaccinated, because she didn't believe in it. The press was happy to report in detail the outrage citizens expressed over one of Drapeau's more harebrained schemes – the scarring of the city's beloved, pristine Mount Royal on behalf of the automobile by building two "speedways" across it, a scheme that was quietly scrapped. There was a further humiliation for the strait-laced mayor when Inspector Armand Courval, head of his police Morality Squad, was found to have been issuing condoms to his officers before they embarked on raids on brothels.

But Drapeau's greatest problems were to emanate from Quebec City, from where Premier Duplessis had been watching him suspiciously, wondering whether the cocky little mayor might not have ambitions to challenge him by graduating to provincial politics. Despite Drapeau's denials, this may well have been the case, and he would have been much encouraged by the letter of congratulation he received, soon after his election, from Lionel Groulx, the bigot-priest who was always looking for a man on horseback to lead Quebec out of the wilderness of democracy. "In time of crisis," Groulx wrote, "people always look for a leader. Why would you not be this man, at some future time and on a wider stage?" But the wily Duplessis was determined to keep Drapeau off that wider stage. And eventually, the premier decided, he ought to be dislodged from the narrower stage as well, from the mayoralty of Montreal.

Drapeau had been irritating Duplessis in a number of ways. To start with, the mayor had been making too many speeches up and down the province, enhancing his reputation. Then he had spoken out against Frank Hanley, the Point St. Charles ward heeler, who was a candidate in the 1956 provincial election and a favourite ally of Duplessis. With a large infusion of cash, Duplessis managed to buy the election for Hanley, but he couldn't forgive Drapeau for his intrusion. But the most momentous clash between the mayor and the premier was over the question of slum clearance and subsidized public housing. The project under consideration was the Dozois Plan, named after Paul Dozois, a city councillor who was its main proponent. Under the plan, ten blocks of slums, among the worst in the city, would be razed and replaced by low-rent subsidized housing. The project had the support of both the federal and provincial governments, but Mayor Drapeau was adamantly opposed. The municipal government, he said, had no role to play in providing this kind of housing, which would only create a new ghetto for the poor. Besides, common hallways in the proposed apartment buildings would facilitate promiscuity; presumably middle-class apartment dwellers, living uptown, could be trusted to refrain from illicit sex with neighbours down the hall, but the lower orders would find it far too easy to hop into the wrong beds. Also, the plan was to be located near the city centre, an area for which Drapeau had more grandiose plans: if the slums were to go, they should be replaced by a large radio-television studio complex.

Drapeau's opposition to the Dozois Plan was again seen, by the public, as heartless, with no compassion for the poor. Charitable organizations spoke up loudly, as did the English newspapers, which were perhaps less concerned with the housing needs of the poor than with their editorial policy of showing support at all times for Premier Duplessis. For Duplessis was a strong supporter of the plan, which would be largely financed by Ottawa. Drapeau's opposition was like a red flag waved in his face. "The Dozois project will not be built as long as I am mayor," Drapeau said, whereupon the ever-resourceful Duplessis hurried a bill through the provincial legislature taking the project out of the hands of the Montreal executive committee and vesting responsibility for it in a newly created Housing Bureau. Now the project could go ahead. And now the battle lines were drawn. As one newspaper observed, Duplessis was less interested in demolishing the slums than in demolishing Drapeau. As the October 1957 election approached, the premier threw his support behind Sarto Fournier, a senator who had been one of the candidates defeated by Drapeau in the 1954 election.

"Never has anyone done so much in so little time," Drapeau proclaimed in his election-campaign literature. It listed two hundred separate achievements, including improvements in many parks, creation of eighty-four miles of new streets, renovation of libraries, the building of a restaurant at Beaver Lake, extending the municipal golf course and planning for a world-class zoo (which would fail to materialize). But Sarto Fournier's election literature was more colourful, featuring doctored photos of Jean Drapeau with his hair slicked down like Hitler's and his arm, with a swastika armband, raised in a Nazi salute. The full weight of Duplessis's Union Nationale electoral machine was thrown behind Fournier's campaign, and in addition the premier authorized the spending of some $200,000 to pay for the Hitler ads and to hire, for election day, a larger than usual force of goons and telegraphers. The invasion of Drapeau committee rooms by thugs resulted in injuries to forty people. It was an unprecedented effort that worked, electing the lacklustre Sarto Fournier by a slim margin of 4,300 votes.

As Drapeau left the scene to lick his wounds, the underworld rejoiced. Its scourge, Pacifique Plante, was also gone, and Albert Langlois, the police chief who had been fired as a result of the Caron vice inquiry, was now back in office, the Quebec Superior Court having overturned Judge Caron's finding that Langlois had tolerated vice. Within a few months an angry Cardinal Léger was complaining that Montreal was again an open city, as in the bad old days. Every form of corruption, moral and civic, was rampant and nightclub shows were more indecent than ever. *Le Devoir*, marvelling that half a million pornographic magazines were being sold every week in Quebec, was charitable enough to suggest that Chief Langlois was more stupid than evil.

Meanwhile Jean Drapeau was already planning his comeback. In January 1958, he rented the St. Denis Theatre and invited citizens to come and hear him denounce the Fournier regime and hear his plans for the future. It was a political meeting with a new twist: there was a one-dollar admission charge. He had been robbed at the polls, Drapeau told his enthusiastic audience, by criminals who had cast twenty thousand false votes. But, he said, speaking for an hour and forty-five minutes, he would rise to fight again. The following month he charged English Montrealers a dollar apiece to hear him deliver a similar message at Her Majesty's Theatre. But here he had an additional theme, his wonderment at the Anglo tolerance of the undemocratic, corrupt regime of Maurice Duplessis.

In the three years that followed his defeat, Drapeau continued his vigorous politicking. He severed his connection with the balky Civic Action League and founded a new party, the Civic Party of Montreal – "at the service of all classes." Campaigning in the 1960 election, he promised a vast array of public works and, of course, he would clean up the vice and corruption that had again flared up in the city. He denounced his opponent, Mayor Sarto Fournier, as an incompetent clown, the man who once took City Hall's Golden Book, signed by kings and other distinguished visitors, and put it down on the floor to receive the paw print of a dog. In the voting, in October 1960, Drapeau swept back into power with almost thirty thousand votes more than Fournier. Members of his party got two-thirds of the elective seats in city council, and the coast was now clear for him to run Montreal without too much impediment.

Jean Drapeau would be mayor for the next twenty-six years and, like Camillien Houde before him, he would come to be known as "Mr. Montreal." His accomplishments – Place des Arts, the subway, Expo 67, the 1976 Olympics – would be considerably more monumental than Houde's beloved comfort stations, but the hard-driving, sober-sided Drapeau would never enliven the local scene the way old Camillien did, with his unpredictable antics. Drapeau's civic style and his personal demeanour would be very much in keeping with the atmosphere of the new Montreal, a serious, self-conscious city so different from the jaunty, rakish church-and-nightclub town it used to be.

∾

When Maurice Duplessis died, in 1959, the *Montreal Star*'s editorial raised the question of whether he had been a dictator. Many Montrealers had thought him to be exactly that, but the *Star* allowed the old premier to defend himself from the grave by quoting a response he had once made to this accusation. "To be a leader is not to be a dictator," Duplessis had said. "To be a leader is to be firm, strong and courageous in bringing to one's people safety, stability and security in their homes and in their jobs." What the *Star* failed to point out was that Duplessis brought security to his people in their jobs by sending in policemen with truncheons to break their heads during strikes and by assuring employers that workers in Quebec would earn less than workers anywhere else in North America. He brought safety by fighting the unions' efforts to improve dangerous working conditions in mines and factories. And he brought stability by keeping his Union Nationale government in office for sixteen consecutive years, winning four elections through methods that were spectacularly fraudulent.

For the 1948 election, after four immensely profitable years in power, Duplessis's Union Nationale government had accumulated the largest election fund in Quebec history, much of it extorted from contractors seeking government work. With perhaps five times as much as the Liberals were able to spend, the UN could be more lavish than ever in bribing voters in rural ridings and, in Montreal, in stealing votes through the time-honoured methods. It could also buy many full-page ads in newspapers and endless radio commercials extolling the premier's policies, and could even hire a small airplane to fly over villages in the country with a loudspeaker that shouted "Duplessis! Duplessis! Duplessis!" With this enormous war chest, Duplessis decisively crushed the opposition. He took twenty-nine seats from the Liberals and put an end to the short life of the Bloc Populaire, the upstart radical nationalist party. He now had 90 percent of the seats in the Legislative Assembly, which he took as a mandate for total autocracy. During debates in the legislature, he would sometimes interrupt one of his own ministers, telling him in a loud voice to shut up and sit down. And the Speaker, before making a ruling, would almost always glance at Duplessis for a nod or a shake of the head.

In the winter of 1949, when five thousand miners went on strike in and around the town of Asbestos, eighty miles east of Montreal, Duplessis seemed to take it as a personal affront. The miners, who were earning eighty-five cents an hour, wanted a pay raise that would bring the rate to a dollar an hour, which would still be less than miners earned elsewhere in Canada. They also wanted something done about the choking asbestos dust that pervaded their workplace, the dust that led to lung disease and early death. Almost everywhere else in Canada, this kind of cleanup in mines was being enforced by law, but not in Quebec. On hearing the workers' demands, Duplessis immediately declared their strike illegal, decertified their union and sent in 150 members of his Provincial Police to quell disorder that did not exist. "On their arrival, a great number of these policemen were under the influence of alcohol," said a resolution of protest passed by the Asbestos town council. "A certain number even rendered themselves guilty of indecent acts in streets of the town, and also were the causes of disorder in public places."

The asbestos strike dragged on for more than four months, with Duplessis constantly supporting the mining companies' obduracy and frequently sending in his police to protect strikebreakers and foment disorder that he could blame on communists. Maurice Duplessis, self-anointed protector of the French Canadian people, was kicking them in the teeth at the behest of the American owners of the mines. In the end, when the strike was settled – with the miners getting a raise of ten cents an hour rather than the fifteen cents they wanted – Duplessis proclaimed himself to be a great mediator of labour disputes. He had used these tactics in fighting organized labour in the past, and would do it again in the future – in the Shawinigan aluminum strike, the Louiseville textile strike, the Murdochville copper-mine strike. But it was the asbestos strike of 1949 that won the sympathies of much of the public for organized labour, and it energized Montreal intellectuals who would become, in the decade ahead, a thorn in the side of this autocrat who ruled from Quebec City.

The asbestos strike probably influenced blue-collar voters in the 1952 election, when Duplessis lost fourteen constituencies to the Liberals; however, he still retained three times as many seats as they did, and so the Liberals could in no way impede his program. Although his greatest strength was in the countryside, his nationalist rhetoric still managed to get him almost half the popular vote in the predominantly French sections of Montreal. In the English parts of the city, in three elections, he averaged a surprising 24.75 percent of the popular vote. In a 1959 article entitled "The Astonishing Attitude of the English in Quebec," André Laurendeau, editor of *Le Devoir*, wondered how English Montrealers, with their supposed reverence for free speech and parliamentary democracy, could give any support at all to a tyrant like Duplessis. Laurendeau came to the conclusion that it was because the Anglos were so consistently misled by their newspapers, the *Star* and the *Gazette*. "Reading regularly this otherwise excellent and expert press," Laurendeau wrote, "is like inhaling an anaesthetic calculated to paralyze the natural distaste of English minds toward Mr. Duplessis. . . . What happened to our Englishmen, at least to their leaders? Because let me state that I am putting a case against the leaders of English-speaking Quebec, not against the people. People know what they are told: they can't guess what their papers systematically hide."

Despite his Padlock Law and other ways in which Duplessis curtailed free speech, the English newspapers adored him. The *Star* gave one of its reasons for this in an editorial on the eve of the 1948 election, when it said, "The present government makes free enterprise an article of faith and in the campaign now proceeding Mr. Duplessis has left no doubt about his attitude on this score." The *Gazette* was equally vocal in its praise and was most appreciative of the way the premier denounced the "centralizers" of Ottawa. "Canada," the *Gazette* said, "with its diversities of regional, racial and religious interests cannot survive under centralizing manipulation." Both papers applauded Duplessis's never-ending denunciation of communism, which he saw as an imminent menace to the province. It was a charge that he backed up with vivid fictions, like his assertion that Bolsheviks were hiding thousands of machine guns in the bushes of northern Quebec. With the exception of *Le Devoir*, all of Quebec's dailies remained loyal supporters of Duplessis well into the late 1950s. Many of them benefited from his government's job-printing contracts, and all of them were happy that his threats to the pulp-and-paper producers kept newsprint prices low. As for the working press, there was always "the envelope" for reporters covering election speeches – ten dollars at meetings being addressed by *Le Chef* and five dollars at meetings with lesser speakers. And two months before one of the elections, Duplessis treated members of the Quebec City Press Gallery to an all-expense-paid junket to New York. With benefactions like these, he assured himself that the press would not be unfriendly.

Speaking of Montreal's French newspapers, Gérard Pelletier, himself a former journalist, wrote that with the exception of *Le Devoir* they were "lacking in courage, imagination and conscience." Their publishers, he said, "held their editorial staff[s] in a reign of . . . stifling terror." On the English side, "most newspaper work was . . . intellectually stultifying, morally degrading and financially unrewarding." These were the words of Brian Cahill, written after he left the employ of the *Gazette*, a paper where, like the *Star*, the advertiser reigned supreme and nothing that might possibly offend him could ever be printed. "It was an era," Cahill wrote, "in which nothing but good things ever happened in or about a Montreal department store, or in any of the major hotels, or to anyone who lived west of Atwater Avenue and might possibly object to having the family name 'in the paper.'" In effect, the English papers were the house organs of the Anglo-Scottish business elite. If someone were to be stabbed to death in Eaton's or in the Mount Royal Hotel, the *Star* would identify these places as "a downtown department store" or "a downtown hotel" – if the event were mentioned at all. When a disgruntled investor took a potshot at Sir Herbert Holt, the richest man in Canada (only grazing him with the bullet), and then went home and committed suicide, the Montreal newspapers ignored the event.

Reporters were constantly frustrated at not being able to report anything unpleasant about Maurice Duplessis and having other interesting stories rejected by their editors. But perhaps there were compensations, as described in *Why Rock the Boat?*, a satirical novel (by William Weintraub) about the journalism of that era as prac-tised at the slightly fictitious *Montreal Daily Witness*. "A newspa-perman is a glamorous person," the book pointed out, "only in proportion to the amount of news he is able to withhold from the public; newspapermen really know what is going on, but once this knowledge is made public it becomes trite. When it came to what was happening behind the scenes in Montreal, no one knew more than Witnessmen and, because of the paper's fortunate policy, they were allowed to keep most of it to themselves. This made them fascinating raconteurs, much sought after for conversation." Throughout the Duplessis years, Montreal newspapermen could tell fascinating stories about the enormities of his regime, but they could never get them into print.

~

On February 7, 1947, University of Montreal students assembled for a gala evening. Responding to their requests, the French Embassy had agreed to give them the much-acclaimed French film *Les Enfants du paradis* for a screening that would be its Canadian premiere. There was great excitement as students and faculty members assembled and awaited the arrival from Ottawa of René de Messière, the embassy's cultural attaché, who would introduce the film. But when M. de Messière arrived, he and the students were informed that the Quebec Censor Board had decided, at the last minute, that the film could not be shown and would be banned in Quebec. The French diplomat stormed out of the university in a huff, leaving the students to ponder this latest edict of their paternalistic government. Georges Sadoul, the eminent Paris critic, called *Les Enfants du paradis* a masterpiece, a "gigantic, philosophical ballet . . . essentially an aesthetic soliloquy on the relations between art and life." But it was not morally fit for Quebec eyes, and in Montreal it was generally accepted that the university had done something to displease Maurice Duplessis and was being punished for it.

The censorship of films was perhaps the most vigorous way in which the Duplessis government accommodated the Church in its efforts to protect the morals of the populace. The word divorce could not be uttered in a movie, and there could be no scenes in which a man and a woman were shown, even standing up and far apart, in a room that had a bed in it. Needless to say the film *Martin Luther*, about a man not beloved of the Church, could not be shown. And when Alfred Hitchcock arrived in Quebec City for the premiere of *I Confess*, which he had filmed in Quebec, he was disgusted to learn that two minutes had been cut by the Quebec censors, who could not tolerate the notion that a man who had once been in love with a woman later became a priest.

Books, too, were withheld from the people of Quebec, much to the satisfaction of the Church, which was always on guard against literary corruption. The provincial government would not fund public libraries, and whereas Ontario had 281 libraries in the early 1950s, Quebec, with a similar population, had only forty-three. In Ontario, in 1949, children borrowed twenty-five times as many library books as did Quebec children. The Carnegie Fund, which financed libraries all over North America, offered to create libraries in Quebec, but its offers were turned down because it stipulated that institutions it supported could not restrict purchases of books that were prohibited by the Catholic Index. The Index and its censorship were part of the traditional Catholicism that pervaded every aspect of life in French Montreal in this era, when families would kneel down in their living rooms at 7:00 p.m., in front of their radios, to recite the rosary, led by the archbishop from station CKAC.

Most members of the clergy, in the 1940s, were deeply suspicious of social change of any kind, and in resisting change they had a strong ally in Maurice Duplessis. In 1940, when his party was in opposition, he voted against a Liberal bill that would, at long last, give the vote to women. His vote was in accord with Cardinal Villeneuve's strong statement opposing female suffrage: "It is contrary to familial unity and hierarchy," the cardinal said, "[and] its exercise exposes the woman to all passions and adventures of electoralism. . . ." Even after they got the vote, women in Quebec continued to be subject to disabilities encountered nowhere else in Canada. Like minors and lunatics, married women were not legally capable of entering into contracts. A married woman could not buy or sell goods without her husband's permission and could not borrow from a bank. Except in a dire emergency, she could not undergo surgery without authorization from her husband.

In 1954 Duplessis permitted a small concession to women in a revision of the Civil Code. Up till then, a husband could demand a separation simply on the grounds of his wife's adultery, but for a wife to get a separation her husband would have had to commit adultery with a "concubine" that he kept on the family premises. In the Civil Code as now revised, the concubine did not have to live under the same roof as the wife, thus making it a bit easier for the wife to get a separation. But it was still only a separation, not a divorce, and there could be no possibility of remarriage. In Quebec there was no divorce to be had from the courts, and persons wishing to dissolve their marriage had to have a special act of Parliament passed to effect it. Divorces for Quebec were handled by the Senate, and the plaintiff (usually the wife) would have to go to Ottawa with her lawyer and appear before a Senate committee. They would usually bring a private detective with them, a man hired to cheerfully perjure himself by testifying that he had caught the defendant (usually the husband) in bed with a woman (usually a fictitious woman) who was not his wife. After listening to this charade, the senators, mostly unhappy at having to do this work, would recommend that Parliament pass an act granting the divorce. But most Montrealers seeking Ottawa divorces were Protestants or Jews; divorce was still one of the greatest taboos of the Catholic Church. As one of the characters in Gratien Gélinas's play *Tit-Coq* summed it up, "When you're married here, it's for a long time. Getting a divorce is not easy in this province. We're a long way from Hollywood. Down there, if you take the wrong train, it's simple: you get out at the next station. But here you've got to go right through to the terminus."

$\sim$

Although Duplessis helped foster the industrialization of Quebec, he wanted above all to preserve the province's traditional way of life, derived from its largely rural past, and he failed to acknowledge that the new society of the cities would of necessity have a different outlook and different needs. Halfway through the twentieth century, the Church still controlled education and social services in French Quebec. It supplied the priests, nuns and lay brothers who did most of the teaching in institutions from elementary schools to universities. Hospitals were owned and staffed by members of religious orders, as was every kind of social service. Moneys raised through private charities were far from sufficient to finance these private institutions, and so they had to depend on funding from the state, which essentially meant the largesse of Maurice Duplessis and his Union Nationale Party. This largesse had to be appreciated by the recipients, and during election campaigns parish priests in the country, speaking from the pulpit, would often remind the voters in their flocks that the sky was blue and hell was red, parishioners being well aware of the traditional party colours, the UN being *les bleus* and the Liberals *les rouges*. At a higher level, Duplessis revelled in the influence he had over the episcopate, thanks to his ability to dole out public funds to Catholic institutions – and to withhold money if those institutions displeased him. "The bishops," he was fond of saying, "eat out of my hand."

But not all the bishops were docile. After the asbestos strike had dragged on for eleven weeks, the archbishop of Montreal, Joseph Charbonneau, delivered an impassioned sermon denouncing the government's collusion with the enemies of labour. "When there is a conspiracy to destroy the working class, the Church must intervene," he said, and he ordered that collections be taken in all churches in his diocese to buy food for the impoverished strikers.

Soon churches throughout the province followed suit, pouring money into the strike fund. This infuriated Duplessis, who for years had detested Charbonneau's progressive views on social policy. The archbishop's support of the asbestos strikers was the last straw, and a few months after the strike was settled he was forced to resign his office and was exiled to a lowly function in Vancouver. It was widely believed that Duplessis had brought pressure to bear on the Vatican to punish this troublesome cleric. But the Church's opposition to Duplessis in the strike helped give the event its enormous symbolic importance. "The social climate of Quebec is no longer what it was six months ago," Le Devoir wrote, soon after the strike. "Today we are beginning to acquire a social conscience." And, as Pierre Trudeau, who was active in support of the asbestos strikers, wrote: "This strike is a turning point in the entire religious, political, social and economic history of the Province of Quebec."

All this was much to the annoyance of Duplessis, who intimated that true Christian justice emanated from his office and not from that of any priest. When Father Jacques Cousineau wrote a number of articles for a Jesuit publication in which he criticized the Union Nationale for consistently favouring the interests of the employer rather than those of the worker, Duplessis did not hesitate to label the priest a communist. Even more damaging to Duplessis was an article written by two other priests, Father Gérard Dion and Father Louis O'Neill, denouncing the outrageous dishonesty of Quebec election campaigns. Their accusations, soon after the 1956 provincial election, did not actually name the Union Nationale Party, but there was no doubt about whom they were talking when they detailed abuses like vote buying, threats of reprisals against persons who didn't support the right party, false oaths, impersonations at the polls and corruption of electoral officers. These abuses, the priests said, "seem to become normal elements of our social life at election time." What troubled them most, they said, was that so many priests, fully aware of this immorality, condoned it and sometimes even applauded it. This, said Dion and O'Neill, amounted to a religious crisis, a breakdown of Christianity.

The two priests wrote their four-thousand-word article for their own newsletter, which had a small circulation and was meant only for other priests. But *Le Devoir* discovered it and reprinted it in its entirety, causing a province-wide sensation. For Duplessis, of course, this was simply more proof that this newspaper was "*un journal bolsheviste.*" (*Le Devoir* had become much changed after the death of its longtime editor Georges Pelletier. Under new direction, it was still strongly nationalist, but it had divested itself of its fascist tinge and the anti-Semitism to which Pelletier had been so devoted. And it became the only newspaper in Montreal that would stand up to Duplessis.)

Although much of the clergy remained wedded to the status quo, Dion and O'Neill represented a growing number of priests who were prepared to work for social reform. In this they drew inspiration from the radical movements that had taken root in the Catholic Church in western Europe after the war. These same ideas inspired many intellectuals in Montreal – students, professors, writers and younger members of the professions. All were becoming increasingly aware, during the '50s, of the stagnation of life in Quebec and were searching for ways to bring the province, belatedly, into the twentieth century. There was a thirst for new ideas, for open and free-wheeling debate, and if the stodgy, servile press could not provide this information it suddenly became available from an unexpected source – the new medium, television. Duplessis and his ministers had made ample use of radio to influence the public, but they seemed unaware of the power of television and largely ignored it. French Canadians, however, were fascinated by the little screen, and from 1952 onwards it brought them not only glimpses of life in an outside world they had never seen before but also a heady flow of political discussion and debate from the studios of Radio-Canada in the old Ford Hotel. Being a federal enterprise, television could not be muzzled by Duplessis or influenced by him, the way he influenced the press, and in bringing about the gradual liberalization of life in Quebec no stimulus would be more important than television.

～

By 1957, the tide was turning against the authoritarianism of Maurice Duplessis. In March of that year the Supreme Court ruled that his infamous Padlock Law was *ultra vires* and must be wiped off the statute books of Quebec. No longer would the police be able to padlock any house for up to a year, throwing its residents out onto the street, on the suspicion that it was a source of communist propaganda (what constituted "communism" never being defined). The battle against this law, which had been in force for twenty years, was led by Frank Scott, the brilliant McGill law professor who was also a leading poet. Vigorous opposition by Duplessis's lawyers did not avail against Scott's forceful arguments that the Padlock Law was not only an invasion of a federal jurisdiction but also an effort at thought control and an abridgement of the basic freedoms of speech, press and public assembly.

Two years later Scott won another victory over the premier, this time by the conclusion of a case that had been bouncing in and out of the courts for twelve years. Soon after his election in 1944, Duplessis began what he called his "war without mercy" against the Witnesses of Jehovah, a proselytizing sect prone to denouncing the Catholic Church. Witnesses by the hundred were arrested for distributing their tracts on street corners, and as soon as they were arrested they would be bailed out by Frank Roncarelli, the prosperous owner of a Crescent Street restaurant. Infuriated by this, Duplessis ordered the cancellation of the restaurant's liquor licence, a move that led to its closing and to Roncarelli's eventual bankruptcy. Roncarelli's suit for damages finally ended up in the Supreme Court, with Frank Scott arguing that political power was not the same thing as legal authority. The court ruled in Roncarelli's favour and ordered Duplessis, being personally responsible for his impoverishment, to pay him, out of his own pocket, forty-six thousand dollars in damages and costs. Scott's victory made him a hero at McGill, and at the law students' annual dance there was a large banner stretched across the hall emblazoned with a knight on horseback and the words "KNIGHT F.R. SCOTT VANQUISHES NIGHT DUPLESSIS." Even the *Montreal Star*, Duplessis's old chum, had to applaud. "The judgement," the *Star* said, in an editorial, "puts a curb on the exercise of arbitrary authority and establishes the supremacy of the rule of law in this country."

Public disapproval of Duplessis was mounting. Quebec universities were starved for funds, but when Ottawa offered them money Duplessis forbade them to accept it, on the grounds that this would be a federal intrusion into a provincial domain, an invasion of Quebec's cherished autonomy. A delegation of university students came to see him, to explain that French Canadians would never be able to compete for jobs with the English unless their educational system was greatly improved, which would require increased funding. But Duplessis refused to meet the students. They waited outside his office day after day for a month, but he still refused to meet them. Meanwhile the universities would have to make do with the meagre funds that he doled out to them, erratically and at his pleasure. At the end of February 1959, he was telling the legislature that he would never weaken in doing his duty to resist Ottawa's "meddling" in education. "As long as I have a breath of life I will not fail," he said. "My last word will be 'I will never surrender.'" Six months later Maurice Duplessis was dead, suddenly, at the age of sixty-nine.

The following year, in the election of 1960, the Liberals came back into power, after being in feeble opposition for sixteen years. Quebec was now on the threshold of the Quiet Revolution that would so radically change life in the province. It was the revolution that was being plotted all along during the years of the Duplessis regime, the revolution that would reflect the struggles of labour leaders, educators, liberal priests, artists and writers, the militancy of people like Pierre Trudeau, Thérèse Casgrain, Jean Marchand, Jacques Hébert and Gérard Pelletier. As Pelletier would write, years later, in his splendid and aptly titled memoir *Years of Impatience*, "Most chroniclers of our recent evolution place the starting line at the beginning of the Quiet Revolution, i.e., in 1960. To my mind, this is the finish line. By the end of the '50s we were already programmed decisively, irreversibly. The play was written; all we had to do was act it out."

Quebec had now firmly emerged into the twentieth century and it was widely agreed that *la Grande Noirceur*, the Great Darkness of the Duplessis regime, was a bad dream that ought to be forgotten. But eighteen years after his death, on the grounds of the parliament buildings in Quebec City, a statue of this odious man was unveiled. The Parti Québécois was now in power and the premier, René Lévesque, officiated at the unveiling. Although his party did not share Duplessis's economic and social policies, Duplessis's xenophobia was a quality that could always warm the heart of a separatist.

13

1960:
"Montreal Is Bursting at the Seams"

Reign on, majestic Ville Marie!
Spread wide thy ample robes of state!
The heralds cry that thou art great;
And proud are thy young sons of thee
Mistress of half a continent. . . .

The poem, entitled "Montreal," resounded with the orotund optimism of the 1880s when it was written by William Lighthall, an
ambitious lawyer who later became mayor of Westmount. In those
days the city might well have been seen as mistress of half a continent, what with the new railway stretching west to the Pacific and
the river, busier than ever with ocean shipping, flowing happily east
toward Europe. The optimism on the part of some writers was even
more bombastic in 1915, when a local business yearbook asserted
that "Montreal will some day rival New York as the centre of the
continent's commerce. Even now, there are indications of nervousness on the part of the residents of Manhattan Isle." As the decades
passed, New York's nervousness abated somewhat, but in Canada
Montreal remained a force to be reckoned with, a city that seemed
forever to be spreading William Lighthall's ample robes of state.
"Montreal Is Bursting at the Seams," an article in *Saturday Night* proclaimed in 1960. Which city in the future would be Canada's greatest? the article asked, and it answered by saying, "Latest trends show
that this title rests firmly where it always did – with Montreal. And
the current growth of this metropolis indicates that the day when

287

the title must be handed over is not yet in sight." In other words, the challenge from Toronto was still faint and distant.

It was the phenomenal pace of new construction in the city that gave rise to all that optimism. To alleviate the cruel post-war housing shortage, some ten thousand new dwellings went up each year between 1946 and 1952, as the city spread out into the suburbs. But it was the dramatic transformation of the downtown area that attracted most attention. It began with the construction of the Laurentien Hotel, a flashy, twenty-three-storey intruder among the venerable grey buildings that surrounded Dominion Square. It was completed in February 1948, and for the first time Montrealers beheld a building clad in aluminum, the hotel's bright skin gleaming in the winter sun, harbinger of a new and dazzling modernity. Construction had gone ahead despite the misgivings of purists who felt that this cocky facade would be an affront to the solemn dignity of the square. But when the Laurentien was torn down, only twenty-eight years later, to make way for a more imposing structure, there was again an outcry from conservationists, who by now had grown accustomed to its face.

The Laurentien was at the corner of Windsor and Dorchester streets, and it was the widening of Dorchester, from Atwater to Delormier, that was the key to the transformation of downtown Montreal. City Hall announced the plan in the fall of 1948: shabby old Dorchester Street would be reincarnated as an imposing Dorchester Boulevard (many years later to become Boulevard René Lévesque), and in the process a score of nondescript commercial buildings and tourist homes would be demolished. Some landmarks would also come down, like the old Roxy Theatre near the Main and, in the east end, the old Italian church, Notre Dame du Mont Carmel, part of it dating back to the eighteenth century, when it was the home of Lord Dorchester, governor of British North America.

On the new boulevard, construction of the Queen Elizabeth Hotel got under way in 1955, and when it was finished three years later special trains and planes brought scores of dignitaries and celebrities to town for the opening ceremonies, three days of glittering, bibulous festivity. There were lunches, dinners, flag-raisings, fashion shows and a charity ball where high society danced to the music of Guy Lombardo's orchestra. A sixty-page press kit emphasized that this was the biggest new hotel in the world and the first major hotel designed especially to accommodate conventions. In the Grand Salon three thousand delegates could sit down together, while other meetings could be held simultaneously in a dozen smaller salons. Montreal would now become a major centre for international conventions.

The hotel would also be the site of banquets of the Beaver Club, revived now after being defunct for almost 150 years. The original club was formed in 1785 by pioneer Montreal fur traders, like the Frobishers and the McTavishes. To be a member, one had to have spent a winter in the hazardous, unmapped Canadian northwest. Back in Montreal, banquets of the Beaver Club were not without their own perils: at the 1808 dinner, the thirty-two gentlemen attending consumed twenty-nine bottles of madeira, nineteen bottles of port, fourteen bottles of porter, twelve quarts of ale "and a little brandy, gin and negus." As the evening progressed, members sang old voyageur songs at the top of their voices and got down on the floor, where they used swords, walking sticks and pokers to paddle their imaginary canoes in time to their songs. Now, in 1959, modern-day executive buccaneers from enterprises like Dominion Textiles and Imperial Oil would do their best to revive that old Montreal jollity, fuelled by brimming beakers of Johnny Walker Black Label and some of that old negus, also known as *loup-garou* – hot red wine laced with rum. No one would enter into the spirit of the evening more heartily than Donald Gordon, wearing side-whiskers and a fur-trader costume. Gordon was president of the Canadian National Railways, which owned the Queen Elizabeth Hotel, and he was renowned for being able to run his railway in the morning, no matter how ferocious his hangover.

Queen Elizabeth herself was in town in 1959, along with Prince Phillip. They had come to open the new St. Lawrence Seaway, the gigantic project, just completed, which would allow ocean-going ships to proceed past Montreal into the Great Lakes. President

Eisenhower was here, too, as the seaway was a joint Canada–U.S. venture, and he joined the royal couple, and Prime Minister Diefenbaker, on the deck of the royal yacht *Britannia* as she went through the locks into Lake St. Louis. There, between Ile Perrot and Beauharnois, fifteen American and Canadian warships were lined up, and they fired a twenty-one-gun salute as the *Britannia* went by. Twelve hundred sailors doffed their caps and cheered as the heads of state looked on from the yacht. But earlier on this sultry June day, at the ceremonies in St. Lambert that officially opened the seaway, only twenty thousand people showed up, although preparations had been made to accommodate four times as many. And during the Queen's speech, there were only a few light bursts of applause, while President Eisenhower's address was interrupted half a dozen times by applause that was prolonged and vigorous.

The tone of the city's reception of royalty was distinctly different now from what it had been twenty years earlier, in 1939, when the queen's parents, King George and Queen Elizabeth, had visited Montreal. Today large crowds still lined the sidewalks as the royal motorcade drove by, but the mood was more one of curiosity than of adulation; fealty to the Crown and reverence for all things British were in decline. In Outremont, two men were arrested for tearing down street decorations welcoming the queen, saying they really didn't want her in town. And in a *Gazette* story headed "Royalty Can Wear Frown," reporter Bill Bantey said that the queen seemed intimidated by crowds and bored by lengthy speeches. "At these times," Bantey wrote, "the face of the queen is not that of a happy woman." A report of this kind could never have appeared in the *Gazette* of twenty years earlier, when the paper devoted acres of print to unquestioning veneration of the queen's parents and urged its readers, in a front-page editorial, to cheer as loudly as possible.

The queen, of course, visited the new hotel that had been named after her, and while she was there she was shown a model of the new building that was going up right across the street, on Dorchester Boulevard. Place Ville Marie, its promoters promised, would become as much Montreal's major landmark as the Eiffel Tower was in Paris. It would rise 550 feet in height, with forty-two floors of office space, making it the tallest and largest structure in Canada. It would house major corporations, four of which would have their own separate ground-floor lobbies. Its unusual cruciform shape would echo the historic cross on top of Mount Royal, little more than a mile away. And the building would finally cover the gaping hole in the ground north of Dorchester, where the railway tunnel emerged from under the mountain. The hole – a huge, soot-stained open cut – had disfigured the area ever since the construction of the tunnel forty-six years earlier, and none of the many projects that had been envisaged, over the years, to solve the problem had ever come to fruition. But now the solution, a visionary solution, was at hand, thanks to an unlikely combination of talents.

In previous years, the major office buildings of downtown Montreal had been put up by the Anglo-Scottish business elite, and designed mostly by Anglo-Scottish architects. But the Place Ville Marie project marked the entrance of new players in the creation of a new cityscape, and a new kind of cooperation between men of very different backgrounds. Of the six major figures who made it all happen, two were Scots, two were Jews, one – the mayor of Montreal – was French Canadian and one – the architect – was a Chinese American. William Zeckendorf, the New York Jew who was the developer and prime mover of the project, would later note in his memoirs that getting these diverse egos to work together was "no honeyed love feast," especially with James Muir, president of the Royal Bank, which would be the project's major tenant, apt to refer to I.M. Pei, the brilliant architect, as "that damned Chinaman." Zeckendorf referred to the belligerent bank president as "that ruffian," but gradually all the collaborators in the project came to respect each other. In the era of the many-martini executive lunch, Zeckendorf came to have particular admiration for Donald Gordon, whose CNR owned the land they were building on, as "one of the few men I know who could outdrink me."

Zeckendorf's vision involved nothing less than creating a new centre of gravity and focal point for the city. For well over a century, big business in Montreal had centred on St. James Street, the Wall Street of Canada, but now the developer from New York proposed to lure it uptown, to where there would be room for expansion, in more modern buildings. Zeckendorf began by persuading the Royal Bank to relocate its head office and become the first tenant of his Place Ville Marie, which he described as "our great masculine building standing up against the Montreal skyline like a man surrounded by boys." The bank's radical move shocked the ultra-conservative business community, but gradually other companies started to follow it up the hill to Dorchester Boulevard, into Place Ville Marie and other new buildings. Canadian Industries Limited moved into a new building at Dorchester and University, and the Bank of Commerce put up its own skyscraper – or cloud-piercer, as one writer described it – at Dorchester and Peel. "Because of what we did," William Zeckendorf announced, "Montreal and Canada will never be the same again."

In 1961, an advertisement in the *New York Times* with the heading "Montreal on the Move!" showed an aerial photo of the city's downtown, with Place Ville Marie in the centre. "Five years ago," the ad said, "sixteen of the buildings appearing in the picture were not there." In its article entitled "Montreal Is Bursting at the Seams," *Saturday Night* noted how Montreal was ahead of Toronto in many respects, with 5,200 industrial establishments as against Toronto's 4,800. "Montreal today has Canada's greatest concentration of industry, largest reservoir of manpower and most extensive retail market. . . . It will require something so far unforeseen to demote Montreal to second best."

It was a time when the city basked in the glow of achievement and international recognition. In 1946, Montreal was chosen to be the headquarters of the International Civil Aviation Organization, winning out over Paris and Geneva, both of which had been contenders for the housing of this United Nations agency. The International Air Transport Association, the airlines' organization, followed suit, also making Montreal its headquarters. The city was now the world capital of aviation, but as such it was ill-served by its airport at Dorval, which was still operating with the temporary wooden buildings put up for the Ferry Command during the war.

After a decade of complaints from passengers, who were now regularly flying the Atlantic, the federal government finally started work on a modern terminal and facilities that would be the equal of any in North America. And a few miles to the east of the airport, on Côte de Liesse Road, another new federal structure was taking shape in the mid-'50s, the massive new studios, laboratories and offices of the National Film Board. The government had decided to move its filmmaking agency to Montreal despite the hostility of Premier Duplessis, who branded the NFB as being communist dominated and forbade the showing of its films in Quebec schools. The board had been located in Ottawa ever since its founding in 1939, but it was moving to Montreal to be closer to French talent and, according to J.W. Pickersgill, the secretary of state, to affirm that even in the Quebec of Maurice Duplessis Montreal was still part of Canada.

The NFB, winner of scores of international awards, was now pioneering in the making of films especially for the new medium, television. One of the first of these films to be set in Montreal was *New Hearts for Old*, a docudrama in which a victim of a heart attack was being treated at the Institut de Cardiologie de Montréal. It was probably the first time TV viewers were able to enjoy squishy close-ups of open-heart surgery. The Institut de Cardiologie, presided over by Dr. Paul David, was the only institution in Canada that was devoted entirely to the study and treatment of heart disease. The work that was being done there was part of the great flowering of medical research that took place in Montreal in the years after the war. In his laboratory at the University of Montreal, Dr. Armand Frappier, a microbiologist, developed vaccines for use in combatting tuberculosis, which was still a menace in Quebec, and led campaigns to immunize children. Also at the University of Montreal, Dr. Hans Selye, an endocrinologist, attracted wide attention with his theories about the role of stress in the development of disease; his book *The Stress of Life*, written for the general public, and many magazine articles about Selye, gave new currency to the word stress in everyday conversation. Meanwhile, many international honours were being bestowed on Dr. Wilder Penfield, of the Montreal Neurological

Institute, for his discoveries about the workings of the brain and the surgical procedure he developed for the treatment of epilepsy. At the Allan Memorial Institute, its founder, Dr. Ewen Cameron, won wide recognition for his innovative treatments of psychiatric disorders and became president of the American Psychiatric Association. Unfortunately, Cameron's ill-advised "deprogramming" experiments left many patients much sicker than they had been before, after undergoing sensory deprivation and massive electroshock treatment, as well as being given hallucinogenic drugs and drugs that put them to sleep for weeks. More humane and fruitful experiments in the treatment of mental illness were being conducted at the Verdun Protestant Hospital by Dr. Heinz Lehmann, who introduced the use of chlorpromazine in North America in 1954. This anti-psychotic drug, the first of the major tranquillizers, helped bring about a revolution in psychiatry and the release of thousands of patients from mental hospitals.

∾

Johnny Vago and his friends, all new immigrants, had very little money in their pockets but enough for coffee at Drake's restaurant, on St. Catherine Street. When they finished their coffees, the waitress asked them if they'd like to have something more. "No," said Johnny, "we just want to sit and talk." Snatching away their empty cups, the waitress said, "I'm sorry, you can't just sit here and talk. If you want to talk, you'll have to have something else to eat or drink." Johnny Vago and his friends were dismayed. Here was another of Canada's cruelties, as harsh as the February wind that was howling outside the restaurant. In Europe, you went to the coffeehouse to meet friends and gossip and spend hours in philosophical discourse. But there were no coffeehouses in Montreal, no refuges from the tiny, cramped apartment Vago was living in, with no furniture to speak of, on Durocher Street. He had come to Montreal from Hungary, via Vienna and Paris. Now he was a student of architecture by day and a dishwasher by night. "When I first came here," he recalled, many years later, "I wanted to leave right away." But he decided to stay and "build my own world." And in doing so, through the 1950s, Johnny Vago changed the flavour of downtown life in Montreal.

The quality of the coffee in Drake's and elsewhere, Vago found, was really bad, and so he imported what may have been the first espresso machine in Canada. He installed it in the Colibri Restaurant on Mansfield Street, and here you were free to sit and gossip as long as you liked. It was the beginning of the new espresso culture, and in subsequent years Vago designed and built them all, the Hungarian coffeehouses – the Carmen, the Riviera, the Pam-Pam, the Tokay, the Coffee Mill. He was the first to put tables on the sidewalk, outside the Riviera, but Montreal was not quite ready to become Europe overnight; the city fathers felt that outdoor drinkers and diners had to be protected from the gaze of passersby, so they made Vago put up a five-foot fence around his terrace.

The European way of doing things that new immigrants like Johnny Vago brought to the city in the 1950s soon caught on with the younger generation of established Montrealers, and in her radio program *Tea and Trumpets* Mary Peate issued a warning, tongue in cheek, about the perils posed by the new coffeehouses on Stanley Street. "Mothers of this city," she said, "heed the telltale signs of bohemianism. When your daughter leaves the house, does she rub off her lipstick? Does she sit cross-legged – *on the floor?* Is there a copy of *On the Road* in her locker? Is she starting to memorize lines from Allen Ginsberg's *Howl?* Are certain words creeping into her conversation – words like "cool" and "like, wow!"? Is she dressing in black skirts, black turtlenecks and black stockings? Mothers, are you aware of the calibre of disaster indicated by the presence of a coffeehouse in your community?"

The waves of immigration from Europe in the post-war period and in the 1950s greatly changed the complexion of that part of the city that was not French. In 1941 there were almost twice as many people on the Island of Montreal who were of British origin than there were of "others," as the statistics defined those who were neither English nor French. But by 1961 there were slightly more of the "others" than of the British. This was due largely to a massive influx of immigrants from southern Europe – Portugal, Italy and Greece. Italians came in sufficient numbers to become the largest of the non-British communities, and they now outnumbered the Jews, who previously had formed the largest group. If the Hungarians brought espresso and exotic tortes to the city, the Italians introduced pizza. And people visiting Montreal from other parts of Canada marvelled at the strange viands that were offered to them – the Boursault cheese, the *babas au rhum*, the *rigojancsi*, the chopped liver.

The more polyglot the city became, the more it pleased David Banks, the self-taught linguist. When he immigrated from Russia, Banks spoke Russian, Romanian and Yiddish, and in Montreal he quickly learned English and French. In the years that followed, the '40s and '50s, he added one language after another, eventually speaking eleven of them fluently. He did this while operating his outdoor newsstand at the corner of Stanley and St. Catherine streets, working fourteen hours a day selling newspapers and magazines, and taking delight in chatting with his customers in Greek, Italian, Hungarian or whatever. Edmund Wilson, the American literary critic, discovered Banks during a visit to Montreal in the late '50s and took note of his linguistic prowess in his book *O Canada*. For Wilson this was more evidence that Montreal had become a uniquely cosmopolitan city. "I was astonished to discover," he wrote, "that Montreal, once the drab and crass provincial town that I vaguely remembered from my youth, had undoubtedly become one of the most attractive cities on the North American continent."

One of the noteworthy things that changed during those twenty years was the aroma of the streets. In 1939, horses pulling wagons were very much in evidence, and each healthy horse could create twenty-five pounds of droppings every day. On some streets, on a hot summer afternoon, this could make for a powerful fragrance. That year, there were seven horse dealers in the city, seventy-two black-smiths to shoe the horses and eleven shops where wagons and sleighs were being made for them to pull. But by 1959 there were no more horse dealers, no more carriage makers and only a dozen blacksmiths. The truck had supplanted the horse; an ancient form of pollution had been replaced by a modern one.

For young boys, this was a disappointment. In winter, frozen "horseballs" made excellent pucks for street hockey. And in summer you might be able to hitch a ride on a bread wagon, like that of Horace Holdgate, who delivered for Wonder Bread in NDG and Hampstead. His horse knew the route so well that Holdgate could doze off to sleep, at six in the morning, as the horse pulled the wagon northward from the bakery with its load of fresh bread and cakes; when the wagon stopped, Holdgate would wake up, knowing that he had arrived at the door of his first customer. From then on, horse and salesman (Holdgate refused to be called a breadman) worked as a team, moving down the streets from customer to customer, the horse always knowing where to stop. Old horses were a pleasure to work with, but training a new horse could be difficult, especially if it was skittish or frisky. Such a horse was liable to bolt and could be dangerous at an intersection, not so much for pedestrians, who could hear it coming, but for cars that were just entering the intersection.

Icemen as well as breadmen and milkmen depended on horses in the '40s. In Verdun, during the war, Graydon Fyckes worked as an iceman at the age of fourteen, straining to lift the heavy blocks into the top of tall iceboxes. As his horse clip-clopped through the streets, he had to keep his eye open for the police, as it was forbidden to shout "Ice!" at the top of one's voice – an iceman's only form of advertising. But after the war the iceman's days were numbered; people had money now and war industries were quickly retooled to foster domestic bliss with things like electric refrigerators. The disappearance of the old wooden icebox was greeted with universal relief; no longer would the iceman have to come clomping up the stairs every other day and no longer would the housewife have to remember to empty the water tray from under the icebox – if this task was forgotten, there could be an overflow and a small kitchen flood, sometimes damaging the ceiling of the people downstairs. Also, with refrigerators, there would be no crises like the great ice famine of August 1947, when a prolonged heat wave practically wiped out reserves of ice, which was harvested every winter, in huge blocks, from the frozen St. Lawrence River. With their icehouses empty, some dealers went as far afield as Boston to look for supplies. Housewives were dismayed to find that the price of a twenty-five-pound block of ice had soared to fifty cents – when it was available.

Besides refrigerators, the new automatic washing machines were helping to diminish domestic drudgery. These marvels would spin-dry as well as agitate, so wet clothes and sheets no longer had to be laboriously cranked through wringers. Makers of the new automatics advertised that the lady of the house could now do her laundry without getting her hands wet. The new technology also made storefront laundromats possible, and by 1958 there were a dozen of them in Montreal, like the Buanderie Automatique on Mount Royal East and the Duluth Automatic Laundry on Duluth. But when it came to shirts, the meticulous gentleman usually preferred to have them done by hand, at a Chinese laundry, where the collars would be deftly starched. In 1958 there were more than two hundred Chinese laundries in Montreal – storefronts with the familiar little red sign, small family enterprises like Woo Yee's on Decarie, George Yip's on Somerled and Happy Charlie's on Pine Avenue West.

A starched collar was an asset in the business world, where it was important to look as spiffy as possible. And an ambitious young man, sitting in the No. 64 streetcar on his way down to St. James Street, might well be staring down at his shoes and fretting that they had plenty of suburban dust on them. In that case, as soon as he got off at the Craig Street terminus he would be well advised to hurry over to the White Palace Shoe Shine Parlor, near the corner of St. Peter, to get his brogues glistening again. If all Steve's chairs at the White Palace were occupied, he might try Nick Campannolo's shinery in the basement of the Insurance Exchange Building. In 1958 there were forty-two shoe-shine establishments in Montreal. Some, like the American Shoe Shining and Hat Cleaning Parlor on Windsor, just south of St. Antoine, dealt with headgear as well as footgear, for a gentleman's fedora had to be spotless, and headbands discoloured by sweat could be a vexatious problem in the hot summer months. There were six establishments in town that specialized in hat cleaning, like Tony Pappas's place on Mount Royal East. Tony was widely known for his artistry with the steam block, and even if your hat was severely battered he could restore it to its original elegant shape.

But new kinds of informality were becoming acceptable in the 1950s, and some businessmen no longer felt they had to wear a hat whenever they were outdoors. The very stiffly starched collar was also in retreat, thanks to a new miracle called the drip-dry shirt. It was a decade in which every year seemed to bring forth some great new modern convenience, from fitted bedsheets to electric can-openers. For the new suburbs, there were power lawnmowers and portable barbecues. Transistor radios made their appearance, as did coloured telephones and hi-fi consoles to replace old gramophones. Substantial increases in earnings gave people the money to buy these creature comforts. At the beginning of the decade the average weekly industrial wage was around forty-five dollars; by the end of the decade it had risen to more than seventy-three dollars, the increase considerably outstripping inflation.

More people than ever could now afford to own automobiles, and a favourite Saturday-night excursion, during the summer, was a spin up Decarie Boulevard to the Orange Julep. Architecturally more innovative than Place Ville Marie, the Julep was destined to become the Eiffel Tower of the new Decarie Strip, north of Snowdon Junction. It was simply a gigantic orange-coloured orange with a counter at the bottom from which glasses of a sweet, foamy, orangey concoction were sold. It was the brainchild of Hermas Gibeau, who always said he wanted to build the biggest orange in the world, from which to sell his secret-formula drink. He and his wife would live inside their three-storey orange, and raise their children there. When the war was over and building materials became available, Hermas, who said he was descended from the Greek god Hermes, finally built his mighty citrus, mostly out of cement, and grinned happily when it was denounced as a monument to bad taste. But it could be seen from miles away, and it dominated the new, garish roadside culture of Decarie Boulevard. For high-school seniors, it was the place to go on Saturday night. They'd sit in daddy's Studebaker in Hermas's parking lot, roll down the window and wait for the carhops to bring them their juleps and hot dogs. The carhops were girls in short white pleated skirts and they operated on roller skates.

More and more Studebakers, Chevvies, Nash Metropolitans and Hudson Terraplanes were heading north on Fridays, to cottages in the Laurentians. Prosperity in the '50s was making summer cottages and vacations available to people who never before had been able to afford them. But the narrow Highway 11 to the north was becoming too crowded and slow, and a wide autoroute, the first of Quebec's new toll-roads, was under construction. It was officially opened in the summer of 1959, the first twenty-five miles of it, and within hours of the opening ceremonies this ribbon of speed hosted its first accident – one man killed and seven persons sent to hospital.

~

"Wrecker, Spare That Cornice!" said the heading on the article in the *Montrealer* magazine. "The process of change," the article said, "is tearing down the Montreal we have known and loved. New buildings, new streets, new storefronts all combine to try to reproduce the appearance of Buffalo or Cleveland or Toronto." The magazine was calling for the creation of a municipal authority that would preserve what was best in "the city of grey stone, of ancient trees, of graceful steeples, narrow streets, many languages and French fried potatoes." A similar sentiment was expressed in John Glassco's poem "Montreal," in which he blamed the mayor for the erosion of the city's beauty in a verse that began with the words "I do not like you, Jean Drapeau." It was Drapeau's "lipless grin / Under the little merciless moustache," Glassco wrote, that revealed how he was conspiring "to make our city – in the modern fashion – / Not beautiful / But only big, and rich, and dull."

"Onwards and upwards" was the principle that spurred on the builders of the 1950s, but the demolition of fine old buildings was a price that had to be paid for progress. Just after the one-hundredth anniversary of its founding, the St. James's Club had to come down

to make way for Place Ville Marie. This elegant old Victorian structure, with its cornices, bay windows and balconies, stood at the
corner of Dorchester and University. Its membership in the nineteenth century had included not only the city's leading businessmen
but also military men like Lieutenant-Colonel Garnet Wolseley, who
one day would lead the government troops in the Riel Rebellion.
Another famous member was Dr. James Barry who, when he died in
1865, was discovered to have actually been a woman in disguise – the
only woman ever to have belonged to this very masculine club for
wealthy gentlemen. But all this history, redolent of fine port and
cigars, faded somewhat when the old building came down and the
club's members, grumbling loudly, made their way across the street
to new quarters in a sterile office building.

The next historic building to go was Drury's Restaurant, which
had been on the south side of Dominion Square since 1887. It was
a restaurant modelled on an old London chophouse, with several
small rooms, dark-panelled walls and high-backed chairs upholstered
in leather with brass studs. Its steaks and chops were the best, and
its wine cellar superb. Visiting dignitaries were often taken to dine
at Drury's, people like Sir Anthony Eden, Charles Boyer, Eleanor
Roosevelt and Fiorello LaGuardia, mayor of New York. But now, in
1959, the City decreed that Drury's must serve its last sirloin before
November 30, and then it had to come down. It was to be another
victim of civic improvement – the extension southward of Dominion
Square and a realignment of two streets. There was a great outcry
from prominent citizens and a petition to the premier of Quebec –
but all to no avail.

Another institution forced to disappear was the *Herald*, published
as a daily newspaper since 1811. It was a tabloid that came out late
in the morning and was bought for five cents by downtown office
workers to read at lunch. It was much appreciated for its coverage of
sports, and its tone was jaunty, even a bit raffish, in contrast to the
solemnity of its two competitors, the *Star* and the *Gazette*. The
paper's revenues had been increasing, but they were outstripped
by rising costs, and its owner, who had been losing money on it for
some time, decided to close it down. And so, on October 18, 1957,

Montrealers bought their last issue of the *Herald*. "Thus with head held high," its final editorial concluded, "with a nostalgic tear and more than a little difficulty we say it at last: FAREWELL."

The front page of this last issue featured a photo by David Bier, the great hockey photographer, showing Maurice Richard ("the Durable Dervish") scoring his 499th goal for the Canadiens in a game against the Maple Leafs. The paper's lead story that day told of an announcement by the chief of police to the effect that everyone arrested for skulduggery during the forthcoming municipal elections would be held in jail until charged. No one would be quickly released without being charged, as had been the case with twenty-eight thugs arrested in the lively elections of 1954. Inside this last *Herald*, readers learned, from Walter Winchell's New York column, that "Aly and Zsa-Zsa have Londoners agog." A few pages later there was an ad informing them that Patachou, "The Rage of Paris," was singing at the El Morocco on Closse Street, across from the Forum. In the movies, *The Sun Also Rises*, starring Tyrone Power, Ava Gardner and Errol Flynn, was playing at the Snowdon, the Strand, the Outremont and the Seville – four theatres all slated to eventually close their doors, victims of television.

Advertisements in the last *Herald* included a full page of offerings by the city's eleven Handy Andy stores, featuring four-year automobile batteries for $15.45 and snow tires for $11.99. Dunn's Famous Steak House had a big ad drawing attention to its twelve-ounce charcoal-broiled rib steak with potato *latkes* for $1.50. Dunn's ad also pointed out that "we are famous for our black radish with onions and chicken fat." Up the street from Dunn's, the English and Scotch Woollen Company was offering made-to-measure suits for men for $66. They were of imported worsteds or tweeds and came with two pairs of pants. And in the classified section, Dr. Melillo reminded readers, for the last time, that his speciality was "genito-urinary, skin, blood, glands, sexual nervous disorders!" It was to the ever-sympathetic Dr. Melillo, who liked to use that exclamation mark in his ad, that a young man would hasten if he suspected that he had picked up a dose of the clap on De Bullion Street.

The last day of the newspaper's existence was a sad one. "Now

The Herald, as we write, is going," Elmer Ferguson, the sports editor, wrote in his last column. "The editorial rooms are filled with staff, editors and writers. Some veterans who were with The Herald years back have dropped in. . . . Ordinarily there would be chatter, badinage, laughter. But the room is quiet, as fittingly becomes what is close to a wake for the dead. A grand old institution is passing. Hearts go with it."

~

The city's growth during the 1940s and '50s was phenomenal. In 1939 there were hundreds of farms on the Island of Montreal, but twenty years later they were almost all gone. By 1961 the population of the island was almost 1,750,000 – 56 percent greater than it had been twenty years earlier. There seemed to be no limit to the city's expansion, and there was talk of a subway to relieve the traffic congestion in the streets. Advocates of a subway got a great boost for their cause from Colonel S.H. Bingham of the New York Transportation Commission when he visited Montreal and told the city fathers that a subway would not only solve all problems of urban transit but would also serve as a handy shelter if the Russians were to lob an atomic bomb at the city. But in 1957 Pierre DesMarais, chairman of the city's executive committee, declared that the proposal to build a subway was impractical. The city was simply getting too big for a subway to provide adequate service at reasonable rates. The population of the metropolitan area, the city's traffic department had estimated, would eventually reach 7,401,500. It was buses that would solve the problem, he said, and buses would eventually replace all the streetcars. The overhead electric trolley lines that crisscrossed the city would all come down, and hundreds of miles of track, embedded in the streets, would be torn up.

Two years later, on the afternoon of Sunday, August 30, 1959, large crowds turned out to say goodbye to the last streetcars, making their last run in a ceremonial procession. There were fifteen cars in the parade and they travelled the No. 54 route, along Rosemount Boulevard, down Papineau, along Notre Dame to Place d'Armes and then back again. First came two of the old Golden Chariots, the open observation cars, bearing Mayor Sarto Fournier, members of the Montreal Transportation Commission and various civic officials and other dignitaries. Then, borne on large trucks, came two ancient horse cars, one with wheels for summer and the other with sled runners for winter. Next came the spunky old Rocket, which made its debut in 1892 as Montreal's first electric streetcar. The old black funeral car, which used to take mourners and the deceased out to the Pointe aux Trembles Cemetery, was omitted from the parade, as was the *panier à salade* car, which used to take prisoners from Bordeaux Jail to the courthouse and back. But there were other historic cars, including some that carried tramways employees decked out in period costume – top hats, loud checked suits, 1920s flapper dresses, feather boas.

The crowds were thickest along Rosemount Boulevard, standing six deep in some places. Some people had brought chairs and picnic lunches. As each car went by, one elderly woman cried out, "Good-bye, old car!" She was old enough to remember the last of the horse cars, sixty-five years earlier. The loudest cheers were those that greeted J.P. St. Onge, the motorman driving one of the oldest one-man cars. He had been with the company for forty-two years and had been on the No. 54 run for decades. Former passengers, standing on the sidewalk, applauded him all along the route and there were tears in his eyes as he clanged his bell and headed down the last stretch of track.

At the end of the line, a ceremonial arch had been erected for the occasion. One by one the old streetcars went under the arch and, for the last time, into the car barns. After the last car had gone through, the mayor and the president of the Transportation Commission pulled shut two large gates that were inscribed with the words *"La Fin d'une Epoque* – The End of an Era."

Acknowledgements

Warm thanks to Mavis Gallant who, during an exchange of letters, said that someone ought to write a book about Montreal in the 1940s, the city she remembers so well. It should be, she said, the sort of book that would take note of the phenomenon of Lili St. Cyr. After brooding about this for some time, I took it upon myself to attempt this task, adding the 1950s to the scheme.

I am very grateful for the assiduous efforts of Suzanne Côté-Gauthier, Serge Durflinger, Terri Foxman, Jordanna Fraiberg and Brenda Leaver, who helped with the research. Serge, Ron Finegold and Herb Whittaker read portions of the manuscript, to unearth any errors, although I must take full responsibility for any errors that may survive.

I am indebted to a number of librarians and archivists for the help they generously extended to me: Phebe Chartrand of the McGill University Archives, François David of the Centre de Recherche Lionel-Groulx, Nancy Dunton of Heritage Montreal, Ronald Finegold and Carol Katz of the Jewish Public Library, Dr. John D. Jackson of the Centre for Broadcasting Studies at Concordia University, Donna MacHutchin of the *Gazette* library, Nancy Marrelli of the Concordia University Archives, Ann Moffat of the Westmount Public Library, Monique Laliberté of the Centre d'Histoire de Montréal, Carole Ritchot and Bertrand Aubin of the Archives Nationales du Québec, and Janice Rosen and Bonnie Borenstein of the Canadian Jewish Congress Archives.

Special thanks to all those persons who consented to be interviewed and whose names are listed on another page. And thanks to many others who helped with information: Christiana Alexander, Stanley Asher, Monty Berger, Ronald Blumer, Caroline Brettell, Alex Cherney, Michel Choquette, Nini Dagenais, Robert Fulford, Ron Gibeau, Aline Gubbay, Fred Hill, Andrew Hoffmann, Stuart Idelson, Louis Jaques, Mary Cox Johnson, Dr. Joseph Kage, Nick Kasirer, Grazia Merler, Hans Moller, Dr. Sean Moore, Meilan Lam, Kevin O'Donnell, Mary Peate, Robert Sabloff, Beverley Shaffer, Norbert Schonauer, Elizabeth Wilson. If I have forgotten anyone, I beg forgiveness.

Many thanks to Beverley Slopen, my literary agent, for encouragement and ideas. And very warm thanks to my wife, Magda, for her constant support – and patience and patience.

A Note on Usage

Persons who may question my use of the term French Canadians are reminded that that was what they were called, and what they called themselves, before the term Québécois came into use in the 1960s. Montrealers who may be puzzled by a reference to St. James's Basilica, next to the Archbishop's Palace, are advised that that's what it was called before it became Mary Queen of the World Cathedral. I have called the streets Delormier rather than De Lorimier, and Rosemount rather than Rosemont, because those were the spellings common to English publications of the time. On one or two occasions I have referred to young women as girls, fully aware that I was on dangerous ground, but to do otherwise would not have been true to the era. Forgive me, *mesdames*.

Persons Interviewed

Arlene Abramovitch
Lionel Albert
Don Albin
Alison Annesley
Irving Aronovitch

Charles Baerman
Bill Bantey
Peter Barry
Evelyn Bessner
Jacques Bieler
Sheila Horn Bisaillon
Joy Boles
Beverley Boyle
Marcelle Brisson
Munro Brown
Pierre Brunelle
Paulette Buchanan

Nick Ciamarra
Frank Conlon
Suzanne Cordeau
Mary Cornell
Audrey Corrigan
Bernard Côté

Sheila Cox
Harold Cummings

Ronald Finegold
Melba Fleming
Jules Foxman
Jacques Francoeur
Graydon Fyckes

Mavis Gallant
Roland Gauthier
Abe Gersovitz
Alan B. Gold
Harry Gulkin

Frank Hanley
Helen Henry
Suzanne Herscovitch
Horace Holdgate

Stephen Jarislowsky
Thelma Johnson
Norma Jourdenais
André Juneau

Joseph Kage
Walter Klinkhoff
Irene Kon
Elena Kruger
Jadwiga Krupski

Anita Lack
Lucette Lagacé
Jean-Claude Lasry
John L. Liberman
Goldie Libman

Helen McPherson
Marguerite Daigle Mercier
Gabriel Miller
Douglas Monk

Nellie Pajackowski
Paul Pantazis
Charles Peters
Jules Pfeiffer
Don Pidgeon
Sadie Polsky

Firmino Ramos
Allan Raymond
Henryk Reizes

Sylvia Reizes
Doris Resnik
Marjorie Reynolds
Stuart Richardson
Peter Rosen
Jean Rowe
Lois Rowe
Frankie Rubinger

Norbert Schoenauer
Helaine Schwam
Betty Scott
Alfred Segall
Harry Ship
Ruth Sohmer
Harry Stillman
Ronald Sutherland

Johnny Vago

Steve Walker
Joseph Walker
Bernard Wexler
Doug Whyte
Betty Whyte
Ruth Williams
William Wolfe

Selected Bibliography

Anctil, Pierre. *Le Devoir, les Juifs et l'immigration*. Quebec: Institut Québécois de recherche sur la culture, 1988.

Anctil, Pierre, and Gary Caldwell. *Juifs et réalités juives au Québec*. Quebec: Institut Québécois de recherche sur la culture, 1984.

Angus, Fred F., and Olive Irwin Wilson. *Streetcars of Montreal*. Montreal: Canadian Railroad Historical Association, 1990.

Auger, Geneviève, and Raymonde Lamothe. *De la poêle à frire à la ligne de feu*. Montreal: Boreal Express, 1981.

Avakumovic, Ivan. *The Communist Party in Canada: A History*. Toronto: McClelland & Stewart, 1975.

Baie d'Urfé 1686–1986. Baie d'Urfé, Que.: Town of Baie d'Urfé, 1986.

Benoit, Michèle, and Roger Gratton. *Pignon sur rue: les quartiers de Montréal*. Montreal: Guérin, 1991.

Betcherman, Lita-Rose. *The Swastika and the Maple Leaf*. Toronto: Fitzhenry & Whiteside, 1975.

Beurling, George F., and Leslie Roberts. *Malta Spitfire: The Story of a Fighter Pilot*. Toronto: Oxford University Press, 1943.

Black, Conrad. *Duplessis*. Toronto: McClelland & Stewart, 1977.

Bliss, Michael. *Northern Enterprise: Five Centuries of Canadian Business*. Toronto: McClelland & Stewart, 1987.

Booth, Philip J. *The Montreal Repertory Theatre: 1930–1961*. Master's thesis, McGill University, 1989.

Bourassa, André-G., and Jean-Marc Larrue. *Les nuits de la Main*. Montreal: VLB Editeur, 1993.

Bourdon, Joseph. *Montréal-Matin: son histoire, ses histoires.* Montreal: Les Editions La Presse, 1978.

Bovey, Wilfrid. *Canadien: A Study of the French Canadians.* Toronto: J.M. Dent and Sons, 1933.

Brisson, Marcelle, and Suzanne Côté-Gauthier. *Montréal de vive mémoire 1900–1939.* Montreal: Tryptique, 1994.

Bryden, Ronald, ed. *Whittaker's Theatre.* Greenbank, Ont.: The Whittaker Project, 1985.

Callaghan, Morley. *The Loved and the Lost.* Toronto: Macmillan, 1951.

Cameron, Elspeth. *Hugh MacLennan.* Toronto: University of Toronto Press, 1981.

Casgrain, Thérèse F. *A Woman in a Man's World.* Toronto: McClelland & Stewart, 1972.

Chapin, Miriam. *Quebec Now.* Toronto: Ryerson Press, 1955.

Charbonneau, Jean-Pierre. *The Canadian Connection.* Montreal: Optimum, 1976.

Choko, Marc. *The Major Squares of Montreal.* Montreal: Meridian Press, 1990.

Clark, Gerald. *Montreal: The New Cité.* Toronto: McClelland & Stewart, 1982.

Collard, Edgar Andrew, ed. *The McGill You Knew.* Don Mills, Ont.: Longman Canada, 1975.

———. *The Saint James's Club.* Montreal: Privately printed, 1957.

Cook, Ramsay. *Canada and the French-Canadian Question.* Toronto: Macmillan, 1966.

Cooper, John Irwin. *The History of the Montreal Hunt.* Montreal: Montreal Hunt Club, 1953.

———. *Montreal, A Brief History.* Montreal: McGill-Queen's University Press, 1969.

CSN-CEQ. *The History of the Labor Movement in Quebec.* Montreal: Black Rose Books, 1987.

Darsigny, Maryse, et al. *Ces femmes qui ont bâti Montréal.* Montreal: Remue-Ménage, 1994.

de Bordes, Eliane Catela, ed. *Le Mémorial du Québec.* Montreal: Les Editions du Mémorial, 1979.

de Grandmont, Eloi, et al. *Dix ans de Théâtre du Nouveau Monde*. Montreal: Leméac, 1961.

Delisle, Esther. *The Traitor and the Jew*. Montreal: Robert Davies, 1993.

Demchinsky, Bryan. *Montreal Then and Now*. Montreal: The Gazette, 1985.

Déry, Gustave. *A la découverte de Montréal*. Ville d'Anjou, Que.: Privately printed, 1987.

Desbarats, Peter. *The State of Quebec*. Toronto: McClelland & Stewart, 1965.

D'Iberville-Moreau, Luc. *Lost Montreal*. Toronto: Oxford University Press, 1975.

Djwa, Sandra. *The Politics of the Imagination: A Life of F.R. Scott*. Toronto: McClelland & Stewart, 1987.

Dorman, Loranne S., and Clive L. Rawlins. *Leonard Cohen: Prophet of the Heart*. London: Omnibus Press, 1990.

Douglas, W.A.B., and Brereton Greenhous. *Out of the Shadows: Canada in the Second World War*. Toronto: Oxford University Press, 1977.

Evans, Gary. *In the National Interest*. Toronto: University of Toronto Press, 1991.

Forrester, Maureen. *Out of Character*. Toronto: McClelland & Stewart, 1986.

Frick, N. Alice. *Image in the Mind*. Toronto: Canadian Stage & Arts, 1987.

Frost, Stanley Brice. *McGill University for the Advancement of Learning*. Montreal: McGill-Queen's University Press, 1984.

Gallant, Mavis. *Across the Bridge*. Toronto: McClelland and Stewart, 1993.

———. *My Heart Is Broken*. New York: Random House, 1964.

Gélinas, Gratien. *Les Fridolinades 1938, 1939, 1940*. Montreal: Leméac, 1988.

Gibbon, John Murray. *Our Old Montreal*. Toronto: McClelland & Stewart, 1947.

Gilmore, John. *Swinging in Paradise: The Story of Jazz in Montreal*. Montreal: Véhicule, 1988.

Gordon, E.J. *E.J. Looking Back*. Montreal: Price-Patterson, 1993.

Gottheil, Allan. *Les juifs progressistes au Québec*. Montreal: Editions par Ailleurs, 1988.

Graceau, Henri-Paul. *Chronique de l'hospitalité hôtelière du Québec*. Montreal: Méridien, 1990.

Graham, Gwethalyn. *Earth and High Heaven*. New York: J.P. Lippincott, 1944.

Granatstein, J.L., and David Stafford. *Spy Wars*. Toronto: Key Porter, 1990.

Grenon, Hector. *Les belles heures de Montréal*. Montreal: Stanké, 1986.

———. *Camillien Houde*. Montreal: Stanké, 1979.

Gubbay, Aline. *A Street Called the Main*. Montreal: Meridian, 1990.

Hart, E.I. *Wake Up! Montreal! Commercialized Vice and Its Contributories*. Montreal: The Witness Press, 1919.

Hébert, Chantal. *Le burlesque au Québec*. Ville LaSalle, Que.: Hurtubise HMH, 1981.

Héroux, Jean-P. *Troisième centenaire de Montréal*. Montreal: Commission du Troisième Centenaire, 1942.

Higgins, Benjamin. *The Rise and Fall of Montreal*. Moncton, N.B.: Canadian Institute for Research on Regional Development, 1986.

How, Douglas. *Canada's Mystery Man of High Finance*. Hantsport, N.S.: Lancelot Press, 1986.

Hughes, Everett C. *French Canada in Transition*. Chicago: University of Chicago Press, 1943.

Hutchison, Bruce. *The Unknown Country*. Toronto: Longmans, Green, 1943.

Jenkins, Kathleen. *Montreal, Island City of the St. Lawrence*. Garden City, N.Y.: Doubleday, 1966.

Knott, Leonard. *La Place*. Montreal: Rolph Clark Stone Benallack, 1962.

Lande, Lawrence M. *The Montefiore Club*. Montreal: Privately printed, 1955.

Langlais, Jacques, and David Rome. *Jews and French Quebecers*. Waterloo, Ont.: Wilfrid Laurier University Press, 1991.

Laporte, Pierre. *The True Face of Duplessis*. Montreal: Harvest House, 1960.

La Roque, Hertel. *Camillien Houde*. Montreal: Editions de l'Homme, 1951.

LaRue, Monique. *Promenades littéraires dans Montréal*. Montreal: Québec/Amérique, 1989.

Laurendeau, André. *Witness for Quebec*. Toronto: Macmillan, 1973.

Lavertu, Yves. *L'affaire Bernonville*. Montreal: VLB Editeur, 1994.

Leacock, Stephen. *Leacock's Montreal*. Toronto: McClelland & Stewart, 1963.

Lees, Gene. *Oscar Peterson*. Toronto: Lester & Orpen Dennys, 1988.

Legris, Renée. *Robert Choquette: romancier et dramaturge de la radio-télévision*. Montreal: Fides, 1977.

Levine, Marc. *The Reconquest of Montreal*. Philadelphia: Temple University Press, 1990.

Linteau, Paul-André. *Histoire de Montréal depuis la Confédération*. Montreal: Boréal, 1992.

Linteau, Paul-André, et al. *Quebec Since 1930*. Toronto: James Lorimer, 1991.

Lovell's Montreal Directory. Montreal: James Lovell & Son, 1939, 1943, 1958.

MacKay, Donald. *The Square Mile*. Vancouver: Douglas & McIntyre, 1987.

MacLennan, Hugh. *Two Solitudes*. Toronto: Collins, 1945.

Marrus, Michael R. *Mr. Sam: The Life and Times of Samuel Bronfman*. Toronto: Viking, 1991.

Marsan, Jean-Claude. *Montreal in Evolution*. Montreal: McGill-Queen's University Press, 1981.

Marsolais, Claude-V., et al. *Histoire des maires de Montréal*. Montreal: VLB Editeur, 1993.

Matthews, Brian R. *A History of Pointe Claire*. Pointe Claire, Que.: Brianor, 1985.

McDowall, Duncan. *Quick to the Frontier*. Toronto: McClelland & Stewart, 1993.

McKenna, Brian, and Susan Purcell. *Drapeau*. Toronto: Clarke, Irwin, 1980.

McRoberts, Kenneth. *Quebec: Social Change and Political Crisis*. Toronto: McClelland & Stewart, 1993.

McVicar, Don. *Ferry Command*. Shrewsbury, Eng.: Airlife Publishing, 1981.

Miller-Barstow, D.H. *Beatty of the C.P.R.* Toronto: McClelland & Stewart, 1951.

Montrose, David [Charles Ross Graham]. *Murder over Dorval*. Toronto: Collins, 1952.

Moore, Brian. *The Luck of Ginger Coffey*. Boston: Little, Brown, 1960.

Morton, Desmond, and J.L. Granatstein. *Victory 1945: Canadians from War to Peace*. Toronto: HarperCollins, 1995.

Nardocchio, Elaine F. *Theatre and Politics in Modern Quebec*. Edmonton: University of Alberta Press, 1986.

Naves, Elaine Kalman. *The Writers of Montreal*. Montreal: Véhicule, 1993.

Newman, Peter C. *Flame of Power*. Toronto: Longmans, 1959.

Nish, Cameron, ed. *Quebec in the Duplessis Era*. Toronto: Copp Clark, 1970.

Nolan, Brian. *Hero: The Buzz Beurling Story*. Toronto: Lester & Orpen Dennys, 1981.

O'Donnell, Brendan. *Printed Sources for the Study of English-Speaking Quebec*. Lennoxville, Que.: Bishop's University, 1985.

Oliver, Michael. *The Passionate Debate: The Social and Political Ideas of Quebec Nationalism, 1920–1945*. Montreal: Véhicule, 1991.

Palmer, Al. *Montreal Confidential*. Toronto: Export, 1950.

———. *Sugar-Puss on Dorchester Street*. Toronto: Export, 1950.

Paris, Erna. *Jews: An Account of Their Experience in Canada*. Toronto: Macmillan, 1980.

Peate, Mary. *Girl in a Sloppy Joe Sweater*. Montreal: Optimum, 1988.

Pelletier, Gérard. *Years of Impatience*. Toronto: Methuen, 1984.

Penner, Norman. *Canadian Communism*. Toronto: Methuen, 1988.

Prévost, Robert. *Montréal, la folle entreprise*. Montreal: Stanké, 1991.

Provencher, Jean. *René Lévesque*. Toronto: Gage, 1975.

Quinn, Herbert F. *The Union Nationale*. Toronto: University of Toronto Press, 1963.

Remillard, François, and Brian Merrett. *Mansions of the Golden Square Mile, Montreal*. Montreal: Meridian, 1987.

Renaud, Charles. *L'imprévisible Monsieur Houde*. Montreal: Editions de l'Homme, 1964.

Richler, Mordecai. *The Apprenticeship of Duddy Kravitz*. Boston: Little, Brown, 1959.

———. *Son of a Smaller Hero*. London: Andre Deutsch, 1955.

Rioux, Marcel, and Yves Martin. *French-Canadian Society*. Toronto: McClelland & Stewart, 1964.

Roberts, Leslie. *The Chief*. Toronto: Clarke, Irwin, 1963.

———. *Montreal*. Toronto: Macmillan, 1969.

Robinson, Ira, et al. *An Everyday Miracle*. Montreal: Véhicule, 1990.

Rome, David, and Jacques Langlais. *The Stones That Speak*. Montreal: Septentrion, 1992.

Ross, Alexander. *The Booming Fifties*. Toronto: Natural Science of Canada, 1977.

Roy, Gabrielle. *The Tin Flute*. New York: Reynal & Hitchcock, 1947.

R.T.L. [Charles Vining]. *Bigwigs*. Toronto: Macmillan, 1935.

Rudin, Ronald. *The Forgotten Quebecers*. Quebec: Institut Québécois de recherche sur la culture, 1985.

Rumilly, Robert. *Histoire de Montréal*. Montreal: Fides, 1974.

Rutherford, Paul. *When Television Was Young*. Toronto: University of Toronto Press, 1990.

Ryerson, Stanley B. *French Canada*. Toronto: Progress Books, 1943.

Salvatore, Filippo. *Le fascisme et les Italiens à Montréal*. Montreal: Guernica, 1994.

Scher, Len. *The Un-Canadians*. Toronto: Lester, 1992.

Schull, Joseph. *The Great Scot*. Montreal: McGill-Queen's University Press, 1979.

Sirois, Antoine. *Montréal dans le roman canadien*. Montreal: Marcel Didier, 1968.

Stanké, Alain, and Jean-Louis Morgan. *Pax: lutte à finir avec la pègre*. Editions La Presse, 1972.

Stewart, Sandy. *Here's Looking at Us*. Toronto: CBC Enterprises, 1968.

Tombers, Matthew. *Ma vie de stripteaseuse*. Québec Arts, 1982.

Trofimenkoff, Susan Mann. *The Dream of a Nation*. Toronto: Macmillan, 1982.

Trudeau, Pierre, ed. *The Asbestos Strike*. Toronto: James Lewis & Samuel, 1974.

Usmiani, Renate. *Gratien Gélinas*. Toronto: Gage, 1977.

Vac, Bertrand. *Jean C. Lallemand raconte*. Verdun, Que.: Louise Courteau, 1987.

Vallières, Pierre. *White Niggers of America*. New York: Monthly Review Press, 1971.

Wade, Mason. *The French-Canadian Outlook*. New York: Viking, 1946.

———. *The French Canadians 1760–1967*. Toronto: Macmillan, 1968.

Waller, Adrian. *No Ordinary Hotel*. Montreal: Véhicule, 1989.

Watt, Sholto. *I'll Take the High Road*. Fredericton, N.B.: Brunswick Press, 1960.

Weisbord, Merrily. *The Strangest Dream*. Toronto: Lester & Orpen Dennys, 1983.

Westley, Margaret W. *Remembrance of Grandeur*. Montreal: Libre Expression, 1990.

Wilson, Edmund. *O Canada*. New York: Farrar, Straus & Giroux, 1965.

Zeckendorf, William. *Zeckendorf*. New York: Holt, Rinehart & Winston, 1970.

Index